AWS FinOps Simplified

Eliminate cloud waste through practical FinOps

Peter Chung

BIRMINGHAM—MUMBAI

AWS FinOps Simplified

Group Product Manager: Rahul Nair
Publishing Product Manager: Yashashree Hardikar
Senior Editor: Tanya D'cruz
Technical Editor: Arjun Varma
Copy Editor: Safis Editing
Project Coordinator: Shagun Saini and Ashwin Kharwa
Proofreader: Safis Editing
Indexer: Hemangini Bari
Production Designer: Shankar Kalbhor
Marketing Coordinator: Nimisha Dua

First published: October 2022

Production reference: 1220922

Published by Packt Publishing Ltd.
Livery Place
35 Livery Street
Birmingham
B3 2PB, UK.

ISBN 978-1-80324-723-6

www.packt.com

To my mother and father, for their sacrifices and for exemplifying the value of diligence. To Jennifer for being my loving partner and encouragement, and to Jeremy and Ezra our stars.

– Peter Chung

Contributors

About the author

Peter Chung enjoys seeing companies leverage new technologies such as the cloud to experience digital transformation. Before his current role as a Senior Solutions Architect at Amazon Web Services, Inc. (AWS), Peter helped customers save on their AWS bill as a Customer Optimization Specialist. Prior to AWS, Peter worked in numerous New York City agencies to help the city tackle complex challenges such as hurricane recovery efforts, responding to street homeless populations, and improving shelter conditions. He holds all AWS certifications, two Google Cloud certifications, and is, of course, FinOps certified.

About the reviewer

With more than 20 years of working in technology, **Felipe Campos**, also known as **KiKo**, started his career as a developer and then migrated into the cloud infrastructure area. When he began working in the FinOps area, he finally managed to bring together all of his passions, such as development, cloud architecture, and evangelization in tech. Always very curious, Felipe participates in several communities, contributing his knowledge in articles, lectures, events, and even long chats with friends!

Surely my journey alone would have ended at the first steps, had it not been for the support I've received from the people I've known in the tech community, and of course, my beautiful family and friends who have been extremely important in defining who I am.

Table of Contents

3

Managing Inventory   31

4

Planning and Metrics Tracking   49

5

Governing Cost and Usage   69

Part 2: Optimizing Your AWS Resources

6

7

8

Part 3: Operationalizing FinOps

11

Driving FinOps Autonomously   209

12

Management Functions   237

Index   259

Other Books You May Enjoy   270

Preface

Enterprises' usage of the cloud doesn't appear to be slowing down. In fact, it seems to only be accelerating. The growth of the cloud has enterprises seeking demand for cloud skills in not only the use of its technology, but in its operations as well. Many enterprises understand that the cloud offers benefits such as the ability to test and develop software quickly, the ability to innovate by offloading the undifferentiated heavy lifting to a cloud provider, and the ability to reach customers globally to essentially expand into new markets.

One benefit of the cloud that enterprises are often enticed by is its cost savings. However, some shake their head at this so-called benefit, arguing that it's more costly to operate in the cloud. At first glance, this might be true if you look at a cost comparison from a certain perspective. But when you're able to tell the whole story in the context of an enterprise's business goals, then there's a lot more to unpack. This book will help you do just that. It will unpack both the tactical ways to optimize on cloud costs, and the strategic approaches that ensure your business is leveraging the full value of the cloud.

This book's focus will be cost optimization in AWS. Although you can adopt some high-level strategies for any public cloud provider, the tactical aspects will be centered on AWS.

Who this book is for

Business, technology, and finance leads will inevitably become involved with FinOps in some way, shape, or form. A thoughtful software architect aims to learn as much of the business domain as possible to ensure that the technology being built supports the goals of the business. Similarly, any person concerned with lowering the variable costs of cloud resources will benefit from the themes and concepts presented in this book.

C-level executives will benefit by learning how they can help shape lean cloud operations to lower costs for the aggregate business. Line-of-business leaders will benefit by learning techniques they can employ within their teams to ensure they are maximizing the value of the cloud.

Technologists can apply the practices within this book to architect their cloud workloads in the more optimal way. Developers can benefit by gaining an understanding of how their deployment decisions impact the bottom-line. However, DevOps and infrastructure engineers will benefit more, as the book will help uncover tactics to lower costs.

Those in financial planning and analysis will benefit by gaining knowledge behind the technology that drives the cloud. These people offer a different perspective from technologists. Observing cloud operations through a financial lens will help technologists see new and optimal ways to build on the cloud.

What this book covers

Chapter 1, FinOps Foundation, defines FinOps so that all readers have the same foundation as they progress through the rest of the book. You will understand the origin of FinOps, as well as its purpose. You will understand the definition of FinOps, the entities responsible, the importance of the discipline, and how to set the foundations for doing so. In other words, it explains the who, what, why, and how of running FinOps on AWS.

Chapter 2, Establishing the Right Account Structure, discusses strategies for organizing AWS accounts allowing you to use AWS Organization for consolidated billing, volume discounts, reserved instance sharing, and others. Everything in AWS starts with the AWS account: this includes cost optimization. You will understand the benefit of consolidated account management in terms of governance and resource management.

Chapter 3, Managing Inventory, teaches you to take an inventory of all your assets now that you have the right account structure in place. This chapter teaches you how to use AWS tools to take inventory, produce reports, and identify anomalies. It also provides guidance on different tagging strategies to have a sustainable inventory-tracking policy.

Chapter 4, Planning and Metrics Tracking, teaches you to baseline your spend. You need this data in order to see where you can reduce waste, and find opportunities for optimization. This chapter teaches you how to use Cost Explorer to see your usage, create reports that can be tracked over time, and set up policies and goals to know how well you are performing to reduce waste.

Chapter 5, Governing Cost and Usage, emphasizes that with inventory, metrics, and baselining in place, you must now know how to govern your usage so that costs do not deviate from expected spend thresholds. You will learn how to use various AWS Management services such as AWS CloudTrail, AWS Config, and AWS IAM to govern your account's spend. You will also learn to tag their resources properly so that you can track resource use effectively.

Chapter 6, Optimizing Compute, covers compute, the most popular use case for customers. You will learn how to choose the right pricing model for your workload. These options are reserved instances, Savings Plans, Spot, SageMaker Savings Plans, and on-demand. You will learn to use AWS Compute Optimizer to rightsize their instances. You will also learn about serverless offerings to maximize efficiency.

Chapter 7, Optimizing Storage, examines another core component of IT: storage. You will learn how to optimize your storage use. You will learn the different storage tiers in S3 to optimize storage costs, including S3 Storage Lens. You will also learn how to optimize on the database services including Amazon RDS, Amazon OpenSearch, Amazon EFS, and DynamoDB.

Chapter 8, Optimizing Networking, discusses the last core IT component: networking. You will learn how to analyze and optimize on data transfer costs. You will also learn to use VPC endpoints to reduce bandwidth costs wherever appropriate for your workload. You will also learn the different hybrid networking architectures and learn how to conduct cost analyses to choose the optimal solution.

Chapter 9, Optimizing Cloud-Native Environments, covers optimization topics beyond compute, networking, and storage. You will learn how to use rightsizing and elasticity such as auto-scaling to maximize the efficiency of your AWS usage. You will learn different autoscaling policies and strategies, and learn which to use for a specific workload. You will also learn to use Trust Advisor to see other opportunities to optimize.

Chapter 10, Data-Driven Fin-Ops, explains that cost optimization is not a one-time activity. You must continually monitor, report, and act upon FinOps best practices at scale if you intend to maximize the benefits. This chapter shows ways to automate reporting and response to adopt a CI/CD practice toward FinOps.

Chapter 11, Driving FinOps Autonomously, goes through different ways individual teams can incorporate FinOps best practices in their daily operations. While the previous chapter focused on FinOps practices centrally, this chapter essentially teaches you about FinOps practices that also need to be managed de-centrally or autonomously. This provides you with the full spectrum of everything you can do to reduce waste from both the top-down and bottom-up perspectives.

Chapter 12, Management Functions, brings together the concepts of the previous chapters to teach you how to integrate both centralized and de-centralized FinOps practices. This will close the gap between all that you have read and bring everything together.

To get the most out of this book

You will need access to an AWS account if you would like to follow along in the exercises. Ensure that you have the proper **Identity and Access Management (IAM)** *permissions to access AWS resources. If you are a first-time user, you can sign up for free at* `aws.amazon.com`.

If you are using the digital version of this book, we advise you to type the code yourself. Doing so will help you avoid any potential errors related to the copying and pasting of code.

Download the color images

We also provide a PDF file that has color images of the screenshots and diagrams used in this book. You can download it here: `https://packt.link/i2fRK`.

Conventions used

There are a number of text conventions used throughout this book.

`Code in text`: Indicates code words in text, database table names, folder names, filenames, file extensions, pathnames, dummy URLs, user input, and Twitter handles. Here is an example: "Mount the downloaded `WebStorm-10*.dmg` disk image file as another disk in your system."

A block of code is set as follows:

```
model = sagemaker.estimator.Estimator(
container,
role,
train_instance_count=1,
train_instance_type='ml.m4.4xlarge,
input_mode='Pipe'…)
```

When we wish to draw your attention to a particular part of a code block, the relevant lines or items are set in bold:

```
model = sagemaker.estimator.Estimator(
container,
role,
train_instance_count=1,
train_instance_type='ml.m4.4xlarge,
input_mode='Pipe'…)
```

Bold: Indicates a new term, an important word, or words that you see onscreen. For instance, words in menus or dialog boxes appear in **bold**. Here is an example: "Select **System info** from the **Administration** panel."

> **Tips, important notes, and use cases**
> Appear like this.

Get in touch

Feedback from our readers is always welcome.

General feedback: If you have questions about any aspect of this book, email us at customercare@packtpub.com and mention the book title in the subject of your message.

Errata: Although we have taken every care to ensure the accuracy of our content, mistakes do happen. If you have found a mistake in this book, we would be grateful if you would report this to us. Please visit www.packtpub.com/support/errata and fill in the form.

Piracy: If you come across any illegal copies of our works in any form on the internet, we would be grateful if you would provide us with the location address or website name. Please contact us at copyright@packt.com with a link to the material.

If you are interested in becoming an author: If there is a topic that you have expertise in and you are interested in either writing or contributing to a book, please visit `authors.packtpub.com`.

Share Your Thoughts

Once you've read *AWS FinOps Simplified*, we'd love to hear your thoughts! Scan the QR code below to go straight to the Amazon review page for this book and share your feedback.

`https://packt.link/r/1803247231`

Your review is important to us and the tech community and will help us make sure we're delivering excellent quality content.

1
FinOps Foundation

Before we embark on a FinOps journey, we must level-set expectations and definitions for us to stay on the right path. We'll begin by justifying the need for FinOps. Operating in the cloud warrants a mind shift from traditional IT procurement practices. For organizations to truly benefit from what the cloud offers, they must align their line of thinking with the variable nature of paying for cloud resources.

We will define what FinOps is and its principles. We'll use these definitions as set boundaries as we dive deeper into the execution and implications of FinOps on AWS.

In this chapter, we're going to cover the following main topics:

- Changing with the cloud
- Rethinking procurement
- Defining FinOps

Changing with the cloud

Cloud cost management is hard. A dynamic cloud environment, autonomous teams provisioning IT resources at will, and even changing prices of the resources themselves all complicate cloud cost management. Layer a multi-cloud strategy on top of that and the complexity increases even more. But how come we see companies such as Lyft cutting costs by 40% in 6 months, Etsy achieving a 42% reduction in computing costs, and MicroStrategy optimizing by 30%? Surely cost management appears to be possible.

Cloud cost management is indeed hard but, even more fundamentally, change management is hard. We get so used to the way of doing things. We set up processes, reports, approval mechanisms, and training sessions, then something changes that forces us to re-evaluate and redeploy all our efforts. We not only have to help people understand why things are changing, but we must help people change their behavior to adapt to what's new.

Cloud cost management is a major change to how organizations think about IT resource procurement. It is a change in the operational processes involving software development, and it is a change in how teams gauge metrics and democratize resource ownership. Successful cloud cost management depends on successful organizational and cultural changes. It requires a mind shift that aligns IT procurement thinking to the variable nature of the cloud.

Cloud cost management calls for increased awareness of how efficiently you use your cloud resources. The on-demand nature of the cloud is convenient in the sense that you can obtain resources at will, but it also requires discipline in choosing the right amount of resources to get the job done.

The business value of cloud cost management is no different from the business value of optimizing any other domain of your business. We can take operation optimization as an example. When you optimize your operations, you find ways to minimize your operational costs while maximizing your operational outputs. With process optimization, you identify areas of improvement in a defined process, implement those changes, then measure the impact of those changes on some business-centric performance indicators. All these efforts are meant to help your business lower costs and increase profitability. Moreover, to ensure that your efforts are having an impact on your business, you define **Key Performance Indicators** (**KPIs**) to validate the outcomes.

The practice of cloud cost management is the application of these optimization efforts in different areas of the business and the use of cloud IT resources. You apply the same discipline of minimizing cloud costs while maximizing the value of cloud resources. Equally important is the measuring of KPIs for intended business outcomes; having data to validate your cloud cost optimization efforts proves your efforts have business value.

Let's unpack a bit more of how we must change the way we think about our use of cloud IT resources to move toward these efficiency gains.

Rethinking procurement

Imagine you grab lunch at a local eatery that provides several culinary options. You can either purchase option A, a sandwich/soup combo at a fixed price, or you can choose option B, the buffet, in a sense, but where you pay based on weight. Given that the buffet has a myriad of food items that you enjoy, you choose to go with the latter. When you select your options, you are sensitive to what and how much you put in the to-go box. On the other hand, if you went with the sandwich/soup combo, there's less mindful calculation required because you know exactly how much you're paying. This juvenile example illustrates the mind shift required to go from option A to B where cloud spending is more like the latter.

Those with cloud cost management success stories have already adopted this new way of thinking and dismissed traditional IT procurement processes. In the past (and even in some cases today), the relationship between technology and finance teams was largely transactional. When developers needed resources, a centralized finance procurement team found the appropriate vendor and approved the request. Oftentimes these approvals took weeks, hampering technology teams' efficiency. Moreover, developers had to wait for the hardware to arrive even after approvals, further extending this waiting game.

With the cloud, things are different. Engineering teams can now procure the necessary IT resources at the click of a button, or even an entire data center through code. The on-demand nature of the cloud enables teams to innovate quickly because not only are they able to obtain resources within minutes, but they can also test and experiment freely without the financial burden of keeping those resources long-term. Teams can easily spin up resources and just as easily remove them when they are done, and not pay for them. Organizations avoid the disadvantages of lengthy procurement cycles and wasted IT resources, especially when they sit idle for a long period of the year.

These all sound like good things to have. But they also sound like they can lead organizations on the wrong path. In fact, it's quite easy to indulge in cloud resources at any moment given the on-demand nature of the cloud, while ignoring the financial consequences, much like piling food on your lunch platter at the local eatery. We will dive into the various strategies around cost control, cost management, and value-driven optimization strategies on AWS throughout this book. But let's first level-set a few things.

> **Important note**
>
> *Cost* throughout this book refers specifically to financial costs. There are other costs to consider such as labor costs, operational costs, and the cost of technical debt. I will explicitly indicate the type of cost when appropriate when I'm not referring to financial costs.

We've established that change is hard but inevitable in today's technological landscape. Modern computer system architectures make teams rethink how they design network communications, databases, and data processing within a cloud computing framework. This also requires teams to rethink how they procure these resources to support their business domains. Although not entirely obsolete, traditional means of procuring computer hardware and software debilitate an organization's need to move quickly. This requires a shift in how teams think and operate financial practices to be more in line with the methods adopted by agile software delivery teams. This is where **FinOps** comes into the picture.

Defining FinOps

To put FinOps into context, let's look at its derivation, **DevOps**. The industry often describes DevOps as a set of practices that combines software development (Dev) and IT operations (Ops). It involves people, processes, and tools that work together in a collaborative culture to accelerate an organization's ability to deliver services to customers. DevOps isn't just one tool, nor is it a one-time event. It's a repeated and ever-evolving practice that serves to ultimately bring value to an organization. Indeed, if it doesn't bring value to an organization, it is not something worth pursuing. At the same time, if it's not bringing value, there might be a chance it's being implemented incorrectly.

Similarly, FinOps is the merging of financial accountability and management of cloud resources with cloud operations. Much like how DevOps is a combination of cultural philosophies, practices, and tools that advocate a collaborative working relationship between development and IT operations, FinOps encourages the same collaboration between technology and finance teams as well as across lines of business. While DevOps increases an organization's ability to deliver applications and services at high velocity, FinOps increases an organization's visibility, cost efficiency, and profitability of cloud resources. Storment and Fuller succinctly define FinOps as *the practice of bringing financial accountability to the variable spend model of cloud, enabling distributed teams to make business trade-offs between speed, cost, and quality.* They aptly proceed to say that FinOps is not about *saving* money. FinOps is about *making* money and using your money in a more effective way.

The ultimate purpose of FinOps is to bring business value to your organization by reducing cloud waste. Simply decreasing cloud costs by purchasing AWS **Reserved Instances** (**RIs**) or using optimal Amazon S3 storage classes is narrow in scope (we will discuss these practices in later chapters). These practices may bring immediate benefits but may fail to bring lasting value if they aren't implemented strategically without measurable metrics and meaningful KPIs.

For the remainder of this book, I'll refer to the term *FinOps* to encompass the people, processes, and tools you use toward your path of eliminating waste in using AWS cloud resources.

> **Important note**
>
> Cloud providers use their own terms when referring to cloud cost management. For example, AWS uses Cloud Financial Management, Azure uses Cloud Cost Management, while Oracle uses Cost Management Cloud. In this book, FinOps refers to all these and more as they all mean to achieve the same goal.

FinOps is the framework within which teams can operate to ensure they are optimizing their use of cloud resources. Conversely, FinOps cannot apply to traditional IT procurement processes – you cannot operate and scale with agility if you are waiting for financial approval for hardware that will be arriving in 3 months. For FinOps to be successful, teams must accept cloud operating principles and expect to dynamically provision IT resources. Let's take a closer look at these principles in the next section.

FinOps principles

An organization with a successful FinOps cadence involves personas from business, finance, and technology actively working as a cohesive team to embed cost management discipline within business domains. And (hopefully!) within your business domains, there exist domain experts. Domain experts are the folks who know the line of business they are working in very well. Whether they are product managers, developers, financial analysts, or architects, they have deep knowledge of the business domain in which they operate.

If you're already familiar with **Domain-Driven Design** (**DDD**), you know how important it is in developing software. DDD is a software design approach that exists to not only help teams build high-quality software but software that meets core business objectives. Without DDD, you may have a scenario such as a developer engaging with a domain expert, but the collaboration is largely transactional. The developer builds software that's based on a list of business requirements that is loosely interpreted rather than truly reflecting what the business needs. The result is a poor representation of the domain experts' mental model and over time, this disconnect between software and the business domain increases.

DDD addresses this disconnect by aligning software to business value. Developers can easily get distracted by technology and technical solutions to business problems. By investing in developers' knowledge of the business domain and creating a common language between domain experts and developers, software becomes more about the business rather than technology.

Within DDD, the domain is the problem space that a business occupies. The business operates within a particular domain. However, regardless of the existence of the business, the domain always exists. Then, a subdomain is a component of the main domain, but it focuses on a specific subset of the business. This usually manifests itself in the form of business departments such as sales, engineering, or finance.

A domain model is an abstraction of the domain in which a business operates. The properties of the domain that are most important to the business constitute the business' domain model. Models oftentimes need to be changed as the domain changes and the business priorities change.

Finally, bounded contexts are the logical boundaries that include the inputs, outputs, events, requirements, data models, and processes. These bounded contexts are a property of the solution space and are, ideally, aligned to the subdomain.

I broach the topic of DDD because DDD's good intentions apply to FinOps' good intentions. FinOps requires a common language among all teams. One of DDD's primary pillars is **Ubiquitous Language**. This is a shared team language among domain experts and developers. This Ubiquitous Language is not meant to be organization-wide and only applies within a bounded context of a business domain. To illustrate, a tomato in the bounded context of nutrition is considered a vegetable, whereas in the bounded context of botany, it is considered a fruit due to the presence of seeds (but let's face it, it's really a vegetable).

Different terms mean different things in different contexts so it's important to have the right language within a FinOps context. It's also nearly impossible to have an established global language within a larger enterprise. So, the best approach is to accept that differences will exist but when speaking within a FinOps context, the language is well-defined and clearly understood.

A common language is a property of a business' communication structure. DDD aims to improve the efficiencies that come with organizing teams by function, which was traditionally how teams were organized when deploying software:

1. Sales teams would request engineering teams build something.
2. Engineering teams would respond with an estimated deployment date of 8 weeks.
3. Sales teams would outsource troubleshooting to support teams.
4. Support teams would request the engineering teams fix a bug.

This transactional type of communication would not facilitate domain knowledge to be shared across the organization. It would, at times, prevent businesses from iterating and innovating quickly since teams and data were siloed with teams having to depend on other teams to make changes and meet customer demand.

Rather, DDD organizes teams into their respective bounded contexts. Teams operate within their own subdomains and make their data and interfaces to other teams through well-defined protocols and processes. Teams better understand how to communicate with each other since this is implied within the software architecture. I'm not saying FinOps is a bounded context in and of itself. What I am saying is that the discipline that comes with maintaining consistent, reliable, and defined communication channels for an organization practicing DDD is a helpful frame of reference when thinking about the communication channels necessary between a FinOps team and the various other teams within a business.

This common language is critical when deciding on going with application design A over B, even when A costs much more. Optimizing application A solely for the purpose of saving money but sacrificing its performance or availability, which leads to system downtime, which can crush revenue, hardly seems like a worthy trade-off. Even language around AWS-specific cost terms such as RI unblended cost, and Intelligent-Tiering can lead to confusion if teams don't have a shared understanding of what they mean, and specifically how they impact the business.

Centralization of knowledge and oversight is key to ensuring that business domain knowledge doesn't sit lazily within the minds of a select few. In FinOps, having a central team driving cost management policies and documenting knowledge helps with this knowledge transfer. In the cloud, this central team is often called a **Cloud Center of Excellence (CCoE)**, composed of individuals from various lines of business. A CCoE drives cloud adoption for the business, instilling cloud best practices in the various teams. A FinOps team derived from, or as part of, this CCoE can drive the adoption of FinOps best practices across the organization, embed them as part of the software development cycle, and report on performance to continually find areas to reduce waste.

What FinOps is...

FinOps is using tools to eliminate waste, whether those are AWS-native tools, third-party solutions, or your own homegrown applications. These tools help you take inventory, track cost performance over time, identify outliers, and assist in automation to remove unexpected waste and maximize the efficiency of cloud resources. However, tools themselves are a means to an end. FinOps also involves education and enablement in using these tools and interpreting the results appropriately so that the tools themselves bring value to the business. We will see how to apply various AWS-native tools to reduce cloud waste.

FinOps is establishing and executing practices that encourage automation to optimize as quickly and as efficiently as possible. Rather than manually pulling RI recommendation reports every few months and determining which instances are worth purchasing upfront, FinOps, at its best, automates the process of gathering RI recommendations, interpreting the results, and communicating to the ones responsible, ranking the RIs by maximum value for the business. FinOps also re-evaluates its practices and iterates on them depending on the use case.

FinOps creates meaningful metrics that you can track to see how well you are achieving your goals. You may have business leaders that worry that "our cloud costs are increasing." However, are increasing cloud costs necessarily a bad thing? What if for every dollar you spend on a cloud application, that application is bringing in 5 dollars? In that case, although your cloud costs are indeed increasing, the costs are nominal compared to the revenue generated. Although AWS itself is ultimately a technology, the cost of building on AWS becomes a justifiable business investment, not just a cost center. But you need to have metrics to prove this. FinOps not only involves these metrics but budgeting and planning so that you can track your cloud cost efficiency over time. The better you get at tracking metrics, the better you can prove your efficiency in reducing cloud waste.

A FinOps approach

You can define a successful FinOps approach broken up into four major practices: identify what you own, optimize resources that you need, plan and track spending, and execute policies that align with your financial goals. The diagram in *Figure 1.1* presents these ideas but in no particular order.

Figure 1.1 – A FinOps approach to waste elimination

Everyone will have a different starting point because everyone's cloud journey is unique. Some may be just starting out and won't have any resources provisioned. Others may have already been using the cloud for years and thus have a huge inventory of cloud resources to manage. Moreover, some organizations may prefer methodological approaches and set budgets before approving any projects, whereas others may prefer to be iterative and adjust budgets as needed. Regardless of your preference, these are important practices that you can incorporate into your FinOps strategy. We'll see how you can apply these practices on AWS.

Identifying what you own is knowing what resources are provisioned and will be provisioned. Imagine you are a company that sells toys online and in-store. You have warehouses storing your assets to ship to customers and deliver to physical stores. It's likely you have an inventory of your assets so you know when to replenish when stock is low. It would be rather difficult to run your business if you didn't know what you own! The same can be said of your cloud resources. It's unlikely that you'll have a successful FinOps strategy if you don't know what you have.

Optimizing the resources that you need means maximizing the efficiency of what you elect to use. Naively, the best way to reduce costs in the cloud is to not use anything – if you pay for what you use, just use as little as possible. Although facetious, it holds some truth. Turning off resources when you don't need them is a great way to eliminate waste (to know what you can turn off, you need to take inventory). Rightsizing resources, choosing the right pricing model, and leveraging the cloud's elasticity are practical ways to optimize the resources that you do need.

Planning and tracking help you see whether you are actually moving toward the ultimate goal of eliminating waste. By setting budgets, you can anticipate what your costs will be on a daily, monthly, and yearly basis. Budgets and reports can help you establish a baseline for your cloud spending. Then you can use features such as anomaly detection to identify events that deviate from expectations. Metrics also inform leadership on how cloud spending is contributing to the business. From that point of view, cloud spending becomes more of an investment.

Executing involves scaling your FinOps practices, incorporating automation, and iterating on your practices as business needs change. It's also important to standardize and communicate these practices to stakeholders, showing how these practices support business goals. Ideally, you want to automate as much as possible to ensure FinOps isn't a blocker to agility and innovation.

The following chapters focus on each practice so you can apply them within your AWS accounts.

> **Important note**
>
> You can apply these practices to any public cloud platform, but this book's focus is on AWS. The tools we use will be dependent on AWS-provided services. You can stay up to date with AWS tools on their Cloud Financial Management website.

We use a fictitious example throughout this book to demonstrate how an organization might apply FinOps to reduce cloud waste. We'll follow VidyaGames in their journey to transform from an organization with little to no FinOps practices to an organization with a mature FinOps practice. Each chapter focuses on a particular FinOps practice and as we expound on each practice, we'll see how VidyaGames applies the practice to its specific business domain.

VidyaGames' cloud cost journey

VidyaGames is an online video game review website with a growing user base. The company's core domain is a social media platform where registered users can share video game reviews, experiences, and photos. The company expects to build a live-streaming application and a vibrant online advertising space as two strategic business initiatives. Originally running on-premises in a data center, the company has migrated most of its applications to the cloud.

The business has been growing but so have its cloud costs. Initially, leadership wasn't concerned with cloud costs. The agility, scalability, and availability of the cloud were reasons enough to justify the move to AWS. Fortunately, the business experienced these benefits immediately, which contributed to its growth. However, as the business adjusts its goals to better manage its assets, cloud cost control has become a priority.

The company recently hired Jeremy as the head of engineering practices for the organization. His immediate directive is to get the organization's AWS costs under control. Leadership expects AWS costs to decrease by 30% within the next 3 months.

Jeremy asks Ezra, from the finance department, for a copy of last month's AWS bill. Ezra sends Jeremy multiple bills, each reflecting cost for a distinct AWS account. Jeremy asks Ezra who are the respective owners of the AWS accounts but Ezra does not know.

Jeremy cannot recognize any spending patterns based on the bills. He doesn't have any visibility into resource use to help him make any optimization decisions. He understands that he won't be able to do this alone.

A successful FinOps practice depends on a decentralized approach where all teams are engaged in practicing resource hygiene, cost awareness, and optimization techniques where possible. Although individual teams drive FinOps practices, a centralized team will evangelize best practices and apply the appropriate governance to ensure teams are operating within bounds that help the business achieve their cost goals.

Summary

In this chapter, you learned about the importance of having to change your mindset when running financial operations in the cloud. You cannot use a traditional, centralized IT procurement approach since cloud operations aren't owned by a single team. Rather, it is much more important to provide autonomy to your business teams to enable them to maximize cloud benefits. We will discuss how to enable your teams to be agile, autonomous, and to bring business value while controlling and managing their cloud spending throughout the remainder of this book.

You also learned that FinOps is a framework and discipline that crosses many teams within an organization. It is a combination of people, processes, tools, and metrics that empowers an organization using the cloud to manage its cloud resources as true assets that bring measurable value to the business. FinOps is not a one-person job, nor should it be owned and managed entirely by scattered teams. Rather, a centralized body such as a CCoE should own FinOps and share best practices with teams, enabling them to embed clean cloud cost hygiene within their operations.

You were also introduced to a few characters from a fictitious company struggling with implementing FinOps. You will encounter these characters and their stories throughout this book. The intent is for you to learn from their experiences and be able to apply their stories to yours. Let's continue on our journey.

Further readings

- *Lyft Uses AWS Cost Management to Cut Costs by 40% in 6 Months*: `https://aws.amazon.com/solutions/case-studies/lyft-cost-management/#:~:text=As%20part%20of%20its%20cloud,engineers%20to%20build%20new%20tools.`

- *Doing More with Less: How MicroStrategy Cut Cloud Costs by 30%*: `https://aws.amazon.com/solutions/case-studies/microstrategy-cost-management/`

- *Etsy: Doing more with less cost and infrastructure*: `https://cloud.google.com/customers/etsy`

- *What is FinOps?*: `https://www.finops.org/introduction/what-is-finops/`

Part 1: Managing Your AWS Inventory

The objective of *Part 1* is to help you understand and track your inventory. This is the first step toward eliminating waste. This part will help you know what you own and what your baseline spending is. If you do not have this information, you won't know what to optimize! This is like knowing your inventory in a warehouse: if you don't know what you have, you are poorly established to grow your business.

This part of the book comprises the following chapters:

- *Chapter 2, Establishing the Right Account Structure*
- *Chapter 3, Managing Inventory*
- *Chapter 4, Planning and Metrics Tracking*
- *Chapter 5, Governing Cost and Usage*

2
Establishing the Right Account Structure

A successful **financial operations (FinOps)** practice begins with the right foundation. With **Amazon Web Services (AWS)**, the organization of your AWS accounts constitutes that foundation. In this chapter, we'll explore ways to establish your account structure. In subsequent chapters, we'll see how an account structure directly impacts your ability to implement successful FinOps practices such as inventory management, governance and control, auditability, and reporting.

But first, we'll learn about the various AWS tools that can help structure your AWS accounts, including **AWS Organizations.** This is the foundation that will direct how successful your FinOps efforts will be over time. We'll then conclude with a brief look at how billing works for a multi-account AWS Organization.

In this chapter, we're going to cover the following main topics:

- Establishing an operating model
- Creating a multi-account environment
- Understanding billing with AWS Organizations

Technical requirements

To complete the exercises in this chapter, you will need:

- A personal computing device (PC, Mac, or Linux) with a web browser installed that has access to the internet
- AWS credentials such as your AWS account name and password
- If you've enabled AWS multi-factor authentication, you will also need your device's authentication code.

Establishing an operating model

We've already established that a successful FinOps practice depends on the foundation of how you structure your AWS accounts. But how you structure your AWS accounts will likely depend on how you organize your business teams. Organizational structure is important because if the way you operate FinOps does not align with how your teams operate, you'll create a chasm that disrupts any well-intended cost-saving initiatives. Conway's law particularly holds true within FinOps:

> *Any organization that designs a system...will inevitably produce a design whose structure is a copy of the organization's communication structure.*

> *(Melvin Conway, How Do Committees Invent?)*

Teams must know which role they play when contributing to projects that yield business value. They also need to know how their team synergizes with others when they collectively work toward set goals. The same ideas apply when implementing FinOps. Rather than having a centralized FinOps entity telling teams what to do and how to optimize, it's much more effective if teams take ownership of cost savings and federate FinOps among teams. By doing so, teams are empowered with information; this data gives teams the information they need to see the kind of impact they have on costs as they gauge how their work impacts the broader business.

Operating models will vastly differ depending on a company's industry, size, team size, and maturity, but we can at least categorize three generalized operating models that apply to FinOps on AWS.

Fully siloed models

When teams expect to operate with their specific function, a company can create silos that make it difficult for cross-team engagements. In the following diagram, we have four teams operating within their functional domains:

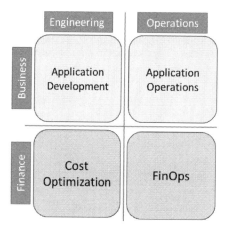

Figure 2.1 – A fully siloed operating model

Business informs *Engineering* of the application's requirements. *Engineering* then passes the day-to-day operations of the application's deployment to *Operations*. Meanwhile, *Finance* works with *Engineering* to find cost optimization opportunities that impact all teams within the organization. These practices can include tagging policies to ensure all cloud resources are tagged with an owner, purchasing reserved instances, executing automation scripts to clean up unused resources, or rightsizing instances.

As described, this model represents a *functional* separation between teams. Although a very common organizational practice, there is one major disadvantage: the lack of agility. By separating an application into functional teams, we expose operations similar to what we outlined previously: the **user interface (UI)** team builds and passes code to the business logic team to ensure functional requirements, then the code passes to the database team to work on storage components.

Each functional team is dependent on the others. This dependency hinders agility since each team cannot build, test, and deploy independently. In order to make a change, all teams must be involved; the change requires the entire application to change as a single unit.

It's common for today's enterprise products to change frequently during a lifetime. Given changing business requirements, changing customer preferences, market dynamism, and changing technologies, it is fitting for companies to move away from this model. Architecturally, this model generally implies a monolithic architecture because monoliths also commonly separate teams by function.

Separated application development with centralized FinOps

This model follows the *you built it, you run it* mantra. Engineering and operations work together as a unit—they perform both development and operations of the software they build to support a business function. Now that teams are working together and don't have to pass off and potentially wait for dependencies from other teams, this enables teams to move faster and meet the demands of both external and internal stakeholders.

A **development-operations (DevOps)** approach has application and operations teams working together to deploy software quickly and iteratively. This removes the need for application developers to ship code to the operations or infrastructure team and wait for deployment. The following diagram shows this silo between engineering and operations removed. Now, the team acts as one enabling quick and agile deployment:

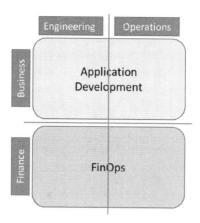

Figure 2.2 – A separated application model with a centralized FinOps function

FinOps, however, is management separated and centralized by finance. FinOps determines policies and governance controls and distributes them to the application teams. This centralized team can be a **cloud center of excellence** (**CCoE**) itself or a sub-team within the CCoE, focused mainly on cost-saving initiatives for the organization.

This model enables more agility than the siloed model in the previous section. Now that teams own the application as a unit, they can operate independently without dependencies on other teams. The trade-off for this is the requirement for organizations to create teams that have full-stack expertise, which can be challenging to say the least. Organizations can operationalize the most common requirements such that some teams can support themselves, while more specialized individuals serve on a cross-team. These best practices are covered in greater detail in *Part 3, Operationalizing FinOps,* of this book.

Decentralized FinOps with autonomous teams

The last model provides the most autonomy to teams. In this model, teams adopt and embed FinOps practices into their day-to-day workings. Although it doesn't preclude the existence of a centralized FinOps team (such as a CCoE), it expects teams to embed FinOps within their operations. This is more easily achieved if there exists a strong culture of autonomy and teams adopting best practices.

In application development, you might see a shared services team that handles networking, security, monitoring, and other cross-domain practices, while the application components are owned by autonomous teams.

This model follows a general format. For example, if you have a workload composed of a microservices architectural style, teams may agree to implement a certain logging standard across all services for consistency and maintainability. In the same way, a centralized FinOps team may establish best practices for purchasing **reserved instances** (**RIs**) or applying rightsizing, but it's up to the teams to implement these practices themselves in a way that makes sense to their specific domain.

As with *Figure 2.2* in the previous section, the following diagram shows engineering and operations as one team. However, the difference lies in how these teams embed FinOps into their practices. You may still have a centralized FinOps team recommending cost-saving practices that apply organization-wide, but you also have FinOps practices that application teams use specific to their domain. Because these teams know their domain better than anyone else, teams know how to apply FinOps, in particular to their context:

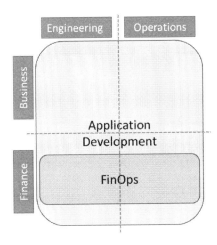

Figure 2.3 – A decentralized FinOps model with embedded FinOps practices

Teams embed FinOps practices within application development. Although we will investigate these practices in the following chapters, some practical examples are tagging resources, rightsizing servers before and after provisioning them, or creating clean-up practices to decommission unneeded services.

The model shows hashed lines representing finance working with other teams to establish best practices for the organization. Finance still centralizes FinOps knowledge and policies, but teams execute autonomously and iterate on them as business needs change.

The optimal model

The common statistical aphorism often attributed to British statistician George E.P. Box, "*All models are wrong, but some are useful*" applies no less here. There won't be strict lines (or dotted lines, for that matter) that physically or conceptually prevent teams from interacting with one another in practice. Nor are these models separate from each other. Real companies are on a gradient where certain pairs of teams may better communicate than others. There may be some centralized policies, while others are decentralized. There may even be one team doing it all, given its size.

It's hard to state one model is better than the other but steering away from a siloed model better aligns with how modern cloud architectures are being developed today. Companies realize the benefits of speed and agility that come from federated operations. The agility that comes with DevOps, microservices, and distributed data architectures such as data meshes results in smaller and autonomous teams. Needless to say, don't just adopt these patterns simply because everyone else is doing it, but rather apply them if the business need exists.

A centralized FinOps team to be the guiding star is still important. A FinOps team may decentralize more of the execution, reporting, and automation to autonomous teams, but a FinOps body composed of stakeholders from business, finance, and technology to drive best practices and share FinOps knowledge will bring success. Moreover, having executive sponsorship to support a FinOps practice ensures efforts are indeed valuable to the business but appreciated as well. This also benefits teams by creating a feedback loop; FinOps provides better visibility into efficient cloud usage, executives trust that teams are using cloud resources effectively in ways that are beneficial to the business, and then cloud usage continues investing in new projects or optimizing existing ones.

Finding a Better Way to Organize AWS Accounts

Jeremy feels overwhelmed by the number of bills he must consolidate manually and by the fact that the accounts associated with these bills have no clear owner. Jeremy sets up a meeting with Ellia, the lead architect at *VidyaGames*.

"Ellia, do you know who owns these AWS accounts?" Jeremy asks as he shares the bills with Ellia.

"Unfortunately, not all of them," Ellia replies. "Some of them were here before I started. And some of them were acquired when we bought *Hi AdTech* two quarters ago."

"*Hi AdTech* is the digital advertising company, correct?" Jeremy asks.

"Correct. It's part of our strategic move to promote more ads on our e-commerce platform. We acquired them but really haven't integrated their projects yet with our current workloads." Ellia pauses and eagerly says, "Everyone knows your priority right now is to cut costs. What are you thinking? Maybe I can help."

Jeremy smiles. "Thanks. That would be very helpful. I'm thinking we need a better way to organize our accounts and build a process to clearly identify account owners. Then, in the future, if we do make more acquisitions, the integration will be much more streamlined."

Siloed models are not conducive to FinOps, primarily because cost saving becomes reactionary. Instead, you want to have FinOps disciplines embedded within the operating models of applications teams, which is easier to adopt within a decentralized FinOps model and autonomous teams. Reactionary cost saving also bears the risk of never implementing cost optimization practices at all due to the risk of decreased visibility and accountability across teams. For example, finance teams may recognize overprovisioned or idle servers at the end of the month. Then, the team might send a message to the application teams to rightsize or turn off servers, but application teams may never end up following through on the tasks.

Having explored the organizational implications teams have on FinOps, let's find out what it looks like when applied within an AWS environment.

Creating a multi-account environment

All resources and services on AWS require an AWS account. After you create an account, you can deploy AWS resources to that account. Hence, the AWS account is the fundamental container that holds your resources. Every month, AWS aggregates usage for each account, and the account holder is responsible for those charges. However, most organizations using AWS have multiple accounts that run their workloads.

Securing your business assets is the primary reason for using multiple accounts. An AWS account provides a natural security boundary for organizations with multiple accounts. Say you were to deploy your entire business' production workload in a single AWS account. If a malicious actor were to obtain certain privileges to that account, that may lead to a large security breach in your business. However, if the threat affects just one account out of many, this significantly limits the threat or blast radius.

Isolating resources by attributing them to specific accounts also simplifies compliance. Imagine you have a payment-processing capability for a certain application. That payment functionality will likely be guarded by regulations that don't apply to other functions of the application. By leveraging multiple accounts, auditors would only need access to the account responsible for payment processing rather than scrutinizing the entire application if it sat in a single AWS account.

You also gain better resource isolation, which results in cost and billing clarity. Because AWS bills resource use at the account level, you can see resource use by account. If you tagged resources (we'll discuss tagging strategies in *Chapter 6, Optimizing Compute*), you can see costs by tags within an account. You can also aggregate tags across multiple accounts, so you can choose different levels of granularity. AWS also assigns quotas to each of its resources. You're likely to reach quota limits more quickly using one account than by using multiple accounts. By breaking up resources across multiple accounts, you can address quota limits incrementally as needed.

> **Important note**
> AWS accounts have default quotas specific to each Region. For resources that have soft limits, you can request an increase by contacting AWS Support. You can check each service's quotas on its respective AWS documentation page.

Another important reason is decentralization of ownership. When teams own their own AWS accounts, they are less likely to interfere with each other and can operate independently. This may increase a team's agility by removing bureaucratic tendencies that stem from centralized control. By decentralizing ownership, administrators can delegate the managing of certain organization-wide requirements to individual teams, one of those requirements being cost control.

Structuring your AWS accounts

This begs the question, "*What's the right multi-account structure?*" The short answer, as is usually the case in software architecture, is: "*It depends.*" A reasonable place to start is to structure accounts by functional business departments. The following diagram provides an example of this:

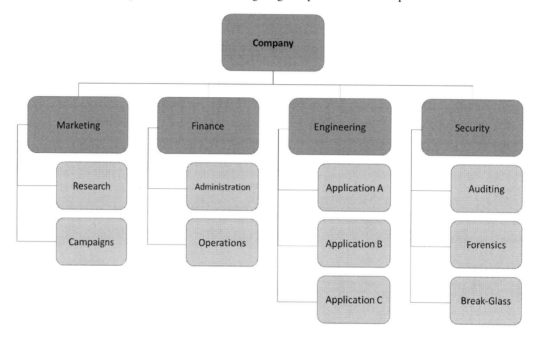

Figure 2.4 – AWS account by business department

A company provides multiple AWS accounts to allow each department to run workloads that bring business value. Users and applications deploy resources in those accounts for a specific purpose. Although minimal, by mapping resource use to a business function, you start to reduce waste. If you had a single account with users and applications provisioning resources without defined boundaries or clear business objectives, it would become difficult to justify the use of those resources. This is very similar to the usually undesirable *big ball of mud* software system anti-pattern. You'll also find yourself reaching AWS service quota limits rather quickly, which can impact your business agility.

You can create an even more granular account structure if it benefits your organization. *Figure 2.4* shows a nested account structure with the first layer separated by department. Engineering teams may create another layer to segregate applications using AWS accounts. Then, they may add a third layer to separate each account, and use an AWS account to host distinct environments, as shown in the following diagram:

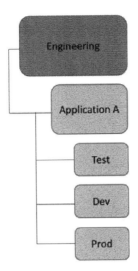

Figure 2.5 – Application segregation by environment

You may also consider structuring your accounts by domain. Architects break down an application by its components or domains. An architect should be able to identify what purpose that domain serves and which dependencies each domain has with others. By breaking an application down by its components, architects and developers can modularize an application, which has different advantages than a single monolithic application. This can also improve your security posture as resources in one environment can be independent of another. This means that if one environment becomes compromised, it won't negatively impact the security posture of another.

For example, if you have an application that processes customer payments and the business saw value in adding a mobile payment capability, under a monolithic application, adding this mobile payment functionality would require the entire application to accommodate this change. However, with a modular approach, you can develop this functionality independently and focus on how this new service would communicate and essentially be *plugged into* the existing application with minimal disruption. Architects compare this kind of microservice architectural pattern to the monolithic architectural pattern. This topic of microservice architecture warrants multiple books, so we won't dwell on it for much longer.

It's worth noting how agility through decentralized ownership in microservice architectures relates to FinOps practices and account structures. Teams own and deliver distinct components of a microservice-based application. They have the operational autonomy to use whichever tool is best suited for their domain. Providing an AWS account to each team enables this practice of decentralized ownership and component-based design. You can see what purpose that account serves because it is directly related to an application's functionality. Teams can further segregate their domain by environment (for example, test, development, staging, and production) if necessary.

Choose the right account structure based on your organization's needs. You could start by mapping your account structure to your organization's structure. You may want to separate accounts by business departments because the tasks and data used by the marketing and finance teams are distinct and there is little reason for any overlap. You may have some monolithic and microservice applications and decide to place monolithic applications in their accounts while creating domain-specific accounts for your microservice applications. You have the freedom to create something that works best for you, and the flexibility to change as needed.

There are no financial costs for creating an AWS account. That means you can create hundreds or thousands of accounts and still not be charged if you don't deploy any resources in those accounts. Hence, there are no direct financial risks to creating multiple accounts. In other words, it doesn't cost anything to open an account.

Conceptually, managing a single AWS account is obviously easier than managing multiple accounts. Cross-account functions such as logging, security, and monitoring are simpler to manage within a single account. You must consider how to manage cross-account functions and coordinate communication between accounts. Fortunately, AWS Organizations helps to reduce the burden of multi-account management.

Managing accounts with AWS Organizations

You group multiple AWS accounts together to form an organization. You designate one account as the management account, while the others become member accounts. The management account is the ultimate owner of the organization. Once you establish the management account, you cannot change which account will be the management account, unless you dismantle the organization entirely and start anew. The member accounts are members of that organization and can only be part of one organization at a time.

You structure your AWS accounts within your organization from the management account. You can group accounts to form an **organizational unit** (**OU**). If you followed the example from *Figure 2.4* in the previous section, you would have four OUs with your organization: Marketing, Finance, Engineering, and Security. Furthermore, you can create nested OUs. Within the Engineering OU, you would have a nested OU for applications A, B, and C, following the example in *Figure 2.5*.

An account can be part of just one OU, but you can move accounts freely from one OU to another. This will help organize your accounts to accommodate changing business needs. If your business decides that an AWS account should switch functions from running marketing campaigns to supporting a financial need, you can simply move the account into the appropriate OU. The following screenshot shows how you can do this using the AWS Management Console:

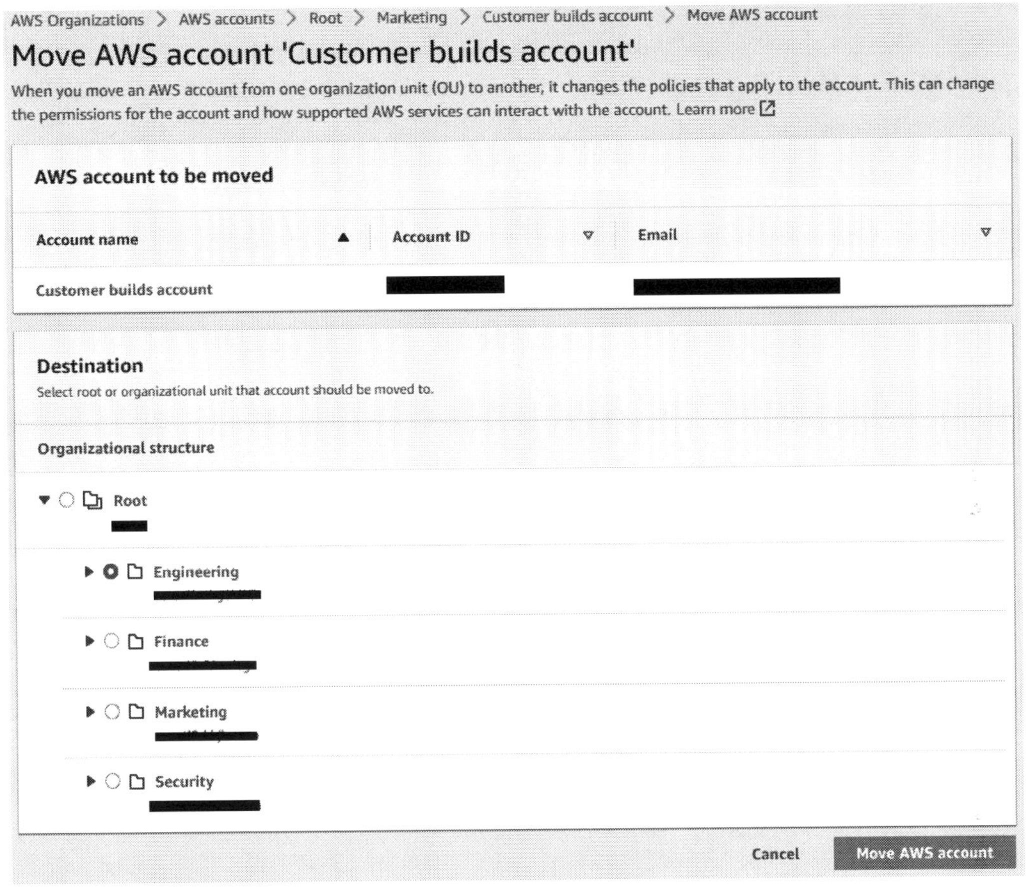

Figure 2.6 – Moving accounts from the Marketing OU to the Engineering OU

You can also expand your account footprint in AWS Organizations. You can create new accounts and invite existing accounts into your organization, as shown in the next screenshot. This provides you with additional flexibility because you don't have to perfect your account strategy from the beginning. As your business grows through acquisition, refactors applications to meet business objectives, and creates new environments to increase agility, you can adjust your accounts accordingly. Knowing each account's purpose helps reduce waste because if an entire workload and its resources within an account aren't contributing to that purpose, then you should eliminate those resources. We'll explore which resources your accounts have in the next chapter:

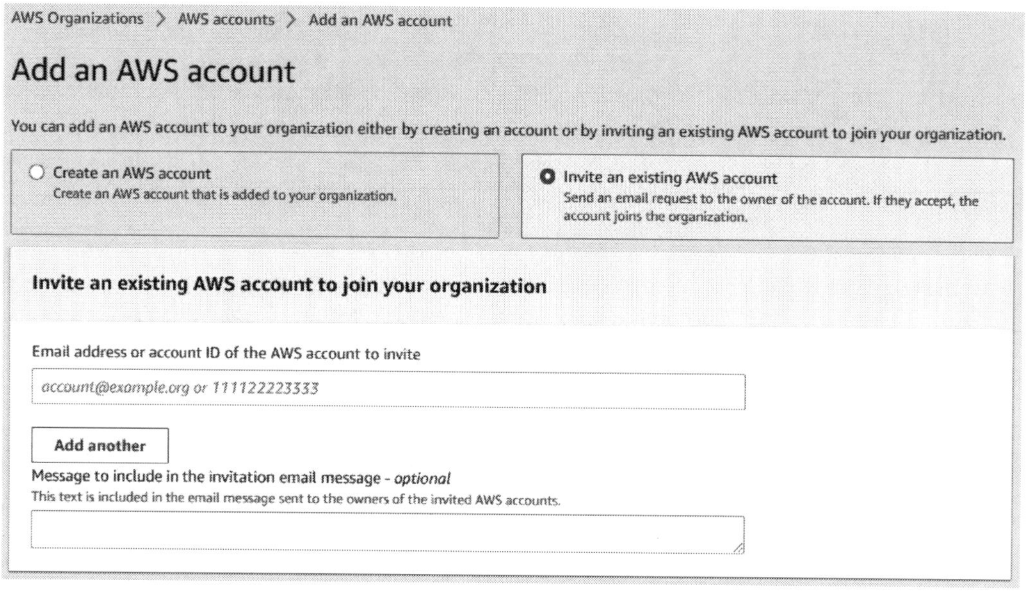

Figure 2.7 – Adding an AWS account through invitation

One important policy decision to consider is defining a process to clean up unneeded or forgotten accounts. You may run into situations where you have an AWS account but the original owner of the account left the organization, or you may have inherited an account that you cannot access. Not only will this incur financial waste if resources are running in those accounts, but it also poses a security issue since a non-registered user in your company's domain has access to resources. Every AWS account must have an associated email. Hence, having a process to change account ownership, update emails, and decommission unnecessary accounts is practicing healthy account hygiene and reducing waste.

> **Important note**
>
> AWS recommends having a catch-all account to help you retrieve password reset emails. This allows an email administrator to record these emails in case an account owner leaves the company. Your administrator would still be able to reset account passwords even if the original owners were unreachable. It's highly recommended that you enable **multi-factor authentication** (**MFA**) on your root AWS account.

Managing your AWS accounts with AWS Control Tower

Managing your multi-account environment with organizations provides you with a lot of flexibility in how you want to structure your accounts. As you scale, however, you may encounter situations where you want to create a centralized logging account or security account to aggregate activity in a single location. This approach is easier than having to access logs for each account individually. You can certainly create your own cross-functional accounts but may find it easier to start with a blueprint and iterate from there.

You can use **AWS Control Tower** to quickly set up a multi-account AWS environment based on best practices. Control Tower establishes a landing zone, which is a blueprint for a well-architected, multi-account environment. For example, if you create your multi-account structure using Control Tower, Control Tower will automatically create a core OU with a centralized logging and security account.

You can modify the **Landing Zones** settings to meet your business needs. Let's say there is no reason for anyone in your organization to use any **AWS Region** that's not in the **United States** (**US**). You can apply **Region Deny** settings to limit what folks can do to certain Regions in your landing zone.

> **Important note**
>
> An AWS Region is a geographic location hosting a cluster of data centers. AWS groups data centers within a Region to form **Availability Zones** (**AZs**). AZs are physically separated from each other for redundancy.

Control Tower helps when you'd rather build your multi-account environment upon already established best practices over starting from scratch. This enables you to quickly set up a baseline environment where you can focus on applying governance and cost controls from a centralized dashboard, which we will cover in greater detail in *Chapter 5, Governing Cost and Usage*.

The following screenshot shows a sample dashboard from the AWS Control Tower console. Here, we see the number of accounts and OUs, including the enabled guardrails for governance. You can also find non-compliant resources, although these are not specifically shown here:

Figure 2.8 – A sample Control Tower dashboard in the AWS console

We've seen how to organize AWS accounts to create an organization. A multi-account environment is easier to manage with AWS Organizations and can help improve your visibility on costs. Let's understand how billing works in AWS Organizations.

Understanding billing with AWS Organizations

When you operate with AWS Organizations, you receive one aggregated bill that shows usage for every account in your organization. AWS calls this consolidated billing. This consolidated bill shows both aggregated usage for the organization and usage per account, enabling you to conduct proper chargeback mechanisms or create showbacks for visibility.

> **Important note**
> In **information technology (IT)**, a chargeback is the practice of charging **business units (BUs)** for their IT usage, whereas a showback is the practice of showing BUs their spending but internally reconciling from a central budget.

If your business requires separate bills for every AWS account, then you should not combine accounts with AWS Organizations. This, however, prohibits you from taking advantage of volume-tier discounts, which will help reduce costs.

Some services in AWS provide a volume-based discount—the more you use, the better the deal. With consolidated billing, AWS regards usage across all accounts in an organization as if it were a single account. AWS then applies discounts for eligible services if the aggregate usage meets those volume thresholds. The following screenshot shows an example of aggregate Amazon **Simple Storage Service (S3)** charges across 12 AWS accounts. Here, we see Amazon S3 pricing for the S3 Standard storage class in the US East (OHIO) Region for individual accounts storing 45 **gigabytes (GB)** of data per month:

S3 Standard Storage Amount	Storage Cost per GB
First 50 TB / Month	$0.023
Next 450 TB / Month	$0.022
Over 500 TB / Month	$0.021

Account Name	Storage (GB)	Cost
Account A	45	$ 1.04
Account B	45	$ 1.04
Account C	45	$ 1.04
Account D	45	$ 1.04
Account E	45	$ 1.04
Account F	45	$ 1.04
Account G	45	$ 1.04
Account H	45	$ 1.04
Account I	45	$ 1.04
Account J	45	$ 1.04
Account K	45	$ 1.04
Account L	45	$ 1.04
Total	540	$ 12.42

Figure 2.9 – An Amazon S3 pricing example for a multi-account environment

Without consolidated billing, each account would be charged **US dollars (USD)** $1.04 (calculated as 45 GB x $0.23 rate) for 45 GB of storage for the month. The total monthly cost would be $12.42 (calculated as 12 x $1.04). With consolidated billing, the total storage is treated as one account, thus the rate would be $0.021 instead of $0.023. Using the $0.021 rate, your total then becomes $11.34, an 8.70% saving. Although this is a simple example reflecting nominal usage, savings accumulate quickly as usage increases. Our goal is to reduce waste, and these are just small steps in that direction.

> **Important note**
> AWS provides a 12-month Free Tier that allows customers to try AWS services free of charge for new accounts. However, if you use AWS Organizations to consolidate payment across multiple accounts, you will have access to only one Free Tier per organization.

The management account can view monthly usage by account in the billing console. Once you select a specific month's bill, you can select the **Bill details by account** tab to see each account's monthly charges within the organization, as illustrated in the following screenshot:

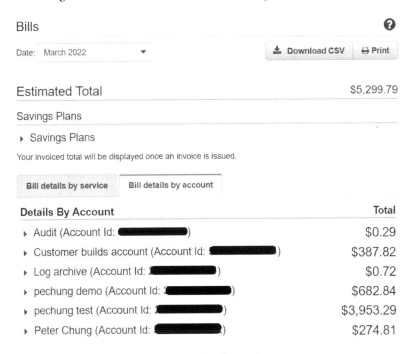

Figure 2.10 – Monthly charges by account

A Multi-Account Structure for VidyaGames

Jeremy and Ellia start to whiteboard a viable multi-account structure for *VidyaGames*. They decide AWS Control Tower is the easiest way to get started with a proven multi-account strategy based on best practices. By deploying a new organization through Control Tower, they establish a multi-account baseline with a log archive and audit account in the core OU provided through Control Tower. From the management account, they move all existing accounts into this newly created organization to leverage consolidated billing, volume-tier discounts, and better cost visibility.

After meeting with engineering teams, infrastructure teams, and business operations teams, Jeremy and Ellia realize that their AWS Organization's structure could be improved by grouping accounts by function. They created the following OUs to support their organization:

Infrastructure: This OU holds AWS accounts meant for shared infrastructure services such as networking and shared message buses.

Security: This OU holds AWS accounts hosting security-related access and services. Jeremy and Ellia move the Control Tower-initiated log archive and audit accounts into the Security OU. They also plan to create a security break glass account for emergency security incidents.

Sandbox: This OU allows developers to test applications and learn about different AWS services in a safe environment, with certain policies applied to the OU to control costs. Having this OU will help *VidyaGames* differentiate between applications that generate revenue and test applications for research and learning purposes.

Workload: This OU holds the bulk of revenue-generating applications for *VidyaGames*. Working with engineering teams, Jeremy expects to have sub-OUs within the Workload OU to delineate between test, development, staging, and production environments. This OU is also where AWS accounts for the software lifecycle are created to make deployed applications more resilient to organizational changes.

FinOps: This OU is where Jeremy expects to spend most of his time. The FinOps OU serves the finance teams. It has cost visibility across all accounts within *VidyaGames* for reporting purposes. It holds accounts that intend to centralize cost-saving mechanisms.

Suspended: This OU holds accounts that have been suspended and are on the verge of being deleted. Having this OU allows *VidyaGames* to differentiate between accounts that need to be cleaned up and do not deliver business value. Jeremy has an idea to use this OU as a black hole where no resources can or should be active.

With administrative privileges and consensus with various teams, Jeremy and Ellia start to create these OUs and move accounts into the appropriate OU. Jeremy makes sure there are no restrictions applied at the OU level. He does not want OU-based governance policies to disrupt any workloads running in the existing account. This is something he intends to address later.

By working with the email account administrator and AWS Support, they map currently active accounts to owners within the organization. Now, Jeremy feels he has a little more control over account assets within the company. With a renewed sense of ownership, he tackles a new challenge.

Ellia meets with Jeremy during the next cadence, then asks, "Now that all our accounts are in one place, what should our next step be?".

Summary

In this chapter, you learned the basics of an AWS account and the benefits of using multiple accounts. Structuring your AWS accounts will depend on your organization. You might segregate accounts by BU, application, application function, or a combination of these, and more.

You learned how to manage your accounts with AWS Organizations, group them through OUs, and use AWS Control Tower to quickly set up a multi-account environment.

You further learned how billing works with AWS Organizations. You can view usage by account from the management account and take advantage of volume-tier discounts through aggregated use.

Organizing accounts is the first step toward reducing waste since all resources are associated with an account. Possessing good account hygiene helps find wasteful and lost resources that may become forgotten due to employee turnover or organizational changes.

Now that we have the foundation set with a multi-account environment, we can begin to understand which resources those accounts own. This is something we'll look at in the next chapter.

Further reading

For more information, refer to the following resources:

- *AWS Organizations now provides a simple, scalable, and more secure way to close your member accounts*, 2022: `https://aws.amazon.com/blogs/mt/aws-organizations-now-provides-a-simple-scalable-and-more-secure-way-to-close-your-member-accounts/`

- *What is AWS Billing?*, 2022: `https://docs.aws.amazon.com/awsaccountbilling/latest/aboutv2/billing-what-is.html`

- *Laying the Foundation: Setting Up Your Environment for Cost Optimization*, 2022: `https://docs.aws.amazon.com/whitepapers/latest/cost-optimization-laying-the-foundation/introduction.html`

3

Managing Inventory

With the right account structure in place, we can begin to work on managing **Amazon Web Services (AWS)** resources—those items that actually contribute to your costs. We will look at several tools that AWS provides that help you see the resources you have running within your accounts. These resources, plus your defined **financial operations (FinOps)** processes, make up your **inventory**.

We will then look at ways to manage your inventory with native AWS tools and explore the necessity of tags and how they increase visibility into your inventory. Cost optimization is not possible when you don't know what you have. Hence, this chapter provides you with the knowledge and tools needed to better manage your inventory.

In this chapter, we're going to cover the following main topics:

- Tracking your AWS resources
- Establishing a tagging strategy
- Grouping tags with AWS Cost Categories

Technical requirements

To complete the exercises in this chapter, you will need the same components specified in the previous chapter.

Knowing what you own

"Now that all our accounts are in one place, what should be our next step?" Ellia asks Jeremy as they discuss the next steps while eating lunch in the conference room.

Jeremy takes a bite of his sandwich and ponders to himself, "We have better control of our accounts… what should we have better control of next?" After swallowing his bite, he says out loud, "Do you know which things are running in our accounts?"

Ellia furrows her eyebrows and responds, "I don't entirely. I have a general idea of what is running but nothing in detail."

"Who would know? Maybe Ezra?"

"Ezra might know. But developers would definitely know since they are in those accounts almost every day. Well… at least, I hope they know. We can ask Ezra first."

Jeremy and Ellia invite Ezra to their next meeting and ask him the same question. Ezra shrugs and tells them, "Yeah, I know in general what the accounts are using. I know costs are rising month over month and I have a spreadsheet that breaks down the cost per AWS service. I've been tracking this information for months because it's easier to do it in a spreadsheet when I have so many bills to consolidate."

Jeremy updates Ezra on all the work that they've done in consolidating accounts, and how it may make Ezra's life easier by getting one bill. "Thanks. That's good news to hear. I think that will help", Ezra tells him.

"Ezra, do you have a way to see what each account is using? Maybe see what we're paying based on which service they are using?" Jeremy asks.

Ezra replies, "Yeah. I use a couple of tools for that. Here, let me show you."

Tracking your AWS resources

If you don't know what you're paying for, you'll find it to be quite tough to reduce waste. All jokes aside, we can take a simple yet relatable example of managing your own personal finances.

You would very likely be unsuccessful at managing your own personal finances if you didn't look at your monthly bill to see where you are spending your money. You may forget that you've been paying for a gym membership or a music subscription service that you no longer use, or the pest control service from your previous home. The same discipline of identifying wasteful spending and reducing unnecessary resource use should also apply to your AWS bill.

Fortunately, you don't have to wait until the end of the month to analyze your bill as you do your finances. You can, and should, track the resources that you are paying for on a regular basis. This is often the first step toward optimization because you must first know what you are using before you can optimize. Better yet, you might even identify resources that you don't need and can turn off entirely.

It's equally important to document your processes as well as your resources. It may very well be that you do not have any FinOps processes. That's understandable and perfectly valid when you are in the beginning stages of your FinOps journey. As you mature, by documenting processes you can iterate upon what works, what does not work, and what the **cloud center of excellence** (**CCoE**) and teams can do to improve waste reduction. The collection of your resources and these documented processes combined constitute your inventory.

A brief primer on tags

Tags are a critical part of inventory management. You can tag a resource by assigning it a key-value pair. In other words, tags are a type of metadata for your resources. For example, a tag key of `owner` with a value of `Peter` helps folks within your organization identify a resource. They may safely assume that Peter is the owner of that resource, and any questions about its use can be directed to him.

Tags are key (no pun intended) because they provide additional context to your resources. When you are managing your personal finances, sometimes you can come across a line item that you don't recognize. If you had a way to provide context to that line item (for example, I paid for gasoline in this city when I went to visit my friend on this date, even though I don't recognize the entity **Gas For Less, Inc**.), then you know that it is a legitimate charge. The same applies to your AWS resources. Tags provide you that justification for a resource's existence to prove that it is valuable to your business.

You can reduce waste by properly tagging your resources. Assuming teams adhere to an organization-wide tagging policy and that any tagged resources have a valid business purpose, then for any resources that are untagged, you might assume they don't bring value to your business. Then, you can work toward deprovisioning those resources in your effort to reduce waste. This is an aggressive, albeit effective, way to manage your cloud resources to maximize efficiency. Most organizations won't be at a level of maturity that reflects 100% of all cloud resources being tagged. However, this is a worthy goal to move toward. Some organizations might set goals that are at 60% and then increase these to higher values when they become more mature. Set whichever goals make sense to your business.

You can apply tags to your AWS resources, but you must know which AWS resources you have. The next section aims to alleviate the feeling of being overwhelmed but not knowing which resources you own and to whom they belong. We'll look at several AWS tools that can help.

Tracking inventory with AWS Cost Explorer

An easy way to track cost and usage for free on AWS is with **AWS Cost Explorer**. Cost Explorer provides a visual interface allowing you to see monthly, weekly, and daily spend on AWS resources. If you access Cost Explorer at the management account, you can see costs per account within your organization, providing you a single pane of glass to see usage for all your accounts.

> **Important note**
>
> Although Cost Explorer is free of charge, you must first enable the service before using it. Follow the instructions on AWS' documentation (`https://docs.aws.amazon.com/cost-management/latest/userguide/ce-enable.html`) to enable the service. You may have to wait up to 24 hours before accessing the service.

Cost Explorer has a simple interface where you can group by and filter on various attributes. For example, you can group by account to see which accounts were the highest spenders within a given period. Then, you can apply filters to see cost and usage for just the account with the highest spend. You can drill down further by seeing which services are costing the most and then drilling down on the **application programming interface (API)** operation used within that service.

You can create custom reports to meet your business needs. The following screenshot shows a breakdown of costs by service for the past 7 days:

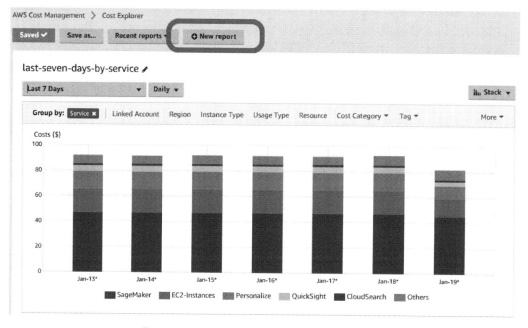

Figure 3.1 – A custom report in AWS Cost Explorer

Because Cost Explorer is free of charge, it's a great starting point to get a better understanding of your inventory.

Important note

If you access Cost Explorer at the member account level, you will only see cost and usage data for that account. You will not be able to see other accounts' usage. Multi-account visibility is only available through the management account.

You may realize a significant portion of your costs comes from a **RunInstance** API action in a Region that has no association with your company. By collaborating with the right teams, you may realize that a rogue server was left running in a remote Region that an individual forgot to turn off after doing some testing. Cost Explorer would provide you that visibility, along with the ability to see trends in usage across and within accounts, which is important in setting a spend baseline.

Using AWS Cost Explorer to Find a Rogue Instance

With access to the management account within *VidyaGames'* AWS Organization, Jeremy uses Cost Explorer to gain a high-level overview of spending patterns for the company's AWS accounts. Jeremy takes a 6-month view grouped by service and finds that Amazon **Elastic Compute Cloud (EC2)**, Amazon **Simple Storage Service (S3)**, and Amazon **Relational Database Service (RDS)** constitute the majority of monthly spend.

Jeremy notices a spike in usage in a particular month, and so he changes from a monthly to a daily view within the given month. This higher charge is coming from the Amazon EC2 service, but Jeremy is unsure of the originating AWS account with this view.

Jeremy then changes the grouping to view by linked account and adds a filter to only show charges associated with Amazon EC2 instances. Using this view, Jeremy narrows down his scope to an account within the Sandbox **organizational unit (OU)**. He cross-references the account **identifier (ID)** to its associated owner and finds that Andrew is the developer that owns the account.

Jeremy schedules a quick meeting with Andrew to review the usage. He communicates to Andrew that he's exercising cost discipline and doesn't intend to police resource use, but rather wants to ensure teams are optimizing their use of AWS.

"Oh, that?" Andrew responds. "That was something I was using to test upload speeds to our website. I purposely used a larger instance type to run a network performance benchmark. I thought I had terminated the instance, but I guess I left it running by accident."

"That's okay," Jeremy replies. "This isn't meant to be a slap on the wrist or anything. It's just something that I noticed when I was looking at the cost reports. Thanks for letting me know! I think it is good that we identified this. We really should be able to find these anomalies quickly and respond accordingly. This will help save on costs."

Using Cost Explorer requires low effort at a minor cost for Cost Explorer API calls. It can be used as a tool to get a preliminary view of your resources quickly, and it's a great starting point when you may not have complex tools or third-party tools available to manage costs.

Cost Explorer provides monthly and daily granularity at no cost. You can elect to have hourly granularity at the cost of **United States dollars** (**USD**) 0.01 per 1,000 `UsageRecord` instances a month. A `UsageRecord` instance is one line of usage. For example, an Amazon EC2 instance running for 24 hours a day will generate 24 `UsageRecord` instances at an hourly granularity.

Another way to obtain hourly cost and usage data is with **AWS Cost and Usage Reports** (**CURs**). We'll learn more about this in the next section.

Tracking inventory with AWS CUR

Cost Explorer is free of charge to a certain extent, and its native integration with the AWS **user interface** (**UI**) makes it easy to get started using it as a tool to view AWS cost and usage. However, it does have its limitations. For instance, you can only see historical data up to a 12-month lookback period. Additionally, you cannot use multi-dimensional queries such as grouping by several layers or visibility such as grouping spend by account, and also by service. Hourly granularity views in Cost Explorer come at a price. Fortunately, there is another native AWS offering at your disposal.

If you have and want to explore your cost data that goes beyond 12 months with support for hourly granularity, you can use AWS CUR. AWS CUR provides hour-level granularity for all charges across all your accounts. It also provides information Cost Explorer doesn't show, such as the unit of charge for your usage (such as **gigabyte** (**GB**) stored, network **input/output** (**I/O**) consumed), at what rates you were charged, and each line item description, all in tabular format. Perhaps the most beneficial is the fact that the tags that you apply are added to CUR. This provides you with a more customized view of your cost and usage that is contextual to your business.

As with Cost Explorer, to see aggregate account usage, you access AWS CUR through the management account. By default, accounts are limited to viewing cost and usage within their own account. Unlike Cost Explorer, however, you must set up CUR to have AWS deliver cost and usage data to a specified S3 bucket. Hence, you will be charged for the data stored in S3. We will discuss ways to optimize S3 storage costs in *Part 3, Operationalizing FinOps,* of the book.

You can activate CUR at an individual account level or the organization level, using the management account. The report includes using columns that help you track inventory, including account identifies, rates and cost, usage amount and unit, and any tags that you specify. CUR provides the most comprehensive way to track inventory with hour-level granularity and API-level tracking, as shown in the following screenshot. With tags appended as columns to CUR, it provides what you need to break down AWS costs by tag. Results show the start and end time of usage, service name, API action, and cost:

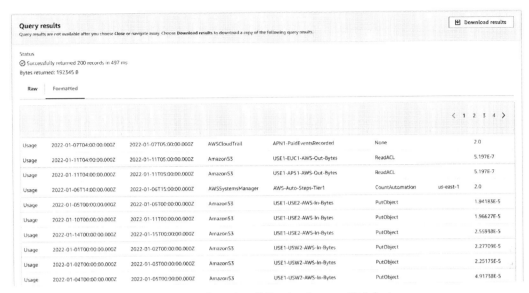

Figure 3.2 – Querying CUR using Amazon S3 Select

You can find the steps you need to take to activate CUR on the AWS website at `https://docs.`
`aws.amazon.com/cur/latest/userguide/cur-create.html`. Because it can take up to
24 hours for AWS to start delivering CUR data to your desired bucket, it will benefit you to have CUR
activated as early as possible. You can configure CUR to send data at hourly, daily, and monthly time
granularities, and if you need to, you can activate the `resource_id` parameter in the information
lines, but this has a cost. Although you can only choose a single-time granularity type at CUR creation,
you are free to create multiple reports to meet your needs. For example, you might set up a monthly
CUR report and a separate daily CUR report to be sent to separate buckets. These reports may serve
different purposes for distinct stakeholders.

Activating CUR for Visibility

Jeremy sees that *VidyaGames* does not have any CUR data, and immediately takes steps to activate
it in the AWS Billing console. Jeremy creates an Amazon S3 bucket in the management account
with the specific purpose of hosting CUR data. Having some data analytics experience in the
past, he understands that CUR data will be delivered to him in tabular format. To ensure that
he can make sense of the data, he needs to use a common query language such as **Structured
Query Language (SQL)**.

Given these requirements, he chooses daily time granularity and enables report data integration
for **Amazon Athena**. Jeremy is aware that Amazon Athena is a serverless interactive query
service. After watching some introductory videos on Athena, Jeremy understands that once
AWS delivers the CUR files to his specified bucket, he will be able to use Athena to query the
data in S3 directly without having to move the data to another data source.

After activating CUR, he waits until the next day to find content in his S3 bucket.

CUR excels over Cost Explorer due to the amount of information it provides in a single dataset. Cost Explorer is a UI for preset queries on grouped costs, while CUR lets you create your own queries if the ones from Cost Explorer are not enough to meet your needs. With Cost Explorer, you must create separate views to see your cost data in the desired grouping. You may save a report that shows spend by service, and another report that shows spend by account. On the other hand, CUR provides all your data in tabular format, so you are free to slice and dice your data using familiar tools such as pivot tables in Microsoft Excel or SQL queries to run aggregations.

Although comprehensive, CUR is just a tabular dataset of your cost and usage. In other words, you must use another tool to visualize the CUR data. Because you can access CUR data as a **comma-separated values (CSV)** file, you can certainly use Microsoft Excel to create basic charts for ad hoc visualizations, but for scalability and shareability, you can use **Amazon QuickSight** as a **business intelligence (BI)** tool. With QuickSight, you can create dashboards using common visual charts such as bar graphs, line graphs, pie charts, and pivot tables. Then, you can save and publish your visuals as dashboards to share with teams. QuickSight has many more advanced capabilities, such as **machine learning (ML)**-based forecasting and insights.

As cost management tools, Cost Explorer and CUR can help you understand which resources you own. Another tool that helps you gain a global view on Amazon EC2-related resources is EC2 Global View. We'll look at this in the next section.

Tracking Amazon EC2 inventory with EC2 Global View

Amazon EC2 provides virtual computing environments on AWS. With Amazon EC2, you deploy virtual servers (also called instances) in minutes to run any kind of workload by specifying the type of instance to meet your business requirements. You can attach block storage to an Amazon EC2 instance. These are called **Elastic Block Store (EBS)** volumes that function like a hard drive on a personal computer.

A major benefit of Amazon EC2 is its elasticity—you provision the number of servers you need and pay for what you use. When you no longer need that compute capacity, you terminate the instance and no longer pay for that instance.

> **Important note**
>
> Amazon EC2 is a fundamental service on AWS. Learn more about it on the service documentation (see the references at the end of this chapter). Having a basic understanding of how Amazon EC2 works will be helpful for the upcoming topics in this book.

When you deploy Amazon EC2 instances, you place them in an **Amazon virtual private cloud** (**VPC**). Much like how you would deploy physical servers in a data center, you deploy virtual Amazon EC2 instances in an Amazon VPC. A VPC is a virtual network contained within your account. You can logically separate the network with **subnetworks** (**subnets**) that define a range of **Internet Protocol** (**IP**) addresses in your VPC. Additionally, you can define firewall settings for resources such as Amazon EC2 servers using security groups.

These services are commonly used by AWS customers. Fortunately, Amazon EC2 provides a global view of an account's instances, VPCs, subnets, security groups, and volumes. When you select **EC2 Global View** in the AWS Management Console, AWS provides a dashboard displaying all your Amazon EC2-related resources, as shown in the following screenshot. You can also run a global search to filter resource ID, tags, or Region, and subsequently download the report as a CSV file for further analysis. Note that these resources are limited to those listed previously. If you want a comprehensive list of AWS resources, then use AWS Cost Explorer:

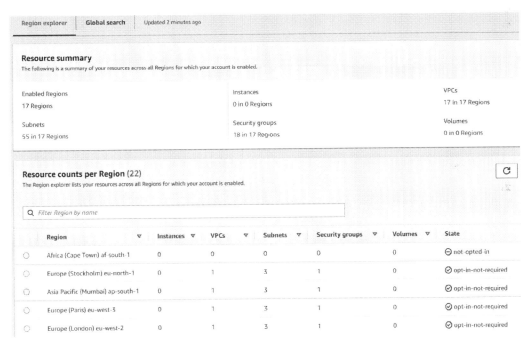

Figure 3.3 – Amazon EC2 Global View

AWS assigns a resource ID for Amazon EC2 resources within a Region. You can reference these resource IDs when searching for resources in Amazon EC2. In *Figure 3.3*, you can see EC2 Global View showing instances, VPCs, subnets, security groups, and volumes in all enabled Regions.

Using EC2 Global View

Jeremy understands that Amazon EC2 is one of the highest-spend services for *VidyaGames* across all AWS accounts, and while the exercise he completed to find a rogue Amazon EC2 server worked in Cost Explorer, it was a bit more cumbersome than he would have liked it to be. Fortunately, with his knowledge of EC2 Global View, he found a much better way to identify Amazon EC2-specific resources.

With read permissions for EC2 resources within the appropriate accounts, Jeremy uses Global View to get resource counts across all Regions. This makes it easier to him to view existing resources, rather than having to set up multiple reports and repeat filtering processes in Cost Explorer, especially when he needs to focus on EC2-specific resources.

Additionally, Jeremy uses EC2 Global View to not only clean up unused instances but unused security groups and EBS volumes as well. As an exercise like spring cleaning, Jeremy gains more confidence in being able to tidy up the company's AWS resources, which provides a renewed sense of control.

With AWS CUR set up for the organization, Jeremy, Ezra, and Ellia have increased visibility into their cloud spend. They've created some reports in AWS Cost Explorer that show spending by member accounts, service, and Region. These regular reports give them a general understanding of how much teams are spending on AWS resources daily.

Jeremy has also set up CUR and has found the S3 bucket being populated with cost and usage data aggregated at the daily level. With the Athena integration, Jeremy can run basic SQL queries on the CUR data to see the top 10 spenders by account, service, and other interesting facts, such as the most used instance types. Having this visibility will help use data to develop cost optimization strategies for *VidyaGames*.

EC2 Global View is a useful tool for viewing EC2 instances, VPCs, subnets, security groups, and EBS volumes across AWS Regions. EC2 Global View is more specific in scope compared to Cost Explorer, but it provides a single pane of glass when you need to view EC2-related resources that are commonly a top spend for many AWS customers.

EC2 Global View helps identify resources within the Amazon EC2 domain. Let's see how AWS Resource Groups can help identify resources across all domains, especially those without tags.

Tracking tagged resources with AWS Resource Groups

You can organize your AWS resources with **AWS Resource Groups**. Resource groups are another way to manage inventory and catalog more resources than what EC2 Global View provides (see the previous section).

Resource groups help organize resources with similar tags. This makes it easy for you to find logically grouped resources. For example, if you tagged an Amazon EC2 instance, an Amazon S3 bucket, and a VPC with the same tag, then you can group those three resources into a resource group. You can query all EC2 instances with that tag and conduct other inventory management tasks. These resources might make up an application. So, grouping resources by a tag-like application allows you to see the total cost associated with running an application.

In the following screenshot, you will see a tag-based query to group all resources in a selected Region with the `Project` tag key and `JupyterNotebook` value. You can then see all resources with this key-value pair:

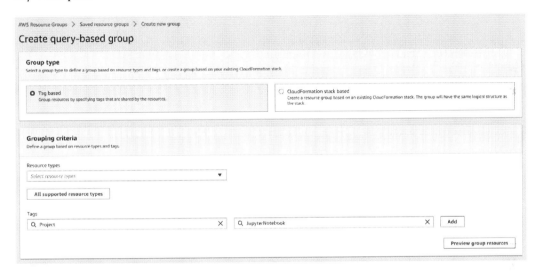

Figure 3.4 – Querying in AWS Resource Groups

Tag Editor is a capability within AWS Resource Groups that helps you find resources to tag. There may be cases where teams provisioned a group of resources pertaining to a specific business case. Perhaps these resources are all tagged by a specific application name, but developers forgot to apply an owner tag. With Tag Editor, you can find this group of resources with a similar application tag, and retroactively apply the owner tag in bulk.

Tag Editor also provides a view of resources that do not have any tags. This could be useful if you wanted a starting inventory to view untagged resources before implementing a tagging strategy. Note that you may not be able to query all resources using this method. AWS updates a list of resources you can use with Tag Editor (see the links in the references section at the end of this chapter).

To obtain a list of resources with specific tags or no tags at all, you can use Tag Editor in the management console. You can choose multiple Regions at once, specify resource types, and optionally select one or more tags (see *Figure 3.5*). Tag Editor will search your inventory, allowing you to export the results to a CSV file. You can also select multiple resources and manage tags directly in the **AWS Management Console** (see *Figure 3.6*).

The following screenshot shows how you can find all supported resource types to tag within the US-East (N. Virginia) Region using Tag Editor:

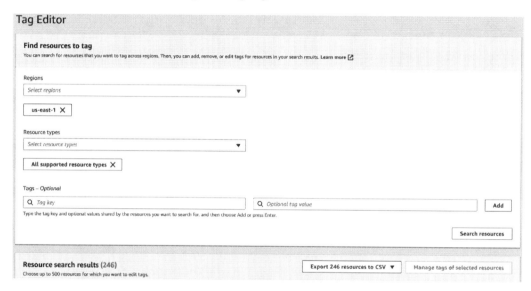

Figure 3.5 – Querying with Tag Editor

After obtaining results from a query, the following screenshot shows applying the owner:peter key-value pair as tags for the resulting resources. This enables you to apply tags to resources in bulk retroactively:

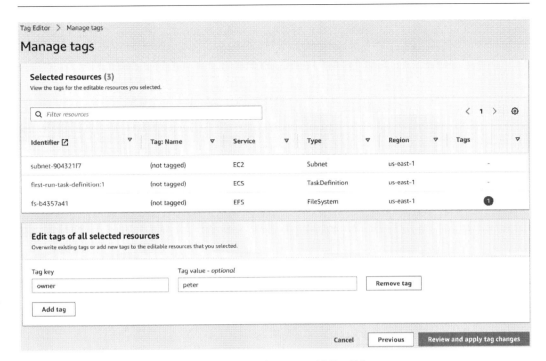

Figure 3.6 – Managing tags with Tag Editor

It's reasonable that not all resources require tags. For example, some organizations may not find value in tagging a resource such as a **Dynamic Host Configuration Protocol** (**DHCP**) option set because that type of network protocol is expected for virtual servers in a network. Apart from that, Tag Editor is a useful tool to expose those resources without tags.

Tag Editor helps you get lists of resources with or without intended tags. You can use the service to understand which resources are running within an AWS account. Then, you can apply tags retroactively, enabling those resources to comply with your organization's tagging strategy. However, Tag Editor cannot enforce any tagging requirements. This calls for another service, which is what we'll look at next.

Tracking inventory with AWS Config

AWS Config is a service that helps you keep track of your inventory and any changes made to your inventory. Imagine AWS Config as a surveillance camera monitoring your AWS resources. For example, perhaps you use AWS Config to see all resources and their configurations in a given week. In the following week when you log back into the **Config** console, you now can see that resources decreased by a certain amount, with slight changes to their configuration. AWS Config provides this view for a single account, but also for your entire organization through the management account.

Unlike the other methods of tracking inventory that we explored in this chapter, you must initialize AWS Config with some setup, although you can set up Config in *one click*. The setup process involves choosing the resources you want Config to monitor and sending those results to an S3 bucket. Then, you specify which rules those resources should follow. Config will monitor your resources according to your defined rules and inform you if those resources are compliant.

For example, if you require all EC2 instances across your organization to be tagged with an `owner` key and the necessary value, you can specify the EC2 resource type and this rule in Config. Config will then monitor your inventory and display those resources as compliant according to the rule, as shown in the following screenshot. Here, we see an AWS Config resource inventory showing all resource types and their respective compliance statuses. For example, we see certain Amazon EC2 subnets marked as **Noncompliant**. We will take a closer look at governing your resources in *Chapter 5, Governing Cost and Usage*:

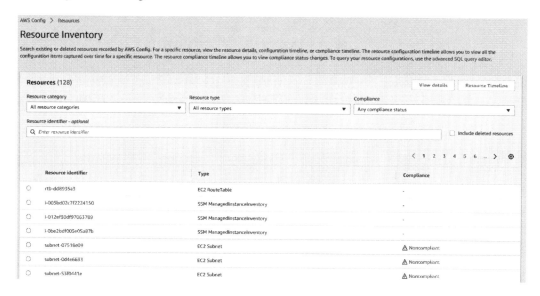

Figure 3.7 – AWS Config resource inventory view

Config is much more valuable as a management and governance tool than it is simply as an inventory management tool. Indeed, Config can help you view your inventory, but it can—and should—be used to do much more than that. We'll take a closer look at how it can help with FinOps controls and governance in the next chapter.

In this section, we looked at Cost Explorer, CUR, Tag Editor, and AWS Config as tools that help you gain a better understanding of all resources running within your AWS accounts. You can use these tools as starting points if you're unsure of which resources you have running. This is required for any cost-saving strategy because you must know what you own before you can optimize. To ensure all teams take ownership of the resources they deploy, it helps to have a tagging strategy, which we'll discuss next.

Establishing a tagging strategy

A clear and clean tagging strategy aligned to the needs of your business will improve your ability to track resources, and subsequently reduce waste. Verifying a resource's purpose will justify its existence in bringing value to the business. At the same time, justifying a resource's termination also brings value to the business by eliminating waste.

The right tagging strategy will change depending on the organization. In fact, the right tagging strategy can change within an organization over time as teams, priorities, and business needs change. However, there are some general best practices you can include to set up a tagging strategy that works for you.

Set up tags for cost allocation. This can be in the form of business tags that help folks see the cost center, BU, or a project the resource supports. You may want to align cost allocation tags to your financial reporting practices. For example, your financial department has reports that cover several dimensions such as BU, cost center, or geographic area. Aligning cost allocation tags to existing processes will help streamline reporting.

Use a common language when naming tags. Include all necessary stakeholders when establishing your tagging strategy. If developers are tagging cost centers in a way that's unexpected to how finance reports on those tags, then the reports may reflect inaccurate data. For instance, if developers are tagging resources using the name of `cost-allocation-center` but finance teams expect the tag name to be `cost-center`, it may lead to a misinterpretation of data. Establishing consistent language and naming standards that all teams adhere to will improve your tagging hygiene and, ultimately, better inventory visibility.

This leads to another important aspect of employing a cross-functional team to identify the right tagging requirements for your organization. Although finance teams may primarily be concerned with cost allocation tags, business teams and application teams may require other metadata associated with resources. Ensure all teams are aligned on tagging requirements and that stakeholders can refer to a **source of truth** (**SOT**) when providing tag names and values. We'll dive deeper into tagging governance in *Chapter 4, Planning and Metrics Tracking*.

Create open channels of conversation, set up a regular cadence among cross-functional teams to discuss tagging hygiene, and consider pivoting on tagging strategies when needed. You may not need to change your tagging strategy, but it's still important to communicate consistent use of tags and tag values.

> **Applying a Tagging Strategy at VidyaGames**
>
> Jeremy and Ellia begin scheduling regular meetings with technology teams to formulate a tagging strategy. Through these meetings, they agree on a common nomenclature to tag resources based on the application name, owner, cost center, and schedule. Through these conversations, teams realize that a tag of `schedule` will help inform teams of how long a resource is expected to run. Delineating between resources that need to be up 24/7 versus resources that only need to be up for a few hours allows the teams to be diligent in reducing waste. Jeremy's mind begins percolating ideas of using automation to stop instances with a `schedule` tag that specifies business-day use.

Keep in mind the downstream effects of changing tags. Changing tag names may lead to inconsistencies in reporting when comparing a resource with a new tag from today to the same resource with an old tag from several weeks ago. Or, if you have policies that require a certain tag, you may need to update that policy to accommodate the new tag. Communicate changes to tagging strategies and create a change management process to minimize adverse effects.

Be aware of AWS tagging limitations. Currently, there is a limit of 50 user-created tags. Choose the appropriate number of tags that provide the most clarity. Sometimes, adding too many tags creates unnecessary noise. Using the fewest number of tags necessary can help keep your reporting clean.

We've seen the importance of tags toward waste reduction and inventory management, but tags can be too granular at times. If you need a coarser way to manage resources or group resources together by tag, use AWS Cost Categories.

Grouping tags with AWS Cost Categories

At this point, you are aware of the AWS tools that can help provide an inventory of resources across your accounts. You know that you can apply tags and associate resources with meaningful organizational assets such as owners, applications, cost centers, and BUs. Combining these strategies and tools can help you start to identify resources that you can terminate.

AWS Cost Categories provides an additional layer of resource management and cost visibility. There may be cases where your tagging strategy is either too granular or too coarse to provide the information you need. For example, perhaps you organize your accounts to support multiple applications. You have a structure that mimics the one shown here:

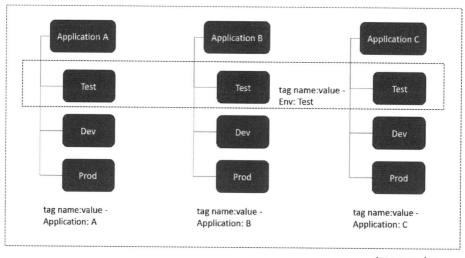

Figure 3.8 – Using AWS Cost Categories to group tags together

Applications **A**, **B**, and **C** are their own OU. Within each OU, there are three accounts to represent different environments. You initially assign tags to both accounts and resources within those accounts to reflect the application name. The tags for resources in application **A** would have a name-value pair as `Application: A`.

Using Cost Categories, you can group these tags to represent different levels of granularity. For example, you may group the tags for applications **A**, **B**, and **C** into one category that presents a full workload. Perhaps all three applications work together to support a specific product (in this case, `OurProduct`). You can use Cost Categories to then group these tags to show the total cost of that product.

Another way to slice and dice this environment is to create another cost category for just the test environments representing all three applications. Cost Categories allows you to create rules using different dimensions such as account ID, resource type, and tags. In this case, you could create a category that encompasses just the test environments for the application to see how much you are spending on testing in total for the product.

Your cost categories will reflect in both Cost Explorer and CUR. Use it to your advantage to help you gain visibility into resource use. Ideally, every meaningful resource should be tagged and categorized into logical groupings. This will allow you to isolate resources that don't have tags under the assumption that tagless resources don't provide value to your business. You can then prioritize terminating these resources to reduce waste.

Summary

In this chapter, you learned about the various ways you can create an inventory of your AWS resources. You learned that you can get started easily by enabling Cost Explorer and using the interface to view your resources. For a more detailed and granular view, you can use AWS CUR to have AWS send you monthly reports on cost and usage across your organization.

You further discovered other ways to gather inventory, including EC2 Global View for resources related to Amazon EC2 and Amazon VPC, Resource Groups and Tag Editor, enabling you to export results to a CSV file, and AWS Config for ongoing inventory management and change.

You gained an understanding of the importance of a tagging strategy that works for your organization. There are certain tagging best practices that you can apply, but it's important to implement your strategy with cross-functional collaboration and streamlined communication.

Finally, you learned about how AWS Cost Categories provides you with ways to group tags to provide another layer of inventory visibility. By combining these concepts, you can begin to map resources to business value and prioritize cleaning up resources that cannot be mapped to a use case. This brings you a few steps closer to eliminating waste.

With a better grasp on the resources you own, you now want to better plan for future costs and usage. This implies a need for proper planning and budgeting, topics we'll explore in the next chapter.

Further reading

Have a look at the following resources:

- *Enabling Cost Explorer*, 2022: `https://docs.aws.amazon.com/cost-management/latest/userguide/ce-enable.html`

- *Filtering and retrieving data using Amazon S3 Select*, 2022: `https://docs.aws.amazon.com/AmazonS3/latest/userguide/selecting-content-from-objects.html`

- *What is Amazon EC2?*, 2022: `https://docs.aws.amazon.com/AWSEC2/latest/UserGuide/concepts.html`

- *Resource IDs*, 2022: `https://docs.aws.amazon.com/AWSEC2/latest/UserGuide/resource-ids.html`

- *Resources you can use with AWS Resource Groups and Tag Editor*, 2022: `https://docs.aws.amazon.com/ARG/latest/userguide/supported-resources.html`

- *Setting Up AWS Config with the Console*, 2022: `https://docs.aws.amazon.com/config/latest/developerguide/gs-console.html`

- *Tagging AWS resources*, 2022: `https://docs.aws.amazon.com/general/latest/gr/aws_tagging.html`

4
Planning and Metrics Tracking

Having a strong knowledge of your AWS inventory enables waste reduction efforts because many teams are often overwhelmed with not knowing what they own. You cannot optimize if you don't know what to optimize. A central FinOps function such as a CCOE can be the enabler that encourages teams to take ownership of their resources while maintaining a high-level view of all the organization's resources themselves. We looked at several tools that AWS provides to help with inventory management in the previous chapter.

Layering planning, budgeting, and tracking on top of your inventory management work can only improve your waste reduction efforts. This chapter outlines how you can add on these layers. We will look at how to monitor costs on AWS, and how to apply budgets to your AWS expenditure to keep your cost and usage in line with your business goals. Finally, we will explore how to respond to anomalies in cost and usage in near real time, using tools such as anomaly detection.

Baselining cloud expenditure at VidyaGames

With an overall tagging strategy set, Jeremy and Ezra meet to discuss baselining their cloud expenditure.

Jeremy asks Ezra, "Now that we have some controls in place, I think I have a general understanding of how much we're spending on AWS daily. Is this consistent with what you've seen over the past few months?"

"Yes, it's within range. Of course, there are days where usage spikes, but they're mostly just temporary," Ezra replies.

"I think it's important that we monitor those spikes in case they last longer than we want. We want to be able to explain our costs consistently, don't you think?"

Ezra sighs a breath of relief. "This is something that we've wanted to implement for a while. I think we should go and talk to Alexander. He's the chief of staff at the office of the CFO. I've talked with him a couple of times. It would be good to get his support on this."

In this chapter, we're going to cover the following main topics:

- Cost monitoring on AWS

- Budgeting on AWS

- Responding quickly with Cost Anomaly Detection

Technical requirements

To complete the exercises in this chapter, the requirements will be the same as the previous chapters.

Cost monitoring on AWS

We will begin by looking at the various tools AWS provides for native cost monitoring and reporting. We'll dive deeper into AWS Cost Explorer's capabilities on this front while introducing new AWS analytics services such as Amazon Athena and Amazon QuickSight for reporting. We'll also see how Amazon CloudWatch, an AWS environment monitoring service, can help with cost monitoring among many other capabilities. Let's dive right in.

Cost monitoring with Cost Explorer

We learned that AWS Cost Explorer is a good tool for getting started with what resources you own. As helpful as this can be, waste reduction is just one aspect of it. Cost Explorer can also help you analyze cost and usage, forecast your expenditure, and detect anomalies. We'll first focus on using it to analyze cost and usage.

Cost Explorer provides a lookback of 12 months for viewing your cost and usage. It also forecasts aggregate expenditure for up to 12 months into the future. Cost Explorer automatically provides forecasting abilities without you needing to set up any configurations. You can easily see a few predictions within the Cost Explorer console.

Reports are useful for saving time, creating repeatable views, and sharing information with stakeholders across your organization. You can access several reports in Cost Explorer that the service provides by default. These default reports provide basic information such as daily costs, monthly costs by service, and monthly costs through a linked account. These can be great starting points to increase your visibility. Furthermore, you can tailor these reports, or create custom ones yourself, to help gather the data that you need to reduce waste.

Let's assume you wanted to track the costs for a new application built on AWS and tag all the application components, granting you the granularity to see how much the business is spending not only on the entire application but also on individual components of it. You can create a custom report, applying a filter using the application tag to have Cost Explorer display the AWS resources associated with that tag.

It's important, and necessary, to activate the tag through the management account. *Figure 4.1* shows how to activate **Cost allocation tags** for Cost Explorer to display on its interface. It demonstrates an **Application** tag. Keep in mind that tag keys are case-sensitive – thus, *Application* will be different from *application*. You have to select **Cost allocation tags** in the **AWS Billing** console and select the tags that you want to activate:

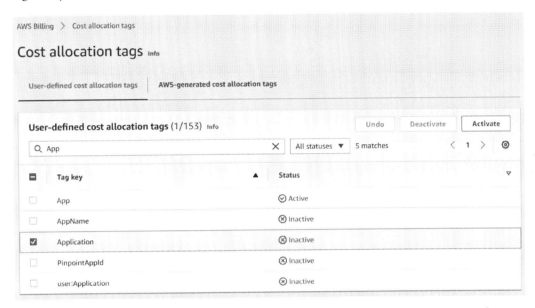

Figure 4.1 – Activating cost allocation tags

> **Important note**
> It can take up to 24 hours for tags to appear in Cost Explorer. AWS does not retroactively apply tags to your reports, so if you activate a tag 3 months after a workload launch, you'll only be able to see costs from the 3-month point onward.

Cost Explorer presents cost data in a few ways. The most commonly referenced term is **unblended costs**. Unblended costs represent the amount charged to you the moment that you used a service. If you used an EC2 instance for 1 hour and it costs $1.00 per hour, the unblended cost is simply $1.00.

Amortized cost is another commonly used term that shows costs accrued over a specific period. We'll discuss reserved instances, Savings Plans, and their pricing mechanisms in *Chapter 6*, *Optimizing Compute*, in greater detail, but for now, simply know that you can purchase compute resources upfront. Rather than paying an hourly rate, you can choose to pay for compute resources in advance at a discounted rate. You can view these upfront purchases amortized over time, in addition to viewing them in their unblended form. To compare, with unblended costs, you would see a relatively large spike in cost that may reflect a large upfront payment, or you can change to an amortized view to see that charge amortized monthly.

For example, suppose you bought a reserved instance lasting 1 year for $1,200. The unblended cost option might show a tall bar reflecting $1,200 at the purchase month. Alternatively, amortized costs will spread out that $1,200 to show $200 every month (for 6 months) beginning on the purchase month. Depending on your needs, you can choose the cost display option that works best. *Figure 4.2* compares the two views, reflecting either **Unblended** as one large cost issued in January or **Amortized,** spreading the cost over 6 months:

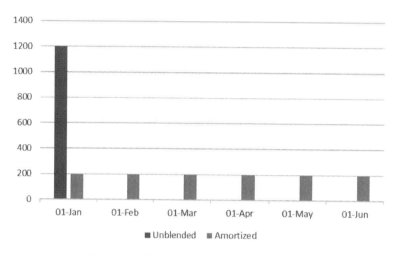

Figure 4.2 – Unblended versus amortized costs

Blended rates show an average rate across accounts, regardless of how much each account used. *Table 4.1* shows a hypothetical example of an organization-wide usage of 70 GB. Each account used a different amount, but we calculate the blended rate by dividing the total cost ($1,000) by the total usage amount (700 GB) to get a blended rate of $1.45. This rate will be different from the actual pricing of the service. Also, the total cost will be the same regardless of using unblended rates or blended rates. The blended rate simply provides another way to allocate costs if the average rate across all users is more suitable for your financing purposes:

Account	Used GB	Blended cost
Account A	100	$142.86
Account B	150	$214.29
Account C	200	$285.71
Account D	250	$357.14
Total	700	
Blended rate	$1.43	
Total cost	$1,000	

Table 4.1 – Blended rates with hypothetical data

> **Important note**
>
> The preceding example does not reflect actual AWS pricing. It was meant merely for example purposes. Blended rates may serve a specific purpose, but unblended rates are likely more applicable.

Because Cost Explorer is free to use, it's a great starting tool to get a baseline of your AWS cost and usage. It provides enough information for you to understand costs for all accounts within your organization if accessing it from the management account. It has out-of-the-box reports, basic filters, and groupings to slice and dice your cost data to meet your needs. However, if you wanted to run custom queries and ask specific questions about your cost and usage, it helps to use analytics services.

Cost monitoring with AWS analytics services

In addition to Cost Explorer, you learned about the **Cost and Usage Report** (**CUR**) in the previous chapter. You can use the CUR to further customize your cost monitoring needs and get another view of your cost and usage in tabular format. AWS provides a refreshed dataset reflecting your cost and usage up to three times a day. It's up to you to determine what to do with that data. Here are a few options.

You can query the data using **Amazon Athena**. Athena is a serverless interactive query service that allows you to query your data stored in Amazon S3 without having to provision and manage any underlying infrastructure (hence, serverless). Because AWS sends the CUR to an S3 bucket that you specify, Athena is an obvious choice for interacting with that data with minimal effort. In fact, you have the option to integrate the CUR with Athena (or Redshift, or QuickSight, for that matter) when you initially create the CUR.

Once you set up integration between your CUR data and Athena, you can query your data directly in the Athena **Query Editor** using standard SQL. As an example, the following query displays the top costs from largest to smallest, associated with the Amazon EC2 product. It outputs the AWS-designated product code (that is, Amazon EC2) and a description to provide some context:

```
SELECT
  line_item_product_code,
  line_item_line_item_description,
  SUM(line_item_unblended_cost) AS sum_line_item_unblended_cost
FROM
  {YOUR_TABLE_NAME}
WHERE
  line_item_product_code LIKE '%AmazonEC2%'
  AND line_item_line_item_type NOT IN ('Tax','Refund','Credit')
AND "month" = date_format(now(), '%c')
AND "year" = date_format(now(), '%Y')
```

```
GROUP BY
  line_item_product_code,
  line_item_line_item_description
ORDER BY
  sum_line_item_unblended_cost DESC;
```

Figure 4.3 shows the results from the preceding query in the AWS Management Console. The bottom section of the page displays the query output, which you can download as a **Comma-Separated Values (CSV)** file. These are the top costs associated with the Amazon EC2 service:

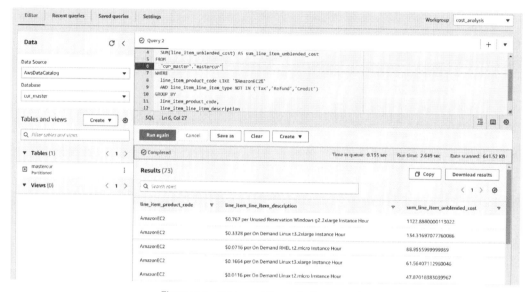

Figure 4.3 – Amazon Athena in the console

You can save queries and create views just as you can create reports with Cost Explorer. However, you must consider your own costs to use the CUR and Athena. Remember, Cost Explorer is free when you are using it to view cost and usage data at monthly and daily intervals. Meanwhile, hourly granularity in Cost Explorer comes with a cost.

Using the CUR and Athena also comes with a cost. You have to pay for storing the CUR data in Amazon S3 and pay per TB scanned when running Athena queries. That said, Athena is best suited for ad hoc reports that don't require long-running queries that scan entire datasets. CUR data can accumulate, especially if you're a large organization. It would be wasteful to use Athena for tasks that you can replicate on Cost Explorer. Use Athena when you need to run ad hoc and more complex queries to find results that Cost Explorer can't otherwise provide.

If you plan to create a data lake of cost data, you can also integrate the CUR with **Amazon Redshift**. Redshift is a fully managed, cloud-native data warehouse. As with Athena, you use SQL syntax to query data, but unlike with Athena, you have to create and manage a Redshift cluster. Also, unlike Athena, you pay per hour for running the cluster, as well as the amount of data stored. There are many other aspects of Redshift pricing available online that I won't detail further. Because the CUR provides you with the option to integrate with Redshift at creation time, you can use Redshift as a data store if you're looking to warehouse your cost data.

Amazon Athena is great for those familiar with SQL. However, it is unable to visualize your data into shareable dashboards. To meet those needs, you can use **Amazon QuickSight**.

Cost reporting with QuickSight

If you want to build your own custom dashboards using the CUR data on AWS, you can use Amazon QuickSight as a visualization tool. As with Athena, QuickSight is serverless, which makes it easy for you to get started. You can connect QuickSight to your CUR data in Amazon S3, or upload a CSV or Excel file directly into QuickSight.

From the QuickSight interface, you can run analyses, create and share dashboards, and use ML and **Natural Language Processing** (**NLP**) to gather insights from your cost data. *Figure 4.4* shows a sample of a QuickSight analysis within a dashboard. Here's a QuickSight visual showing the potential savings if you were to use Amazon EC2 Sopt Instances instead of on-demand instances. You can see savings by account and instance type. We'll take a closer look at the mechanics of EC2 Spot in *Chapter 6*, *Optimizing Compute*. A dashboard can have an analysis in the form of a bar chart, another analysis in the form of a pivot table, and a third analysis representing the data in a pie chart:

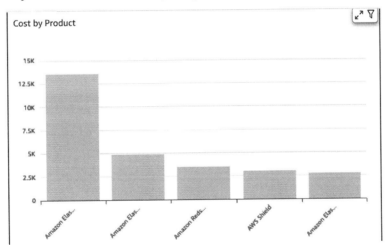

Figure 4.4 – A sample QuickSight dashboard

QuickSight provides more customization options than Cost Explorer. For example, you can create a custom-calculated field that Cost Explorer might not provide otherwise. Indeed, the CUR has more fields by default than Cost Explorer. Hence, if you wanted to create visuals using CUR data, then QuickSight is a natural choice due to its native integration with the CUR.

QuickSight also provides embedding capabilities. Organizations that are further along in their FinOps journey might create their own custom reporting tools using the CUR while embedding QuickSight into an application. Just ensure that the means justify the end, considering QuickSight's cost implications and the work hours involved.

> **Helpful hint**
>
> If you are interested in a sample CUR-centric QuickSight sample, you can explore AWS' **Cost Intelligence** dashboard for inspiration (see the *Further reading* section at the end of this chapter).

Visualizations and queries help us understand historical data. These tools can be used for forecasting and monitoring, but we often want to respond to events that happen within our AWS accounts quickly. For that, we need to turn to active monitoring with **Amazon CloudWatch**.

Cost monitoring with Amazon CloudWatch

The first thing that should come to mind when you hear the terms *logs*, *metrics*, and *events* on AWS is Amazon CloudWatch. CloudWatch is AWS' unified logs platform, used to monitor everything from application to infrastructure to events happening in your account. Clearly, cost and usage data are a form of metric data for your infrastructure. As it turns out, you can monitor billing in CloudWatch.

Monitoring billing activity in CloudWatch makes sense if you are already using CloudWatch for infrastructure and application monitoring. You can create dashboards in CloudWatch containing various widgets that display a desired metric, as shown in *Figure 4.5*. You can apply different functions on these metrics to represent your data in different ways, whether that's an average over a period, the total, or the minimum and maximum values of a metric:

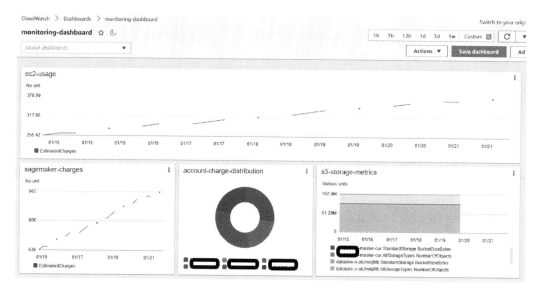

Figure 4.5 – A CloudWatch dashboard

Because CloudWatch encompasses all metrics, it's most useful when you are monitoring cost next to other metrics. For example, you may create a dashboard that monitors autoscaling activity for EC2 instances. You might include a widget to monitor autoscaling metrics such as `GroupInServiceInstances` and `GroupTerminatingInstances`, while also monitoring costs for EC2 instances that belong to the autoscaling group. Having the information in one place is more convenient than having to reconcile autoscaling activity with Cost Explorer reports.

> **Important note**
>
> Consider using CloudWatch metrics for billing when you are already using CloudWatch for monitoring your workload. This removes the waste of using CloudWatch specifically for billing purposes when you can do this more cost-effectively with Cost Explorer.

You can also incorporate alarms and even anomaly detection into your CloudWatch metrics. A simple example would be to create a billing alarm in CloudWatch to notify you when a metric such as **Total Estimated Charge** exceeds a certain price threshold. When this is triggered, CloudWatch sends an alarm to an Amazon **Simple Notification Service** (**SNS**) topic. You can subscribe to this topic and be notified of the billing alarm.

> **Important note**
>
> Think of Amazon SNS as a messaging service. SNS provides topics that you can subscribe to, as you might subscribe to an RSS feed. If the topic interests you, every time there is an update, you receive a notification.

You are charged for using the metrics, dashboards, alarms, and anomaly detection features in CloudWatch. For this reason, it's a less cost-effective method than using Cost Explorer, but can still provide value to your teams if they want to monitor costs next to other application metrics.

We looked at the ways you can monitor your cost and usage using Cost Explorer, the CUR, and CloudWatch. These tools largely perform the same function but accomplish them in different ways.

Cost Explorer is the easiest to get started with because it is AWS' native cost management and visibility tool. It provides default reports and filters that you can use to drill down on cost and usage, and see trends over time. The CUR provides you with the data you need for granularity and additional details. Although the CUR itself doesn't cost anything, storing the data incurs financial costs, and making sense of it requires allocating time and resources. CloudWatch is AWS' native monitoring tool but unlike Cost Explorer, its purpose isn't solely to provide cost and usage visibility. You can use the data CloudWatch provides to monitor costs, but CloudWatch excels when used with other forms of monitoring, such as application and system logs.

These tools help look at cost and usage primarily from a historical perspective. Let's explore the other side of cost management, which is to plan for the future through budgets and forecasting.

Budgeting on AWS

The principles of budgeting your cloud expenditure are not much different from budgeting in other financial contexts. When you budget, you normally identify a reasonable baseline. You cannot budget $5 for food in a month while budgeting $5,000 for entertainment. I suppose in extreme circumstances this may work, but not for most of us. The point is that you set a reasonable variable target and measure your actual costs to that target. You track performance over time and, as your needs change, you re-evaluate your budget to accommodate new situations.

You can use **AWS Budgets** to apply the same discipline to your cost and usage of AWS resources. AWS Budgets provides budgets for cost, usage, reserved instances, and Savings Plans. (We'll learn about the mechanisms of reserved instances and Savings Plans in *Part 2*.) Setting up cost budgets helps you track costs and set targets so that you can see how well you are performing daily, monthly, quarterly, and annually. Setting up usage budgets helps track the use of a service, which can be especially helpful if you are tracking usage to see how close you are to reaching a free tier limit.

From previous chapters, we know that we can establish a cost and usage baseline from Cost Explorer and the CUR. These data sources will help your organization set reasonable budgets. *Figure 4.6* shows a simple bar chart of the daily expenditure for an organization across all Regions. In a simplified view, you baseline your AWS spend to be about $100 per day. You can use this information to set budgets and configure alerts when AWS expenditure meets or exceeds a certain threshold:

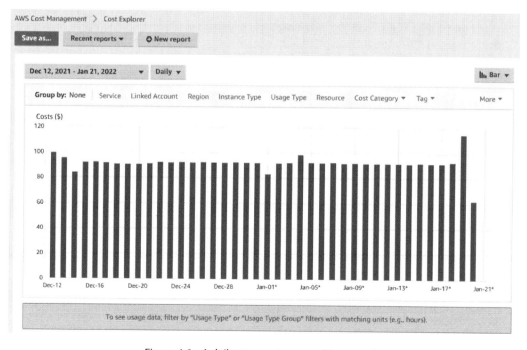

Figure 4.6 – A daily aggregate expenditure graph

Having budgets and alerts allows you to respond quickly to unexpected costs. If these alerts lead to a poorly provisioned server that can be terminated the next day due to notifications, then that helps to reduce waste, rather than you finding out about the resource months later. You can configure AWS to send you alerts not only to an email address but also to chat channels such as Amazon Chime or Slack, depending on the types of messaging and communications service your organization uses.

In *Figure 4.7*, we configure AWS to send an email to recipients when our expenditure exceeds 20% of our budgeted amount (e.g., $120). We see a cost bar graph showing aggregate daily expenditure across all the AWS Regions. A user sets a daily budget when the AWS expenditure exceeds 20% of a budgeted amount. You might have different cost thresholds. You can configure alerts to meet your thresholds and be notified of events that help you meet your financial goals.

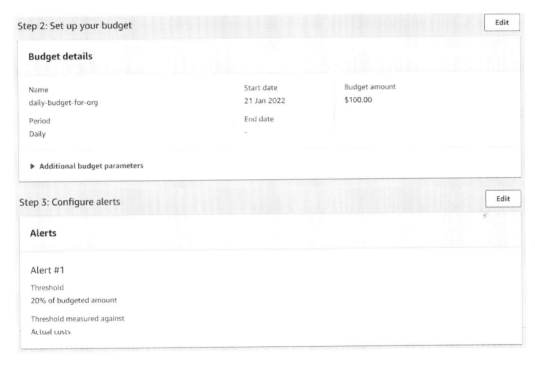

Figure 4.7 – Budget notifications in AWS

Amazon SNS natively integrates with AWS Budgets, making it a natural solution to integrate messaging into your budget alerts. With Amazon SNS, you configure AWS Budgets to send notifications to an SNS topic. You then subscribe to that topic using various protocols to receive those notifications. A common example is to subscribe to a topic via email. Whenever AWS Budgets sends a notification, any email addresses subscribed to that topic will receive the notification.

Setting up expenditure reports at VidyaGames

Jeremy and Ezra schedule time with Alexander to get executive alignment on their efforts. During a meeting, Jeremy explains the work they've done so far in their efforts to identify and eliminate waste on AWS. Alexander appreciates Jeremy's initiative in bringing more structure into VidyaGames's AWS accounts and increasing the visibility of cloud costs.

As the chief of staff to the CFO, Alexander knows that one of the CFO's biggest challenges is daily cost visibility. The CFO has decades of experience in a traditional enterprise setting where IT costs were calculated and reviewed annually to support business needs. As the CFO adapts to the new variable cost model approach, she needs daily visibility into VidyaGames' expenditure and dynamic budgeting where appropriate.

Alexander: "I'm glad we're aligned on the need to actively track our AWS expenditure. What have we done so far and what do you need from the financial side?"

Jeremy shares some reports with Alexander that show the organization's aggregate usage and cost by service and AWS account, ranging from the past week to the past year.

Alexander: "This is good. We already know what we're spending, but it's helpful to see the distribution across accounts and services. Are we able to see costs by team?"

Jeremy: "We've started on that. We have a tagging strategy in place. We're in the process of tagging our resources retroactively and will work with teams to get resources moving forward. When we tag our resources, we'll be able to see our expenditure by team."

Alexander: "That's great to hear. That's something missing from what we have now. Also, we usually view our AWS spend at the end of the month – can we do something more frequently?"

Jeremy: "If the CFO needs daily reports, we can set something up with AWS Budgets to make that happen. We can send these reports via email if needed."

Alexander: "Well… on second thought, that might be a bit much. I know for certain that after a week or two of reports, they are going to become redundant. I don't think people will really pay attention to these reports in the long term, especially if they end up showing the same information."

Jeremy: "That's fair. Perhaps we don't need to send daily reports. Would monthly reports make more sense?"

Alexander: "I believe so. I think what our CFO really needs is to be informed when costs exceed what we know is normal."

Ezra: "I think there is a way to do that. Let me get back to you."

In scenarios where you want to inform multiple folks at once, you can use **AWS Budget Reports** to deliver reports to up to 50 email addresses. This will help you streamline communications to show teams how performant they are in managing expenditure. It's as simple as selecting the budget you want to report, selecting the frequency as either daily, weekly, or monthly, and designating its recipients.

With a firm understanding of how budgeting works on AWS, it helps to differentiate between the various budgeting methods on AWS.

AWS budgeting methods

Budgets are important but they are rarely static. Changing business needs, external market factors, and unexpected product successes (or failures) can all impact the budgets of applications. AWS Budgets provides three methods for setting the budget amount for each budget period.

The **fixed budget** sets one amount to monitor every budget period. This is the method we used in the previous section when we set the budget to $100 per day. A fixed budget is useful in cases when you want to aggregate expenditure into a target number for an organization or AWS account. You can set a recurring fixed budget to renew on the first day of every monthly billing period. Alternatively, you can expire a budget at a given time, which can be useful when setting budgets for a specific project that you know will end. You can set fixed budgets at daily, monthly, quarterly, or annual intervals.

The **planned budget** sets different amounts to monitor each budget period. You cannot set planned budgets at daily intervals. Doing so will likely cause more headaches than is good! Instead, set planned budgets for each month, quarter, or year.

You can use planned budgets when you want to set different budget amounts at a set time interval. For example, you may know that a specific application gets significant usage during the holiday season. You can set different budget amounts for months that make up the high-demand season to differentiate between other months. *Figure 4.8* shows an example of a planned budget set for $100 for most months, but $1,000 for October, November, and December.

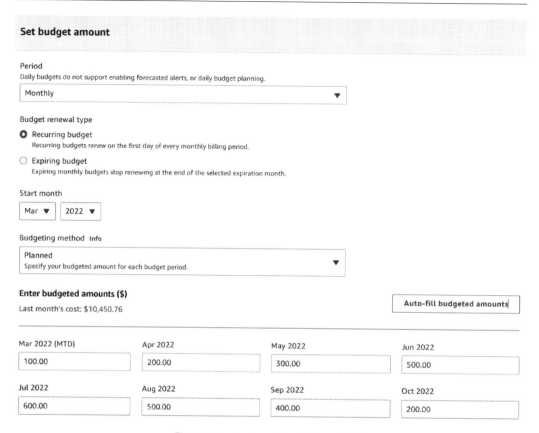

Figure 4.8 – A planned budget method

AWS provides an **auto-adjusting budget** feature to help remove the guesswork in setting up budgets for your teams. Auto-adjusting budgets update as your AWS expenditure patterns change. Auto-adjusting budgets work well when you want to catch spikes in your AWS expenditure.

You can use auto-adjusting budgets with your existing budgets or use them entirely on their own. This helps eliminate the time and effort used to set budgets because the feature will do it on your behalf. For example, you can create an auto-adjusting budget based on your expenditure patterns from the last month. If the average expenditure over the past month was $100, then the auto-adjusted budget for the next period will be $100.

Auto-adjusting budgets will also update your notifications automatically. In the previous section, we looked at an example of setting a notification when the AWS expenditure exceeded 20% of the budgeted amount. If you incorporate auto-adjusting budgets into your budgeting process, the feature will update your budget amount, including all budget alert notifications. Subscribers will receive a notification of the change and future alerts based on the change.

AWS provides native budgeting capabilities to help you on your FinOps journey. Budgeting allows your organization to operate within financial thresholds. Budget alerts can also help notify you about unexpected cost patterns. Budgets ensure that your costs are in line with expectations. However, it's impossible to plan for every scenario, especially anomalous ones. This is something we will address in the next section.

Setting up AWS Cost Anomaly Detection

We looked at an example use case from our friends at VidyaGames in using Cost Explorer to see anomalous usage in *Chapter 3, Managing Inventory*. In the example, Jeremy applied grouping and filters to past expenditure data and saw that the Amazon EC2 service and `RunInstance` API action were contributing significantly to costs. If a bar chart representing daily expenditure shows a sudden spike on a specific day, you can drill down to that day to see what account, service, or API action contributed to the spike. This is a legitimate, albeit manual, approach to detecting unusual expenditure activity.

AWS Cost Anomaly Detection helps to alleviate this manual approach. Cost Anomaly Detection monitors your spend patterns to detect unusual activity using ML. Using this service can help you find anomalies more quickly than doing so manually.

An undesirable effect of anomaly detection is the noise produced from false positives, which tell you that an occurrence is an anomaly but you know for a fact that it is not. You can create monitor types to mitigate these false alerts. You have different options for choosing monitor types, which include monitoring by AWS service, linked account, cost category (see *Chapter 3, Managing Inventory*), and tag.

Once you select a monitor type, you create an alert subscription, informing AWS who to alert, when, and under what circumstances. *Figure 4.9* shows an example of alerting the finance team when AWS detects an anomaly for any expenditure greater than $400 for AWS services:

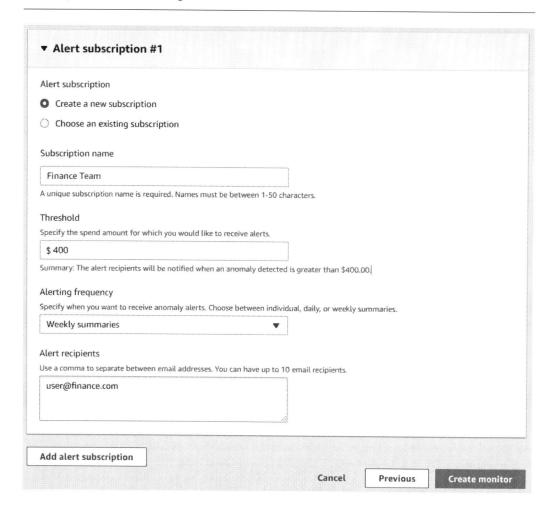

Figure 4.9 – A cost anomaly monitor

Allow some time (usually 24 hours) for the service to learn your spending patterns. Once the service has a baseline of activity, it will send alerts according to your configurations and will also save detection history through an event log. You can use the log to analyze individual events, including finding the root cause and understanding the financial impact.

Figure 4.10 – The Cost Anomaly Detection history log

The **Detection History** log shown in *Figure 4.10* lists the anomalies detected over the time frame you have specified, which was a week in this case. Observe that for 5 days, a cost anomaly detected an increase of roughly $34 in the Amazon QuickSight service. If these anomalies provide value to your efforts, you can submit an assessment to indicate whether the anomaly is not an issue or is an accurate anomaly. The service will then take your provided input and improve the way that it detects anomalies for future cases.

Tagging the VidyaReviews application

From his conversation with Alexander, Ezra takes ownership to learn more about Cost Explorer's Cost Anomaly Detection service and implement it into some AWS accounts. Ezra first sets up a cost monitor for AWS services. This helps him monitor each AWS service individually, allowing smaller anomalies to be detected. Ezra learns that by doing so, the service will automatically adjust the anomaly threshold based on historical spend patterns.

Although useful at a high level, Ezra works with Jeremy and the application teams to set anomalies for several cost categories and cost allocation tags. For example, VidyaGames' highest user engagement application, named VidyaReviews, is tagged with the application name. This enables the teams to see the normal cost to keep the application operating.

VidyaReviews is a video game review platform allowing users to share videos, images, and reviews of gameplay experiences. Given the rich community of users, this platform helps consumers trial a video game from the community before purchasing it. It also allows the community to share experiences, provide helpful hints, and shape the direction of the game since game developers actively monitor user engagement.

From Jeremy's tagging efforts, the teams now have a better understanding of how much it's costing the company to keep the application running. Ezra sets up a cost anomaly monitor based on this tag to help application teams monitor unexpected costs attributed to the application. This also helps the teams test new features, as they can better estimate the impact of pushing changes to production.

Cost Anomaly Detection is a free service and easy to implement. Therefore, it is a must-have tool within your FinOps toolkit. The service detects both gradual spend increases and one-time cost spikes, so it can help you address several scenarios.

CloudWatch also offers a way for you to implement anomaly detection.

Anomaly detection with CloudWatch

CloudWatch anomaly detection follows the same approach as Cost Explorer's Cost Anomaly Detection. CloudWatch analyses a metric that you specify over time and creates a model of the metric's expected value. Training a CloudWatch Anomaly Detection model can take a few weeks, but after the data collection period, it can determine normal ranges for a given metric.

CloudWatch anomaly detection makes it easy to incorporate ML into your metrics without having to train, tune, and deploy your own model. AWS will automatically adjust the model to retain a high level of accuracy. *Figure 4.11* shows anomaly detection in CloudWatch for Amazon EC2 estimated charges. You can see the graph displaying a band of normal values:

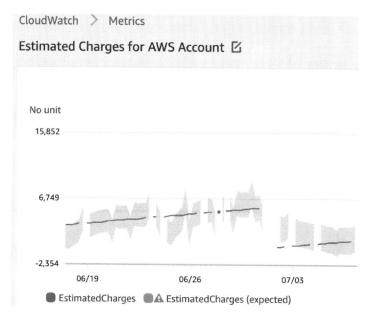

Figure 4.11 – CloudWatch anomaly detection

However, CloudWatch anomaly detection incurs CloudWatch-related pricing. For example, you're billed at $0.30 for every 10,000 metrics and $0.10 per alarm metric in the US East (Ohio) Region at the time of writing. Thus, if you enable CloudWatch anomaly detection, the metrics and alarms contribute toward your monthly usage.

I recommend prioritizing Cost Explorer's anomaly detection feature over CloudWatch. There may be cases where you want to use CloudWatch instead, for example, if you're using CloudWatch to monitor and alert on application logs and want to integrate cost anomalies with existing dashboards. Or perhaps you're aggregating CloudWatch logs into a third-party solution and want to aggregate cost metrics as well as anomalies.

In this section, we incorporated anomaly detection with our budgets and cost and usage tracking. Anomaly detection helps you respond quickly and automatically to unexpected cost spikes, saving you the time and effort of manually searching through reports to find the culprit. Use Cost Explorer's Cost Anomaly Detection to your advantage, as it doesn't add to your financial costs and setting it up requires little effort.

Summary

In this chapter, we explored the features and capabilities of Cost Explorer. The service allows you to baseline your AWS expenditure, allowing you to set budgets, forecast, and find anomalies. These data points assist you with knowing your spending patterns, which is necessary when planning to reduce waste.

We saw how the CUR provides a comprehensive and granular level of understanding of your entire organization. The CUR has the data you need to cover the who, what, and when related to your AWS spending. We saw how the CUR can be integrated with Athena, Redshift, and QuickSight to help you mine that data for insights.

Finally, we learned how CloudWatch adds another layer of cost visibility, especially when combined with infrastructure and application monitoring.

With greater knowledge of our AWS inventory, we now can proceed to the next step of governing and controlling our usage to keep our costs in line with budgets.

Further reading

Have a look at the following resources:

- *Querying Cost and Usage Reports using Amazon Athena*, 2022: `https://docs.aws.amazon.com/cur/latest/userguide/cur-query-athena.html`
- *Amazon Redshift pricing*, 2022: `https://aws.amazon.com/redshift/pricing/?nc=sn&loc=3`

- *How do I ingest and visualize the AWS Cost and Usage Report (CUR) into Amazon QuickSight?*, 2022: `https://aws.amazon.com/premiumsupport/knowledge-center/quicksight-cost-usage-report/`

- *Visualize and gain insights into your AWS cost and usage with Cloud Intelligence Dashboards and CUDOS using Amazon QuickSight*, 2021: `https://aws.amazon.com/blogs/mt/visualize-and-gain-insights-into-your-aws-cost-and-usage-with-cloud-intelligence-dashboards-using-amazon-quicksight/`

5

Governing Cost and Usage

The previous two chapters explained the need to practice proper inventory management and thoughtful budgeting in your FinOps efforts. We explored native AWS tools that can help you implement these practices. Although these practices have good intent, good intentions alone do not yield long-term benefits. You must also have controls in place to ensure your good intentions produce the desired results. *Controls* mitigate financial risks and detect deviations from intended results, while *governance* accomplishes the good intentions proposed in the previous chapters.

We will see how to apply governance to your cost optimization efforts. These methods do not equate to stifling agility, rather, they are there to provide the proper guardrails for teams to be productive within reasonable boundaries. We explore governance at both the AWS Organizations level as well as the account level and the tools you can use at both levels.

In this chapter, we're going to cover the following main topics:

- A quick primer on IAM
- Governance with SCPs
- Implementing tagging policies
- Governance with Service Catalog
- Auditing with CloudTrail

Technical requirements

To complete the exercises in this chapter, we'll continue with the same components we've been using in the previous chapters.

A quick primer on IAM

Until now, we've been acting as though creating anomaly detection monitors, running queries on the CUR, and even creating an entire organization is as simple as logging into the management account and doing as you please. Fortunately (or unfortunately?), it's not as simple as we'd like it to be. In fact, even logging into the management account shouldn't be as easy as logging into your preferred social media platform.

First, you have to prove who you are. We're all familiar with the process of authentication by providing a username and password. There's no shortage of web applications that follow this commonly accepted practice – it's not much different on AWS. You can associate usernames and passwords to AWS accounts, allowing *principals* to authenticate their identity using *what they know* (i.e., a password). You can (and should) enforce an additional layer of authentication using *what they have*, namely a **Multi-Factor Authentication (MFA)** token or a mobile phone to strengthen your security posture.

We're familiar with this process but we're also familiar with how cumbersome it can be to remember all your passwords. Among other things, **Identity and Access Management (IAM)** roles help save you the time and effort of having to type and remember all your accounts' usernames and passwords. AWS roles help to streamline this process by allowing principals to *assume* an identity. You're essentially *being someone else* for an amount of time.

Whether you are authenticating as a user or a role, the next check involves authorizing *what you can do*. Even if you entered the door to get inside AWS, you may not be allowed to do anything once inside unless you are authorized to perform certain actions. *Figure 5.1* provides a simple illustration showing the workflow for an entity authenticating as a user:

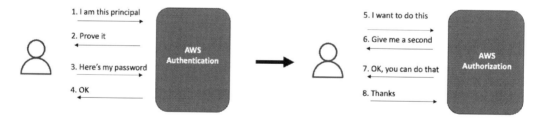

Figure 5.1 – An authentication workflow for an IAM user

Important note

It is always best practice to exercise the **principle of least privilege (PoLP)**. The PoLP only grants the minimum permissions required to conduct a task. For example, rather than giving an IAM entity more permissions than it needs, it's best to chart out which API calls an entity needs and then set the IAM permissions to meet those needs.

IAM users and roles can have more than one policy that outlines their allowed actions. However, entities that want to use a role must first have the permissions to assume that role. Once they assume the role, they can execute the actions allowed for that role. The entity may not have direct permissions to perform an action, as illustrated in *Figure 5.2*. At step **9**, the entity is denied an action. However, the action is allowed when executed through the assumed role:

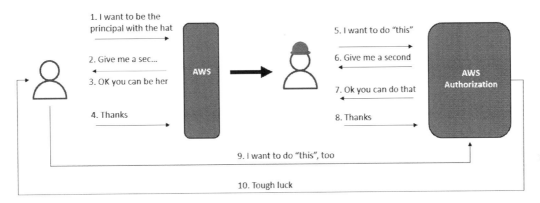

Figure 5.2 – An authentication workflow for an AWS IAM role

Roles simplify your personas' ability to perform cross-accounts actions without having to remember usernames, passwords, and MFA devices. For example, if a financial analyst in one account needs to access Cost Explorer reports in another, you can provide a role that the analyst can assume in the target account to pull only those reports. Furthermore, AWS Control Tower, which we explored in *Chapter 2*, *Establishing the Right Account Structure*, also provides a **Single Sign-On** (**SSO**) experience so that entities can find all their accessible accounts and roles in one place.

We've established that you need to be the right entity and have the right permissions to access anything within AWS. Given these permissions, let's see how you're able to view and access other accounts' cost and usage data within your AWS Organization.

Access to member accounts in Cost Explorer

To simplify things, when you enable Cost Explorer at the management account, all member accounts get access to their cost and usage data by default. This removes the burden of all the accounts within an organization needing to activate Cost Explorer individually.

Once active for member accounts, the management account has further control to grant different levels of access to the member accounts. For example, the management account can choose to show or hide refunds and credits for the member accounts, which may help when centrally managing chargebacks to avoid confusion. Alternatively, the management account may choose to disable hourly and resource-level data to prevent accounts from enabling the extra cost feature. *Figure 5.3* shows how you can change the view options for member accounts under **Preferences** within the **AWS Cost Management** console:

Figure 5.3 – AWS Cost Explorer preferences

Once you enable Cost Explorer for the Organization, all accounts have access. You cannot grant or deny access individually. Whereas the management account has access to view all member accounts' cost and usage data, member accounts can only see their own. If you wanted to specify users or roles in a member account to view or access Cost Explorer's data in another account, you must explicitly configure the proper roles and permissions, as outlined in *Figure 5.2*. Fortunately, you don't have to do this for management accounts since they already have access to view cost and usage data for members' accounts.

With a better understand of how IAM roles and permissions work for individual entities, let's see how the same principles apply to entire accounts or OUs within an AWS Organization.

Governance with SCP

You learned how you can set up a multi-account structure using AWS Organizations in *Chapter 2, Establishing the Right Account Structure*. You also saw how to group accounts into OUs to model your organization's structure and separate your AWS accounts. This helps to logically organize your AWS accounts and cloud assets to make things easier for chargebacks, application boundaries, and governance.

Governance helps you apply the right permission boundaries to logically grouped AWS accounts. For instance, a group of AWS accounts meant for sandbox and AWS service exploration should comply to different rules than a group of AWS accounts meant to hold production workloads. AWS Organizations helps you apply these governance rules using permission boundaries.

You can apply permission boundaries to an OU to govern what actions principals can take under the OU. Any policies applied to an OU trickle down to affect any accounts tied to the OU, and even sub-OUs and their associated accounts. These policies are called **Service Control Policies (SCPs)**.

Let's use Jeremy from VidyaGames as a simple example. Access from the management account provides Jeremy with the permissions to view Cost Explorer for linked accounts A through F. However, accounts A through F are part of an OU and Della is the owner of this OU. As the owner and lead, Della has permission to view and access Cost Explorer for the accounts in her OU. If Jeremy applies an SCP to this OU that denies actions to read Cost Explorer reports for accounts A, B, D, and F, Della will not be able to view Cost Explorer for these accounts, even though she has permissions to view herself. The SCP affects Della's permission boundaries. Although Della has permissions for all accounts, the net allowed permissions is the union between the IAM policy and the SCP. Thus, Della can only read Cost Explorer for accounts C and E.

> **Important note**
>
> In AWS, an explicit deny overrides an explicit allow. In other words, if one policy explicitly states that you can `LaunchInstance`, but another policy explicitly states that you cannot, you ultimately cannot `LaunchInstance`. AWS explains the policy evaluation logic in their documentation, which can assist you when defining your own permission boundaries.

Figure 5.4 shows an example permission boundary for an IAM principal. The overlap, which represents the union of the two policies, represents the allowed permissions for the principal:

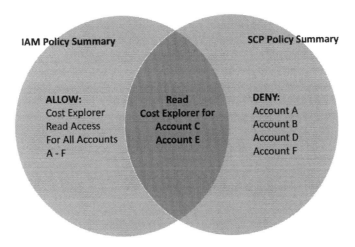

Figure 5.4 – Allowed permissions between two policies

You can use SCPs to enforce and prevent actions across your AWS Organization or within subsets of your accounts. From what you've learned in previous chapters, taking inventory of your cloud assets, sharing reports, and incorporating anomaly detection are all good FinOps practices. Applying SCPs to help govern your resources is another good practice to share within your organization. For instance, you may find from analyzing historical usage and through conversations that you have with developers that teams may be provisioning larger servers than they need for testing or sandbox purposes. To save on costs, teams can collaborate and decide that smaller instance types provide more than enough compute power to run simple tests; restricting developers to smaller instance types poses no business risk nor does it hamper developer productivity. You can use SCPs to implement this organizational initiative to promote smaller instance types for testing and sandbox workloads. We can look at an example SCP that provides this governance. Here, we can see a sample SCP in JSON with the condition to allow only the t2 instance types and the t3 instance types, and the .nano, .micro, and .small instance sizes.

```
{
   "Version": "2012-10-17",
   "Statement": [
      {
         "Sid": "RequireMicroInstanceType",
         "Effect": "Deny",
         "Action": "ec2:RunInstances",
         "Resource": [
            "arn:aws:ec2:*:*:instance/*"
         ],
         "Condition": {
            "StringNotEquals": {
               "ec2:InstanceType": ["t2.nano", t2.micro", "t2.
small", "t3.nano", "t3.micro", "t3.small"]
            }
         }
      }
   ]
}
```

The policy aims to require smaller instance types. The policy denies starting any instance that is not one of the instance types listed in the Condition string. In other words, accounts or OUs that have this SCP applied can only launch t2.nano, t2.micro, t2.small, t3.nano, t3.micro, and t3.small. This kind of policy ensures minimal costs for running instances because relatively, these instances have a lower hourly rate charge.

It's important to define the workload and the users' requirements so that SCPs don't hinder the speed, scale, and innovation expected by teams. But once you define these expectations, and communicate the goals and benefits of having SCPs, they are useful tools to apply to your FinOps practice at scale.

Consider using SCPs in cases where you need to enforce blanket preventative actions. We talked previously about lost or inaccessible AWS accounts due to, say, an employee leaving the company. To place a temporary restriction on any use of that account, you could create a holding OU that restricts any action until you figure out an appropriate owner and the right placement for the account within your organization. In this way, you control costs and are secure knowing that no other resources can be provisioned while that account is contained in that OU.

Applying SCPs at VidyaGames

From his experience working with Andrew, Jeremy suggests the idea of applying an SCP to the sandbox OU for VidyaGames' AWS Organization. This SCP would only allow developers to deploy instance types that are relatively smaller for testing and exploration purposes. The teams agree that such an SCP would not hinder their development efforts.

However, Jeremy learns of several edge cases where developers may need larger instance types to support efforts. Because these cases do not happen very often, Jeremy and the teams establish an exceptions process that would allow developers to launch specific instance types that are larger. This allows administrative teams to maintain control and visibility into the resources deployed in the sandbox OU while granting developers the flexibility to use the resources they need.

Jeremy also meets with the security teams and application teams to identify SCPs for the workloads and security OUs. Controls for public-facing applications such as VidyaReviews require different controls from internal-facing applications. The teams identify only the approved services needed for the production environment supporting VidyaReviews. This helps lock down the workload environment and provide greater control and security boundaries. This also prevents unneeded resources from being deployed in a production environment that would otherwise contribute to waste.

Lastly, the teams collaboratively identify the AWS Regions in which the application teams operate. Jeremy learns that all VidyaGames cloud assets are deployed in two Regions. There are no immediate plans to expand their AWS footprint. Hence, it is reasonable to create a boundary around these two Regions preventing users from deploying resources in Regions other than these two unless the business needs change. Jeremy can use AWS Control Tower to easily apply **data residency** guardrails. Control Tower uses APIs through SCPs to limit resource use to specific Regions. This improves VidyaGames' security posture, as well as its financial control, removing the risk of leaving idle resources in unknown Regions.

AWS also provides a way for you to centrally view and update the alternative contacts for your AWS accounts. In cases where an employee who owns an AWS leaves the organization, or changes teams and makes it difficult to identify the original owner, having an administrator with privileges to manage alternative contacts reduces the risk of idle resources running in an AWS account when you struggle to gain access to the account. *Figure 5.5* shows how you can set up alternate contacts in AWS Organizations for billing, operations, and security purposes. This will improve your control over the account in cases where employees leave or when you cannot identify the owner:

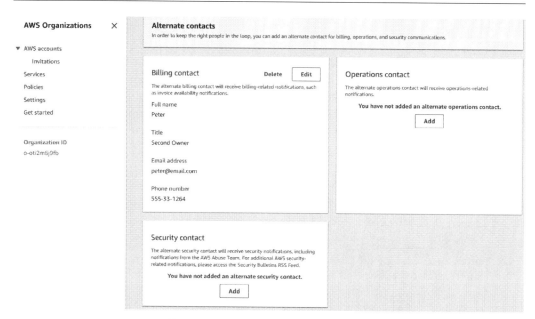

Figure 5.5 – Setting up alternate contacts

You must enable **AWS Account Management** from the **Services** option within AWS Organizations. Enabling **AWS Account Management** allows you to programmatically modify your account information and metadata within the AWS Organization.

SCPs help you enforce governance across your AWS Organization. Although our focus is on governance through cost controls, it's also useful to increase your security posture and improve operational efficiency. We looked at a simple example of using SCPs to limit the types of Amazon EC2 instances accounts within an OU that can launch, but you can apply the same principle to apply the SCPs that are most useful to your organization. We'll look at another example SCP in the next section, emphasizing the importance of tagging to control ongoing costs.

Implementing tagging policies

We've already seen how tagging helps you know your AWS inventory better and report on it to see cost and usage. Once you've defined your tagging strategy, you can improve the level of resource and cost visibility by applying tagging policies to SCPs across your organization. You can write your own JSON as SCP policies and apply them to OUs. But you can also create and apply *tag policies* within AWS Organizations in the AWS Management Console.

Tag policies are related to service control policies in that they can help you standardize actions across an OU, but tag policies specifically govern *how* and *what* to tag. You will need to attach a tag policy at the OU or account level through AWS Organizations. If applied at the Organization root, then all accounts within that Organization will be subject to the policy.

Let's assume you wanted to apply a tagging policy to ensure that EC2 instances are tagged with an owner tag. This allows your teams to contact the individual with any questions about the use of the instances. You can create a policy in the AWS Console, as shown in *Figure 5.6*, then apply this policy to targets whether they are OUs, accounts, or a combination of both. The example tag policy in AWS Organizations requires the owner tag key and a value of either alice, bob, or charlie for any EC2 instance.

Figure 5.6 – A sample tag policy

To measure your teams' tagging success through their compliance with an effective tag policy, use the tag compliance report accessible through AWS Resource Groups. We explored this service in *Chapter 3, Managing Inventory*, when we learned to obtain a list of untagged resources within an AWS account. The same tag compliance report provides a full view of your tagged resources based on your tagging policy. This can help you quickly find untagged AWS resources.

Because it can take up to 48 hours for changes to a tag policy or resource to reflect, this service may not meet real-time requirements. However, it can still be a useful tool when you need to take a snapshot of how your resources are compliant with tagging policies. For faster response times to non-compliant resources, integrate tag governance with AWS Config, which we'll look at in the next section.

Tag governance with AWS Config

Once you apply a tag policy, you can use AWS Config to see how well your accounts are compliant with a tag policy. Within AWS Config, you can configure an AWS-managed rule named *required-tags* to evaluate your resources and see which are not compliant with your desired policy. In this case, the policy is to apply an *owner* tag key to all EC2 instances within an account. *Figure 5.7* shows an application of a `required-tags-managed` rule to check for EC2 instances with the `owner` key of the required tag:

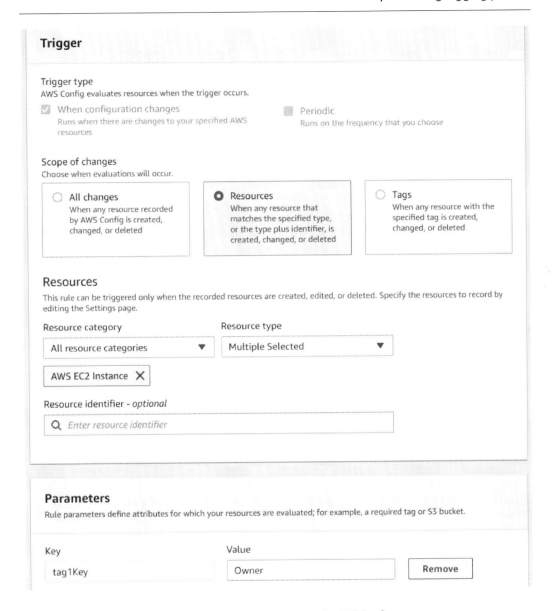

Figure 5.7 – Selecting resources in AWS Config

Once active, AWS Config will regularly evaluate your resources according to these defined rules. Config will mark any resources as non-compliant. After you identify a non-compliant resource, you can take the appropriate action to change its status.

If you need a service to help you manage changes to data within your AWS services, then a good choice is to use **Amazon EventBridge**. EventBridge is a serverless event bus that gathers data about events that occur within your AWS environment (and third-party services as well). As it's a serverless service, you don't need to manage any servers. As an event bus, EventBridge streams real-time data from event sources, such as AWS Config, to targets such as AWS Lambda, Amazon SNS, or other **software-as-a-service (SaaS)** applications. *Figure 5.8* shows an example workflow using the *required-tags*-managed rule to check for EC2 instances with the owner key of the required tag.

Figure 5.8 – Integrating EventBridge with Config

In our case, as illustrated in *Figure 5.8*, we can use AWS Config to ensure AWS resources are tagged according to a tagging policy. AWS Config evaluates the environment and identifies a resource as **non-compliant**. Then, EventBridge will route the finding to a target such as an Amazon SNS topic. This enables you to view and respond more quickly than you would from running a report every few days and parsing through the data. It's important to note that EventBridge will cost money. For example, you will be charged for the storage events used per month, and for any custom events published to EventBridge. However, you will not be charged for any state changes published by AWS services.

Applying tags at VidyaGames

Jeremy's tagging efforts have not only increased VidyaGames' visibility into their AWS resources, but it has also given the teams a fresh sense of ownership over their cloud assets. The company established a tagging strategy that, at minimum, has the teams include an owner, application name, and cost center. The owner tag helps identify either the team or individual that owns the resource to encourage folks to take responsibility over what they provision. The application name provides visibility into how much each application is costing the company. The cost center helps the finance team charge back costs and perform monthly reconciliations.

Jeremy creates and attaches an SCP per OU with this baseline tagging policy requiring these three tag types. For certain individual accounts, such as the production accounts within the workloads OU, he adds an additional *schedule* tag to help developers differentiate between long- and short-running resources. This is implemented in collaboration with developers.

Ultimately, as your maturity in FinOps grows, you'll want to automate the process for evaluation and response. For instance, instead of manual processes, AWS Config's discovery of a non-compliant resource can trigger a workflow to automatically apply a tag, then notify the team that a tag was missing and a default value was applied. This can help streamline your operations and enable you to respond quickly to the dynamic nature of a cloud. We'll explore automation in greater detail in *Part 3, Operationalizing FinOps*.

In this section, we looked at how to define your tag policies, apply them to your AWS Organization, and ensure compliance with services such as AWS Config and Amazon EventBridge. These methods require you to formulate your own governance strategies and respond when resources deviate from your good intentions. Another way to ensure compliance is to use predefined resources that are already compliant with good intentions. This is what we'll explore next.

Governance with Service Catalog

At the beginning of this chapter, we looked at identity-based policies that permit actions for individual entities. We unpacked how permissions work through authentication and authorization. Then, we looked at permission boundaries, primarily in the form of SCPs that are applied to an AWS account or multiple AWS accounts via an OU. These SCPs define the permission boundaries that impact all users and roles associated with the AWS account, the OU, and perhaps the entire AWS Organization.

Another way of governing access to AWS resources is by providing a pre-approved list of resources that users can launch with **AWS Service Catalog**. You can think of Service Catalog as a vending machine of goods – users choose which resource they want to consume. And since you're the one placing the items in the machine for users to vend, as long as you know the items that you place are secured, compliant, and approved for use, you can operate with the assurance that all resources will be used as intended.

Service Catalog helps from both a governance and cost perspective. You standardize how users will use AWS resources by creating a portfolio of products. In the case of *Figure 5.9*, we created a portfolio called *FinOps Portfolio* with two products, an Amazon S3 bucket and an Amazon EC2 Linux instance. You then assign who can provision these products by managing permissions for groups, roles, and users to have access to that portfolio:

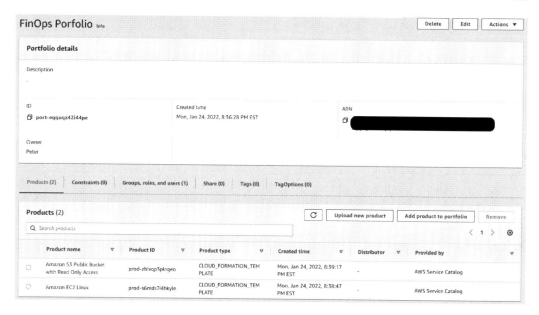

Figure 5.9 – A portfolio in AWS Service Catalog

Even if these users or roles aren't explicitly allowed to launch EC2 Linux instances or create Amazon S3 buckets, they can do so through Service Catalog if they have permission to use Service Catalog and the portfolios therein. Once a user accesses Service Catalog, they can choose to launch resources as defined by the portfolio's product collection. This is illustrated in *Figure 5.10*, where we see someone launching an Amazon EC2 Linux instance through the **Service Catalog** portal:

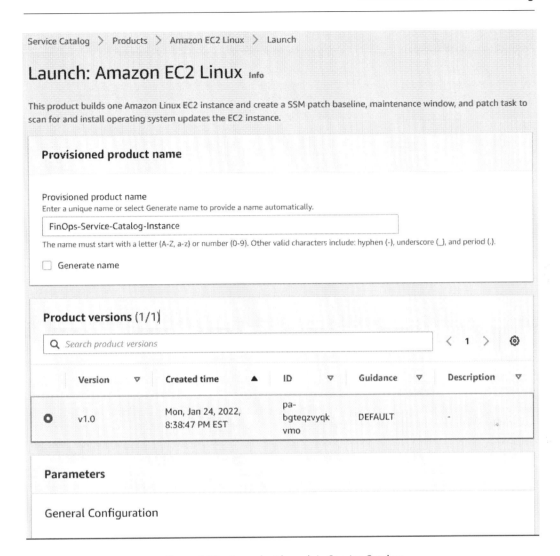

Figure 5.10 – A product launch in Service Catalog

In the preceding scenario, the user may not have IAM permissions to specifically launch an Amazon EC2 instance. Instead, the user has access to Service Catalog and the products within a portfolio. The user essentially accesses AWS resources through a portal. From this portal, users can discover and use products that comply with organizational policies and budget constraints.

From a cost perspective, Service Catalog provides a mechanism to better predict your AWS expenditure because of the predefined nature of products. As a simple example, if you require the use of Service Catalog for all testing workloads that use EC2 instances, you can create a portfolio of products for testers and define the instance settings. A predefined Service Catalog portfolio of EC2 instances that are only certain types and sizes gives you a more accurate cost assurance than if you did not know which instance types your developers would be launching.

AWS provides public pricing for all its services and a pricing calculator to estimate your AWS expenditure. If you predefine a list of approved instance types for testing, you can estimate the lower and upper bounds of how much testing workloads would cost based on how many instance types, total running hours in a month, and expected number of users there will be. You can create budgets and anomaly detection measures against these estimates while, at the same time, setting tagging policies such as adding a *schedule* tag. Users can then specify a key of a set number of planned hours, or specify *24/7*, to indicate how long they expect the instance to run.

Although I am presenting a very simplified example here, you can see how the ideas presented so far can be layered together to form policies that might be useful for your organization. The breadth of AWS services means that you can use a combination of services to meet the changing needs of your organization. Service Catalog may be useful for a business unit, a specific project, or even for an entire organization. You don't have to feel as though you need to use one service over the other. You have the flexibility to use whichever service or services you need that will bring you the most value.

In the last section, before we conclude this chapter, we'll briefly look at **AWS CloudTrail**, which provides a way for you to audit your AWS accounts. CloudTrail allows you to see exactly who did what within your AWS accounts, granting you visibility and auditability into your resources.

Auditing with CloudTrail

AWS CloudTrail is primarily used to audit, secure, and track user activity and API usage for your AWS accounts. CloudTrail continuously monitors and retains account activity for all actions performed within your AWS environments. Although not directly related to cost optimization, CloudTrail is an important governance tool nonetheless and it's worth mentioning here.

When you use the default AWS Control Tower settings to deploy a multi-account AWS environment, Control Tower automatically creates a CloudTrail baseline and a logging account that aggregates API activity across all your accounts. The CloudTrail service collects and retains this log information for you to query and analyze at the required time. If you're not using Control Tower, you have to enable CloudTrail manually for the AWS account.

CloudTrail is helpful for seeing the activities that are taking place to track their cost and usage. This is especially helpful if certain resources are not tagged properly and you cannot identify the owner. The following event record shows a login activity for a user. CloudTrail records the date and time, as well as the source IP address and agent.

Here's a sample CloudTrail console login activity and its associated metadata:

```
{
    "eventVersion": "1.08",
```

```
    "userIdentity": {
        "type": "AssumedRole",
        "principalId": "AROAZBQHLPM42D7PFT36K:user ",
        "arn": "arn:aws:sts::xxxxxxxxxxxx:assumed-role/
developer/user",
        "accountId": " xxxxxxxxxxxx ",
        "sessionContext": {
            "sessionIssuer": {
                "type": "Role",
                "arn": "arn:aws:iam:: xxxxxxxxxxxx:role/user",
                "accountId": " xxxxxxxxxxxx "
            }
        }
    },
    "eventTime": "2022-01-20T15:50:18Z",
    "eventSource": "signin.amazonaws.com",
    "eventName": "ConsoleLogin",
    "awsRegion": "us-east-1",
    "sourceIPAddress": "0.0.0.0"}
```

You can see from the sample CloudTrail event record in the preceding code block that the first few lines of the event display the principal performing the action, who, in this case, is a developer using an assumed IAM role. CloudTrail shows the user and the account ID, and shows that this user did not use MFA for authentication. Then, the event logs the source IP address and a successful login event.

CloudTrail records all event activity and stores the log in an Amazon S3 bucket. The previous example shows a type of management event, a user logging into the AWS Console. You can configure CloudTrail to record data events and insights events as well. These are events related to resource operations on a resource (such as uploading and deleting items from an Amazon S3 bucket) and identifying unusual activity, errors, or user behavior in an account, respectively. As you can imagine, the storage costs can add up if you are logging many users' activities across many AWS accounts.

Depending on your business needs, you may want to create a CloudTrail trail that only logs data events for specific accounts. Configuring more specific trails can help lower your costs. For example, you may only want to log that items are deleted from an Amazon S3 bucket if and when that happens. You can use advanced event selectors when configuring CloudTrail. *Figure 5.11* shows an example of setting this up in the AWS Console. We use advanced event selectors to set more granular configurations on CloudTrail and reduce costs:

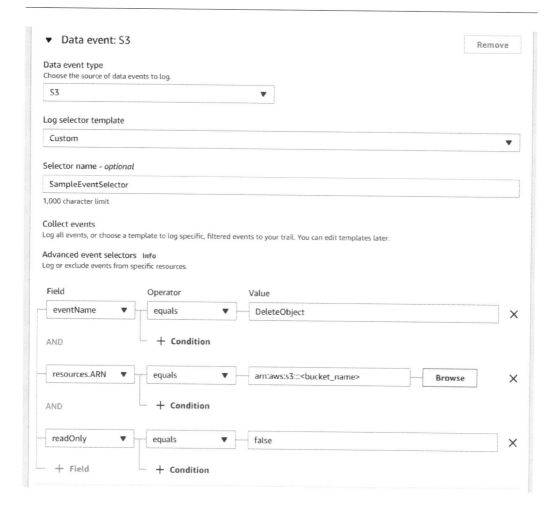

Figure 5.11 – Using advanced event selectors

Here, we set advanced event selectors to only log activity when the `DeleteObject` action occurs on a specific Amazon S3 bucket. This helps reduce costs by only logging the events that matter most to you.

CloudTrail can be a helpful tool for monitoring and auditing your AWS accounts. But depending on your needs, auditing everything may produce more noise than required. Only logging the information that matters can not only help reduce the operational burden of having to sift through logs of information but also reduce your costs in the long term.

Config helps with managing the configurations of your resources. We specifically looked at ensuring all resources are tagged with Config. Config helps set the rules with CloudTrail and helps identify what's in fact happening within your accounts. Using these services together increases the visibility of and control over account activity, which ultimately reduces your waste.

Summary

Governance is a crucial part of your FinOps implementation. Without governance, all you have is good intent. Governance provides guardrails for your FinOps practices to be executed in a standardized and scalable way.

Authentication and authorization are both required for any activity within AWS, FinOps-related or otherwise. It's important to streamline cross-account access via roles and IAM policies that adhere to the principle of least privilege.

You can use SCPs and tagging policies to enforce compliance for the accounts and OUs. All accounts and associated entities are subject to any SCPs. Thus, the allowed permissions are the union between the permission boundary and IAM policy for an entity.

For day-to-day operations, AWS Config, AWS Service Catalog, and AWS CloudTrail are governance-focused services that help with enforcing compliance and auditing account activity.

We have established the right foundation by setting up a multi-account environment, analyzing our cost and usage, setting up budgets, and implementing controls. We can now work toward practical methods for reducing costs, which will be the focus of the next chapter. We will explore cost-saving opportunities in key IT domains and we'll begin by looking at compute as the focus for the next chapter.

Further reading

Have a look at the following resources:

- *How do I allow users or roles in a separate AWS account access to my AWS account?*, 2021: `https://www.youtube.com/watch?v=20tr9gUY4i0`.

- *Managing Users and Access Through Single Sign-On*, 2022: `https://docs.aws.amazon.com/controltower/latest/userguide/sso.html`.

- *Policy evaluation logic*, 2022: `https://docs.aws.amazon.com/IAM/latest/UserGuide/reference_policies_evaluation-logic.html`.

- *AWS Pricing Calculator*, 2022: `https://calculator.aws/#/`.

- *How can I be notified when an AWS resource is non-compliant using AWS Config*, 2022: `https://aws.amazon.com/premiumsupport/knowledge-center/config-resource-non-compliant/`.

- *How to optimize AWS CloudTrail costs by using advanced event selectors*, 2022: `https://aws.amazon.com/blogs/mt/optimize-aws-cloudtrail-costs-using-advanced-event-selectors/`.

Part 2:
Optimizing Your
AWS Resources

In *Part 2*, we will learn about the levers we can pull to realize actual cost savings and move toward eliminating waste. We will break this part into four categories. In *Chapter 6*, we will look at how to optimize compute costs. This means leveraging reserved instances, Savings Plans, spot instances, and AWS Compute Optimizer. *Chapter 7* shows how to optimize storage costs using the right S3 storage tier, Ultra Warm storage, RDS Proxy, and EFS colder tier storage. *Chapter 8* explores networking optimization such as lowering data transfer costs, leveraging VPC endpoints, and using Transit Gateways to reduce bandwidth. *Chapter 9* provides other ways that customers can reduce costs beyond compute, networking, and storage.

This part of the book comprises the following chapters:

- *Chapter 6, Optimizing Compute*
- *Chapter 7, Optimizing Storage*
- *Chapter 8, Optimizing Networking*
- *Chapter 9, Optimizing Could-Native Environments*

6
Optimizing Compute

Compute generally refers to power used by machines to process data and execute tasks as defined by a software program. Cloud computing delivers this compute power over the internet to consumers on demand. And while pay-as-you-go is the de facto means of paying for these resources, AWS provides other means to pay that can help lower costs. You can also configure these compute resources to perform optimally, which helps lower costs.

We now focus on the mechanisms and levers you can pull to reduce waste in the compute domain on AWS. We will look at AWS' different pricing models and how you should be thinking about your workload to take advantage of them. We also explore ways to size your compute resources appropriately to minimize the waste associated with overprovisioned resources.

In this chapter, we're going to cover the following main topics:

- Leveraging steady state discounts
- Maximizing savings for flexible workloads
- Right sizing compute

Technical requirements

To complete the exercises in this chapter, we will continue with the same components we've been using in the previous chapter.

Leveraging steady state discounts

Paying for the IT services you need when you need them is the very nature of paying for AWS cloud resources. This embodies the on-demand nature of the cloud and essentially comprises the trade-off of capital expenses for variable expenses. However, this isn't the only way you can pay for what you use. In fact, Amazon EC2 instances provide you with several choices: on-demand, **reserved instances (RIs)**, **Savings Plans (SPs)**, and Spot.

On-demand pricing is just as it sounds – you pay for however long the instance runs at an hourly rate. AWS provides the on-demand hourly rate for each of their numerous instance types on their **Amazon EC2 pricing** page. The hourly rate will depend on several instance parameters such as the Region where you launch your instance, the **operating system (OS)**, the type of instance, and the size. Intuitively, you will be charged at a higher hourly rate for a larger instance than a smaller instance.

How RIs work

On-demand pricing makes sense – you pay for what you use when you use it and the pricing for the on-demand rate is publicly available to view. But is there any way to pay at a lower rate? There are two ways, as a matter of fact. One is by way of RIs and SPs, and the other is through Amazon EC2 Spot. We will focus on RIs and SPs first. Although technically different, we'll group them together because they have the same discount rate and are both meant for steady state use. We'll focus on reserved instances in this section.

RIs provide a discounted hourly rate for running EC2 instances given several agreed upon terms. There are two types of RIs: standard and convertible.

Standard RIs have stricter terms than convertible instances but the discount rates are greater. When you commit to a standard RI for a term of either one or three years, you are committing to the Region that you'll deploy the instance to, the instance type, the OS, and the tenancy. For example, if you purchase a standard RI for a single t2.small, Windows-based OS under shared tenancy in the US-EAST-1 Region, whenever you launch an instance with those specific parameters, you will be billed at the standard RI discount rate, rather than the on-demand rate. If you launch a t2.small, *Linux-based instance* under shared tenancy in the US-EAST-1 Region, you *will not* get the discount because the OS does not match the parameters of your reserved instance.

Figure 6.1 illustrates an example of the RI configuration mentioned earlier, applying to one specific instance because it matches the RI configuration. **Instance 3** receives the discount rate given the standard reserved instance purchases, as it's the only instance configuration that matches the commitment parameters. **Instance 1** is in the different Region. **Instance 2** and **Instance 4** do not match the instance type:

Reserved Instance Parameters	Standard	Instance 1	Instance 2	Instance 3	Instance 4
Region	US-EAST-1	US-EAST-2	US-EAST-1	US-EAST-1	US-EAST-1
Instance Type	t2.small	t2.small	t3.small	t2.small	m5.large
Operating System	Windows	Windows	Windows	Windows	Windows
Tenancy	Shared	Shared	Shared	Shared	Shared
Discount Rate?		✗	✗	✓	✗

Figure 6.1 – Instance 3 receiving the RI rate

Convertible RIs offer more flexibility at a smaller discount rate compared to standard RIs. During the convertible RI term, you may change the commitment parameters at any time given that the new RI commitment is of equal or greater value. From the preceding example, if you first purchase a `t2.small` convertible RI and, given your business needs, want to change that to a `m5.large` convertible RI, with everything else staying the same, you will be able to do so, assuming that `m5.large` instance types will be more expensive than `t2.small` instance types. Keep in mind that when converting to a new instance type, you should launch instances that match the new configuration; otherwise, you will be adding to your waste! In other words, once you convert to an `m5.large` instance, be sure to actually deploy an `m5.large` instance for your workloads; otherwise, you'll be paying for something you're not using.

Billing for RIs comes in three forms: all upfront, partial upfront, or no upfront payments. When you elect the all upfront payment, you pay for the total amount of the RI cost at your next billing cycle. You get the best discount compared to the other payment options, but you put up more cash upfront to pay for that RI. Partial upfront is similar in that you can pay a portion upfront but the remainder of the cost is amortized monthly. You cannot choose how much you want to put upfront for the partial upfront payment type. You can with SPs, but more on this later. No upfront is just as it sounds – you don't need to pay anything upfront. You will be billed monthly instead for the duration of the RI term.

All three options indicate paying for a resource at a discounted rate whether you use it or not. If you had not purchased an RI and instead used on-demand pricing, you would see the bill for the on-demand instance charged based on the number of hours used. But with RIs, you'll see the RI charge on the bill even if you don't launch an instance matching that configuration. But when you do launch an instance matching that configuration, you're not charged the on-demand rate, but a monthly discount rate covers that usage instead.

A simple example of the RI billing mechanism is gym membership. Most gyms offer two methods of payment to use the facility: you can either pay every time you go (on-demand), or pay a yearly membership and go as many times as you want during the year (RI). Perhaps you do the math in your head and determine that if you pay for the membership, as long as you go to the gym three times a week, you'll be getting a better rate than paying every time you go. Now, it's up to you to actually go to the gym. I'm not one to give motivational speeches, so we can stop here.

RIs act in the same way – it's use it or lose it. If you don't *use it*, you are in fact contributing to your waste. In other words, if you don't launch instances that match your RI commitment, it would have been better to pay the on-demand rate, because now you're paying for the on-demand rate for running instances in addition to a year-long (or 3 year-long) commitment for something you're not using. The way to remedy this is to ensure that your running instance configurations match the RI configurations. By doing so, your running instances won't be charged the on-demand rate since they'll be covered by your RI commitment.

Now with a better understanding of how RIs work, the challenge then becomes knowing how well you are utilizing the RIs that you've purchased. You can find the answer in Cost Explorer.

Understanding RI performance

You can access the **RI utilization report** in Cost Explorer. This report helps you minimize wasteful use of reserved instances by showing you how well you're taking advantage of any RIs owned by the account, or for the entire AWS organization if viewing from the management account. The report shows *what you would have paid, whether you used on-demand instances*, and compares this to your actual RI costs. It then summarizes your net savings by subtracting these values. Ideally, you want the total net savings to equal total potential savings to achieve 100% utilization. I show a bad example of this in *Figure 6.2*.

Low utilization is just as it sounds. You're not using the RIs that you paid for — you're not going to the gym even though you paid for yearly membership. An RI utilization report showing low utilization means that you would have saved money if you had just used on-demand instances and paid for those instances when you used them. In gym terms, you should have not purchased the membership and just paid to use the facility since you only went to the gym twice that year. Used in this way, RIs that were intended to be cost-saving tools turn out to be waste-inducing tools.

Figure 6.2 shows how well you used the RI (i.e., how often you went to the gym) visually. This is an example of poor utilization. The RI costs exceed the on-demand cost equivalent, which reflects wasteful use of RIs. In other words, you paid for gym membership, but you never went:

Figure 6.2 – Poor RI utilization

To avoid these situations, use this report to match the purchased RI configurations to the launched instance configurations. If you happened to make a mistake and launched t3.small instances when you purchased RIs for t2.small instances, then change the instance configurations for your workload to match the RI instance configurations. This will be difficult for standard RIs because you are unable to change the RI configurations for the length of the standard RI terms.

We've seen how you want to ensure you are maximizing the use of your RIs. The RI utilization report in Cost Explorer can help you track how well you are using your RIs. But in some cases, you might need to change your RI configurations. So, what can you do if you need to change your standard RI?

Modifying RIs

One of the ways to modify standard RIs is to change their scope. A standard RI can either be Regional or Zonal. When you select a Zonal RI, you specify which **Availability Zone (AZ)** you want to reserve for your instance(s). If you specify an RI for US-EAST-1A, then you'd selected a Zonal RI. To get the discounted rate, you must launch the instance in US-EAST-1A. Assuming you have no other RIs, if you launch an instance in US-EAST-1B, your instance will be charged the on-demand rate.

Zonal RIs have the additional benefit of reserving capacity in the specified AZ. If there was only one instance left, and you and another AWS customer happened to choose the same remaining last instance to deploy, then the customer with the Zonal RI for that specific instance would have the priority to use it (if you both own the RI, then whoever requested the instance first would win). You can choose Zonal RIs if your workload requires specificity in choosing an AZ to launch instances and when reserving capacity is important.

You can also change the instance size for standard RIs using the Linux/UNIX OS. Each RI has an *instance size footprint* that defines its normalized size. For example, a small instance has a normalization factor of 1, while a medium-sized instance has a normalization factor of 2. If you started off with a single medium-sized Linux/UNIX RI but wanted to change to *two* small-size Linux/UNIX instances, you could do so because it's a Linux/UNIX OS.

Figure 6.3 provides an example of this in the Amazon EC2 page. Here we see an RI modification from a t3.micro, Linux/UNIX, Regional RI to two t3.nano, Zonal RIs applicable to US-EAST-1a:

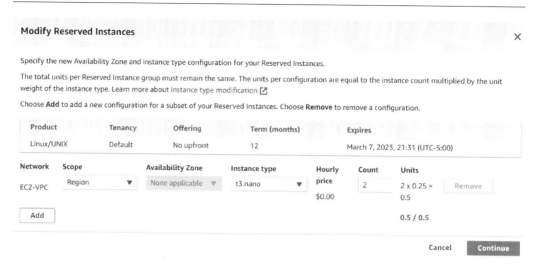

Figure 6.3 – Modifying an RI in the Amazon EC2 console

Modifying the zone and/or size does not provide too much flexibility because you still need to use a particular instance type, OS, and tenancy. However, you cannot change these configurations with a standard RI. If you find that you have no further need for a standard RI and there is still a significant amount of time left in the term, you can try to sell the RI in the RI Marketplace to another customer that might be seeking an RI with your configuration. This is akin to another party taking over your lease. AWS will transact the change of ownership and payment to the new owner.

Although we learned that you could modify some aspects of your standard RI, there are some limitations. In the next section, we'll see how we can exchange RIs for entirely new configurations with convertible RIs.

Exchanging reserved instances

Standard RIs provide minimal flexibility. The better way to deal with uncertainty and to increase the utilization rate of your reservations, and hence decrease waste, is to use convertible RIs.

The trade-off for a better discount with standard RIs is decreased flexibility. Conversely, you have increased flexibility with convertible RIs but at a lower discount rate than standard RIs. Arguably, convertible RIs may save you more costs in the long run if your workload configuration needs to change. From our previous example, we saw poor RI utilization over a 12-month period. Business can experience both internal and external changes such as new business requirements or new product and service launches from AWS. Sometimes, it's worth paying the premium to have that flexibility to change the terms of a commitment given how quickly both business and technology changes.

When you purchase a convertible RI, you can exchange the RI to match a new workload requirement. As stated before, the new RI must be of equal or greater value than the existing RI. If you need to change to a cheaper RI configuration, you may need to purchase additional convertible RIs to cover the difference.

Figure 6.4 and *Figure 6.5* demonstrate exchanging an existing convertible RI for a new reservation. You can exchange a convertible RI for a new RI on the Amazon EC2 page:

1. Select the RI you want to exchange. Select **Exchange Reserved Instances** from the **Actions** menu. You can then select the desired RI configuration that you want to exchange to. The new RI expires on the same day as the old RI but with different configurations:

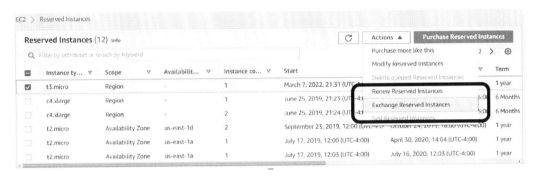

Figure 6.4 – Selecting the RI to exchange

2. Select the desired target RI configuration.

3. Select **Find offering** to find new RIs to match your configuration.

4. Select **Review**, then **Exchange** to execute the change.

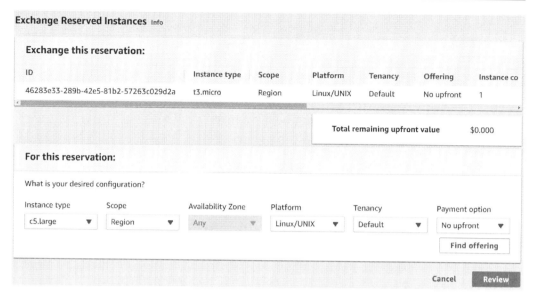

Figure 6.5 – Exchanging a convertible RI for a new RI

There will be a cost involved for the exchange unless you exchange for an RI with the same value. As with standard RIs, convertible RIs can also be modified from Regional to Zonal (and vice versa) and by instance size at no charge, assuming it's Linux/UNIX. You can imagine things get complicated quickly when you exchange RIs at scale. The operational burden to purchase, monitor, and manage your reservation fleet and coordinate with teams to ensure that they are using the right instance types to match your reservations can overwhelm the team.

Managing RIs to maximize your savings necessitates time and resources, which are difficult to spare especially if you're a large organization. Fortunately, at the time of writing this book, AWS is moving to a different approach with the same mechanisms and discount rates, but much less management on your part. The approach is to use SPs.

Improving utilization with SPs

SPs provide the same discounts as RIs but require less management, such as the need to exchange or modify RIs. SPs still come in two types, **EC2 Instance SPs** and **Compute SPs**, and the discount rates are equivalent to standard RIs and convertible RIs, respectively. Where they excel is in their flexibility. Remember, with standard RIs, you are committed to specific instance configurations tying you down to using instances to match the RI configuration for many months. With EC2 Instance SPs, you are only committed to the Region and instance family. This means you can change the OS, tenancy, and instance size and still get the discount rate.

Compute SPs provide even greater flexibility at the same discount rate as convertible RIs. Compute SPs don't even require a Region or instance type selection. Instead, you commit to an hourly dollar rate. Based on the instances you used, AWS will apply the discount rates to your launched instances until it reaches your committed hourly dollar rate. AWS does this automatically for you, removing the need to modify and exchange your RI fleet to optimize savings.

As a simple example, say you commit to a $10 hourly rate for a Compute SP. *Figure 6.6* shows a hypothetical pricing chart for different instance types for demonstration purposes. Given your $10 per hour commitment, AWS will rank your instances based on the savings percentage, and then draw down the SP hourly rate from your commitment amount. For this given hour, **Instance 1** was running with a savings rate of 60%. Since this is the highest savings percentage out of the five instances, it is ranked first. The instance consumes $2 from the $10 commitment. Now, you have $8 left. AWS then sees **Instance 2** as the next greatest savings percentage and subtracts $3 from the remaining $8. By the time it reaches **Instance 5**, you've exhausted your hourly commitment. Thus, **Instance 5** will be billed at the on-demand rate. All the instances before **Instance 5** were billed at the SP discounted rate instead of the on-demand rate. In other words, you saved on those instance costs automatically without needing to match your launched instances to an RI configuration:

Hourly Commitment: $	10.00		
	SP Hourly Rate	OD Hourly Rate	Savings %
Instance 1	$ 2.00	$ 3.20	60%
Instance 2	$ 3.00	$ 4.50	50%
Instance 3	$ 4.00	$ 5.60	40%
Instance 4	$ 1.00	$ 1.20	20%
Instance 5	$ 3.00	$ 3.50	17%

Figure 6.6 – Applying SP rates to usage

The purchase options for SPs are the same as the purchase options for RIs, with one slight difference. You can still choose between three payment options. However, for SPs, you can choose your partial upfront amount to be 50% due upfront. The total amount of the SP is based on the term, either one or three years.

What differs between RIs and SPs is how AWS applies the discount on your behalf. With RIs, essentially AWS would see EC2 instance usage, then see whether you have any RIs with configurations that match that usage, and finally, apply the discount rate if there's a match. If there's no match, it charges the on-demand rate. With SPs, rather than matching usage to an RI instance configuration, AWS simply takes your dollar commit and applies it to all applicable instances.

SPs and RIs can be shared across accounts within your organization, which can help reduce the overall expenditure. SPs and RIs prioritize the account that purchased them. For example, if you purchase an SP at the management (payer) account, then AWS will prioritize the SP rate to any compute use within the management account first before applying the discount rate to any other compute use in the other accounts.

If you develop your account strategy so that you don't have any compute resources running in the management account, or perhaps a dedicated SP/RI purchasing account, then the discounts can disseminate freely across all your accounts. In this way, AWS will rank savings percentages for all compute use across all accounts as in *Figure 6.6* and apply discounts accordingly.

You can elect to turn off sharing for specific accounts if your business requires you to do so. Or, you can purchase SPs/RIs in a specific account if you want to prioritize discounts for that account. This may be desirable to ensure that certain workloads get a discount. By purchasing SPs/RIs in an account, AWS will first do the ranking exercise within that account before seeing whether any remaining commitment can be applied to other accounts. For example, even if a savings percentage is greater for an instance in account B than an instance in account A, if account A purchased the SP, AWS ensures that account A uses the same amount of the hourly commitment before applying the discounted rate to instances running in account B.

Figure 6.7 shows sharing options in the AWS **Billing** console. Once you navigate to the AWS **Billing** dashboard in the **AWS Management Console**, you can select **Billing preferences** from the left-hand menu. The accounts in the left-hand box will share RIs and SPs, while the accounts listed in the right-hand box will be excluded from sharing:

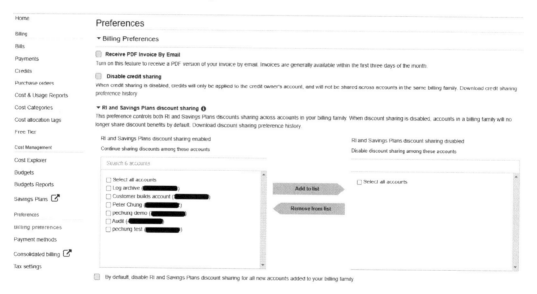

Figure 6.7 – RI and SP discount sharing in the AWS Billing console

Consequently, achieving high utilization with SPs is easier than with RIs. Because now, instead of the question being "are you using this instance type?", the question simply becomes, "are you using compute?" Compute SPs also provide discounted rates on AWS Lambda and AWS Fargate usage as well. Lambda is a serverless compute service in which the underlying server is abstracted from you entirely. By using Lambda, developers tell AWS what to do via code, and let AWS handle how to do it. Fargate is also serverless and tasks AWS with the same level of responsibility but is specifically used for containers. With Compute SPs covering these types of compute uses and instances regardless of Region, they provide better coverage with less management than convertible RIs.

Cost Explorer can provide suggestions if you're unsure of what your hourly commitment should be. Cost Explorer assumes your historical usage will continue, and provides recommendations from a 7-, 30-, or 60-day lookback period. You can use these suggestions as a baseline if you want to further refine your analyses.

Figure 6.8 shows the console view with options to tailor the recommended amount. Here we see Cost Explorer SP recommendations for a **Compute Savings Plans** type at the **Payer** account level for a **1-year** term:

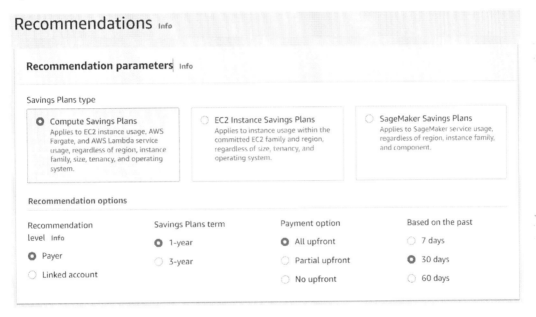

Figure 6.8 – Savings Plans recommendations

Once you've selected a desired SP configuration, Cost Explorer provides details of the SP terms, as shown in *Figure 6.9*. Here, we see that after committing to a $0.19 per hour amount to compute, the estimated savings is around $136 per month. AWS will apply the discount rate to all eligible compute uses, removing any need for you to manage it yourself.

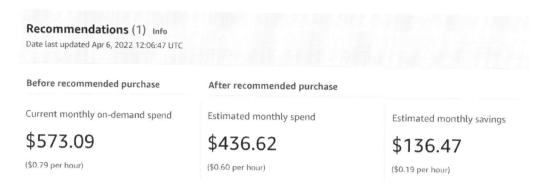

Figure 6.9 – SP terms

SPs offer greater flexibility than RIs. We saw how AWS applies the SP rate discount to your instance usage automatically, saving you the time it takes to exchange convertible RIs. We also learned how to enable and disable RI/SP sharing across accounts, and how to get SP recommendations from Cost Explorer. We'll learn more about another useful SP report in Cost Explorer next, namely the SP Coverage report.

Knowing when to buy more SPs

You can find the SP (and RI) Coverage report in Cost Explorer, which provides insight into how much of your instance costs were at the SP discounted rate for a given period. A coverage of 0% means that you did not benefit from a SP discounted rate, while a coverage of 100% means that AWS applied the SP discounted rate to all your instance usage. In other words, you didn't pay the on-demand rate for any instance usage under a 100% coverage rate; all instance usage was optimized.

Achieving a 100% coverage rate should be the goal to maximize your cost savings potential. However, not all organizations can obtain and sustain that goal due to competing priorities, lack of personnel, and different levels of FinOps maturity. From my experience, aiming for a coverage rate between 60% to 80% is a good start and reasonable to attain. I find that many AWS customers that act on the SP recommendations in Cost Explorer reach that range.

In practice, use SP Coverage report to help analyze your SP commitment amounts before a SP purchase, and use SP utilization reports to quantify how well you optimize from the purchase. You can also start with a small SP commitment and purchase additional ones incrementally. With SPs, you can immediately start reducing waste by optimizing your compute expenditure without a significant upfront financial cost when choosing the no upfront option. Moreover, there isn't the need to manage them as much as with RIs since AWS takes care of the billing and applies the discounts to your instance use during the month.

You can also use SPs and reservations budgets to track coverage and utilization rates over time. With these budgets, AWS will notify when a target coverage rate goes below a threshold. This can be a signal to purchase more SPs, assuming continued use of compute resources. AWS will also notify you when you set a utilization target to inform you when a SP or RI is being underutilized.

Figure 6.10 shows a user setting a utilization rate of 75% for a SP when creating a utilization budget. This means you will be notified if your utilization rate is less than the target 75%:

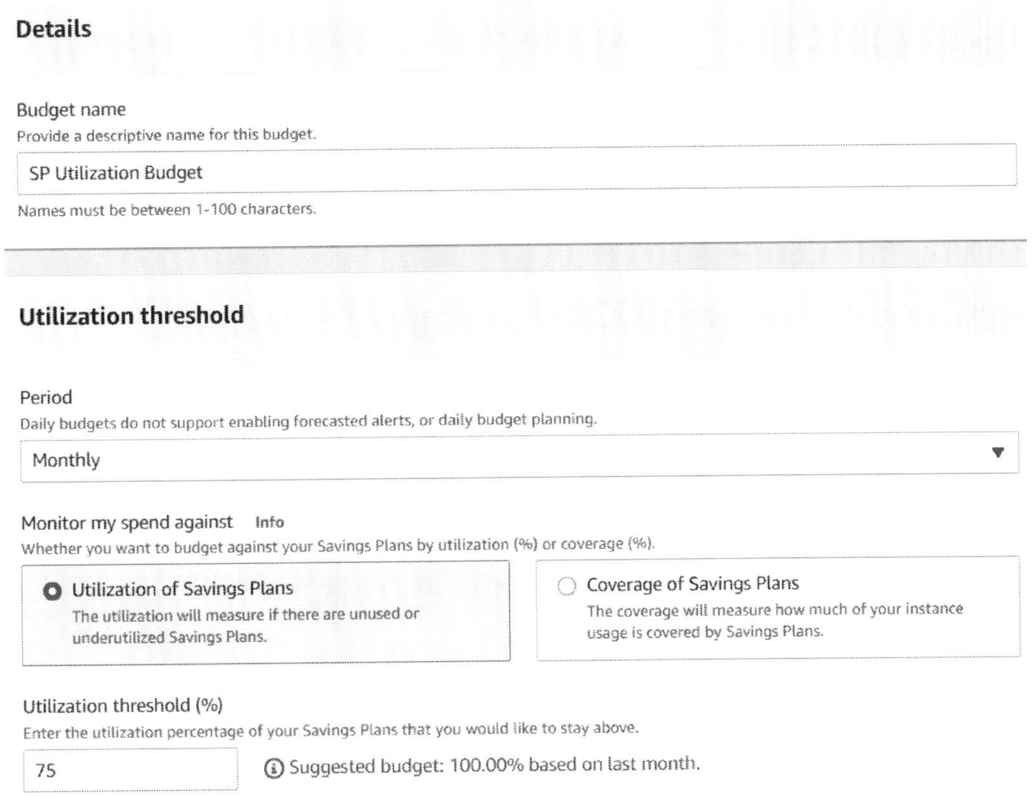

Details

Budget name
Provide a descriptive name for this budget.

| SP Utilization Budget |

Names must be between 1-100 characters.

Utilization threshold

Period
Daily budgets do not support enabling forecasted alerts, or daily budget planning.

| Monthly ▼ |

Monitor my spend against   Info
Whether you want to budget against your Savings Plans by utilization (%) or coverage (%).

○ **Utilization of Savings Plans**
The utilization will measure if there are unused or underutilized Savings Plans.

○ **Coverage of Savings Plans**
The coverage will measure how much of your instance usage is covered by Savings Plans.

Utilization threshold (%)
Enter the utilization percentage of your Savings Plans that you would like to stay above.

| 75 | ⓘ Suggested budget: 100.00% based on last month.

Figure 6.10 - Setting a utilization rate of 75%

RIs are ideal for steady-state workloads such as instances that need to be available and running 24/7. The on-demand price for these types of instances makes little financial sense when you can be paying for them at a lower price. Even if they don't run 24/7 for the entire length of the committed term, the break-even point tends to be around 8 to 9 months in a 1-year commitment or around 18 months in a 3-year commitment. In other words, even if you only use the reserved instances for 10 months out of the 12 months you paid, you're still getting a better rate than paying the on-demand price and hence, still saving money. Compute SPs make this even easier because you are no longer tied down to an instance type. AWS will apply the discount rate to any form of compute you use during the term.

Though not all workloads are steady-state, organizations commonly run batch workloads that require compute for short periods of time, or teams need to temporarily use compute to run some experiments for testing purpose. It may not be a big deal if the compute isn't available for some reason because teams can just restart the job or relaunch an instance with a different instance type. **Amazon EC2 Spot** is ideal in cases such as these where you can sacrifice availability for an even cheaper price.

Purchasing SPs at VidyaGames

Jeremy speaks with Ezra to learn more about VidyaGames' RI purchasing strategy. During their meeting, Ezra shares with Jeremy that his team has been the lead when it comes to purchasing RIs for the organization. Some application teams purchase RIs themselves while others do not. Ezra and his team work to fill in gaps where VidyaGames can benefit from increased coverage.

Jeremy and Ezra agree that the current operating model is inefficient and does not lead to long-term optimization. Purchasing RIs should not be a concern for applications teams. They should rather be focused on building software for customers. Ezra states that centralizing RI purchases makes sense, but his team needs more information from the application teams to know which RIs to purchase.

Ezra: We need to know what the developers' plans are so that we can buy the right RIs. There have been many cases where they say they are going to use a certain instance type but after a few months, they end up changing it. Then, it's up to me and my team to exchange them for the right RIs, which is a daunting task.

Jeremy: How many RIs do we have now and when are they expiring?

Ezra: I don't know how many we have off the top of my head, but I do know that they are expiring at the end of this month because I have a purchase queued up for a new fleet.

Jeremy: Have you considered using SPs instead? I heard they're much more flexible and you don't have to spend time doing exchanges.

Ezra: I haven't. What are they?

Jeremy enlightens Ezra on SPs. Ezra heaves a sigh of relief, as he's hopeful that SPs can eliminate his need to exchange RIs on a regular basis. They decide that at the end of the month, they will purchase a small Compute SP to see how it works.

In this section, we unpacked how RIs and SPs work as billing mechanisms. We saw how SPs can improve your utilization and thus optimize your AWS expenditure by removing a lot of the operational work of matching the instance launches to the RI configuration. We looked also at related reports in Cost Explorer that tell you how much you're benefitting from these mechanisms and how you can benefit further by purchasing more to improve your coverage. In the next section, we'll look at another way for paying for Amazon EC2 compute resources using Spot.

Maximizing savings for flexible workloads

As with RIs and SPs, Spot provides you a discount on EC2 usage but with a different rate. Unlike RIs and SPs, Spot is ideal for workloads that can withstand interruption and can be instance-flexible, meaning you generally don't care which instance type you use to complete a task. For these trade-offs, Spot provides steeper discounts than SPs.

AWS first offered the `m1.small` instance type back in 2006. At the time of writing, AWS now provides over 400 different types of instances to use. We can safely assume that AWS has a lot of spare capacity. AWS offers this spare capacity to customers with a steep discount compared to on-demand instances on the condition that AWS can retake that spare capacity back when needed. AWS provides a 2-minute warning, so this process doesn't abruptly terminate your running workload.

Spot terminations were more prevalent in the earlier years of AWS. Today, given the growing number of instances available, Spot terminations are becoming less likely but they still can occur. But think of choosing the instance types as though you were choosing a parking spot in a shopping mall. Everyone will want to choose the parking spot closest to the mall (they want to walk less.) If you also choose to minimize walking, you'll be waiting for capacity to become available, potentially circling the lot several times to find that ideal spot. If instead you choose less desirable spots, you'll likely encounter interruptions (sometimes it's just worth parking far away so you're not near anyone else.)

Although parking spots and EC2 Spot aren't necessarily the same other than being linked by the word itself, the idea is applicable. If you architect your environment so that you can run your application whether it's on an `r5`, or an `m5`, or a `m4`, or a `C5`, or a `C6g` instance type, then you'll be less likely to encounter interruption. You can create a Spot Fleet, configuring the instances types that constitute your Fleet. The more diversely you create your Fleet, the less chance there is of interruption because the chances of AWS taking capacity back for six different instance types are lower than taking capacity back for one instance type.

You also define an allocation strategy as part of your Spot Fleet configuration. This strategy tells AWS how to fulfill your instance requests from the specified Spot capacity pool. Say your pool consists of the following instance types: `c3.large`, `m3.large`, `t2.large`, `c4.large`, and `r3.large`. The (default) lowest price strategy chooses instances based on the lowest price from your pool, whereas the capacity-optimized strategy chooses based on the available capacity and hence, minimizes chances of interruption. Choosing the lowest price may be desirable from strictly a cost perspective, but you may want to choose another strategy based on the workload at hand, particularly if availability is more important than cost savings.

When you request Spot, you indicate the maximum price you are willing to pay. This is not a bidding system. You are not bidding against other customers and it's not a system where the bidder with the highest price wins. Rather, Spot prices fluctuate based on demand, and the prices can be different depending on which AZ you choose. *Figure 6.11* shows a Spot price history for a `c5.large` instance type to show the variance in price. If the price for an instance goes above your price threshold, then that triggers an interruption. Spot will then give you 2 minutes before taking the capacity back. By default, the maximum Spot price is the on-demand price for the instance.

Figure 6.11 shows the price history for `c3.large`, Linux instances over a 3-month span in the EC2 console. The price history chart also shows Spot prices by AZ:

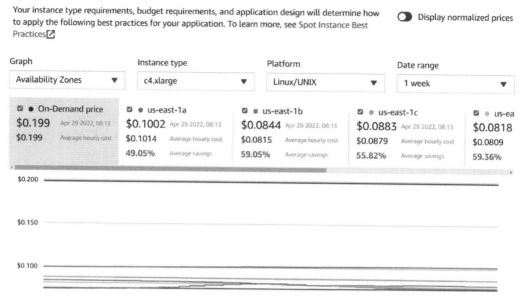

Figure 6.11 – Spot Instance pricing history

Using Spot with your compute is a great tool to utilize for your optimization efforts. Mixing Spot and on-demand instances within a Fleet is another quick way to reduce costs since by mixing these pricing models, you get the best of both worlds, maintaining availability through on-demand instances, while reducing costs where you can with Spot.

Choosing the right pricing model will depend on the type of workload. *Figure 6.12* shows typical usage patterns where each pricing model may be applicable. Choose SPs for steady-state workloads that are presented. This allows you to pay at a consistently lower price. Then, for workloads that are unpredictable and cannot tolerate interruptions, choose on-demand because using SPs would otherwise result in lower utilization and therefore wasteful expenditure. Finally, use Spot for workloads that can be interrupted, such as batch workloads, which may run over the weekend.

Figure 6.12 – Amazon EC2 pricing models

Many customers see Spot as a risky choice due to the likelihood of interruption. However, AWS has helped alleviate this fear in several ways, including increasing the total number of instances available, increasing the number of AZs steadily, and providing mechanisms such as *rebalance recommendations* for Spot. A rebalance recommend signals when a Spot Instance is at a high risk of interruption. You can use this signal to proactively manage Spot Instances prior to the 2-minute warning. You can also use the *Capacity Rebalancing* feature in Spot Fleets that helps you augment your Spot Fleet with new Spot Instances.

The best way to test the stability of Spot is to actually use them. You can follow AWS best practices to minimize risk of interruption by testing Spot with smaller projects, in sandbox environments, or time-insensitive batch processing. Using on-demand instances for these workloads at scale contributes to waste since they are not critical to your business. Be sure to include Spot in your compute workloads, as they can significantly lower costs.

EC2 Spot and RIs/SPs are great tools to optimize your compute usage. But we also want to reduce waste when choosing the right amount of compute. This is called right-sizing and is the topic of the next section.

Right sizing compute

An important question that arises is "do I first need to right-size my instances before reserving them?" Indeed, we don't want to reserve an instance when it turns out it wasn't the right instance to reserve in the first place! Doing so would contribute to waste. With SPs, this question becomes less relevant because with Compute SPs, you have more flexibility in the type of instances you launch. Even if you're launching one instance type today, and you launch a different instance type tomorrow, you still benefit from the SP rate on the new instance type as long as you have enough in your cumulative hourly commitment to cover usage.

Right sizing is still a critical component of cloud waste management. Right sizing leverages the elasticity of the cloud. When you provisioned servers in a data center, you provisioned for peak. To maintain your service, you purchased enough servers (and beefy servers at that) to handle maximum capacity, even if this only constituted a few hours in a year. For other times during the year, the beefier machines would run overutilized. You would not efficiently use your resources. On the other hand, the trade-off was to provision appropriately sized servers that ran efficiently during most of the year, but during times of high requests, you would just deal with an outage when needs exceeded capacity. With right sizing, you can dynamically provision compute to meet demand as and when needed. There's no need to guess your capacity requirements and be locked in to a specific server and fleet size for the lifetime of the machines.

AWS provides you with a wide range of different instance types to meet your workload requirements. General purpose instances provide a balance of compute, memory, and networking power, and are a good fit for flexible workloads, or if you're unsure about where to start. You can also choose between compute-, memory-, or network-optimized instances. There are also accelerated computing instances as well for specialized workloads. Given the wide range of instance types to choose from, it's likely that you will iterate on different instance types and sizes to choose the optimal one. Fortunately, Cost Explorer can help with this.

Cost Explorer provides right sizing recommendations to help you efficiently run your resources. This helps reduce your overall waste when the resources meet your computing needs. Similar in its approach to recommending RIs and SPs, right-sizing recommendations will analyze your historical EC2 usage and identify idle and underutilized instances. For example, if Cost Explorer identified a number of `c5.xlarge` instances that were running at less than 5% CPU consistently for 2 weeks, you could consider changing those instances to a smaller instance type and benefit from the savings.

You can select from two finding types with right-sizing recommendations. You can select between idle and/or underutilized instances. *Figure 6.13* chooses both. Cost Explorer recommends changing instance size from `t2.small` to `t2.micro`:

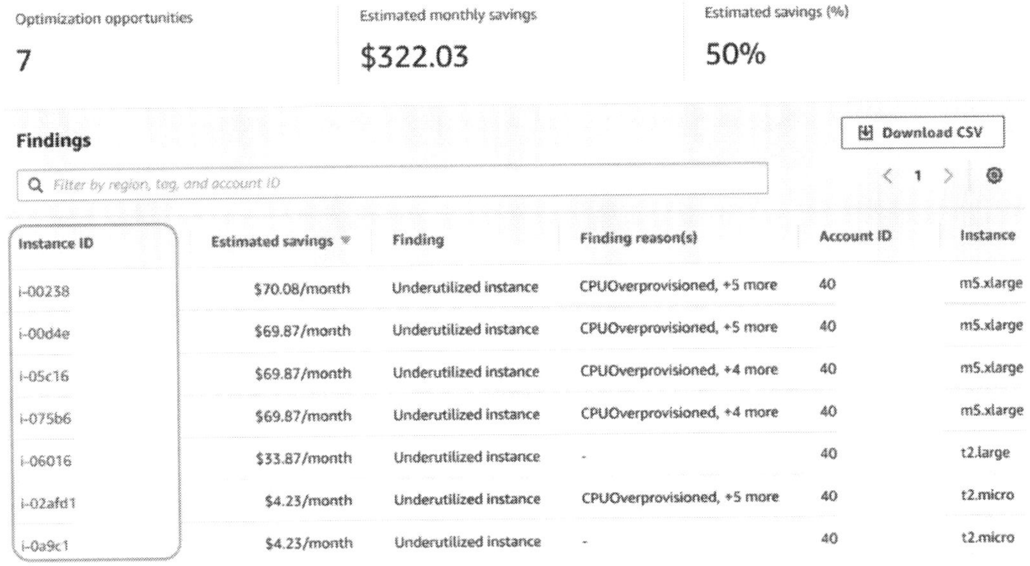

Optimization opportunities	Estimated monthly savings	Estimated savings (%)
7	$322.03	50%

Findings   ⬇ **Download CSV**

Q Filter by region, tag, and account ID   ‹ 1 › ⚙

Instance ID	Estimated savings ▼	Finding	Finding reason(s)	Account ID	Instance
i-00238	$70.08/month	Underutilized instance	CPUOverprovisioned, +5 more	40	m5.xlarge
i-00d4e	$69.87/month	Underutilized instance	CPUOverprovisioned, +5 more	40	m5.xlarge
i-05c16	$69.87/month	Underutilized instance	CPUOverprovisioned, +4 more	40	m5.xlarge
i-075b6	$69.87/month	Underutilized instance	CPUOverprovisioned, +4 more	40	m5.xlarge
i-06016	$33.87/month	Underutilized instance	-	40	t2.large
i-02afd1	$4.23/month	Underutilized instance	CPUOverprovisioned, +5 more	40	t2.micro
i-0a9c1	$4.23/month	Underutilized instance	-	40	t2.micro

Figure 6.13 – Right-sizing recommendations in Cost Explorer

AWS Compute Optimizer performs a similar function as right-sizing recommendations. However, while right-sizing recommendations only suggest actions that size down, Compute Optimizer also suggests actions that size *up*. Perhaps this works against cost savings efforts but the trade-off may be necessary depending on the business requirements.

Figure 6.14 shows the AWS Compute Optimizer dashboard reflecting one optimized EC2 instance. You can access Compute Optimizer from the management account to view optimization recommendations for all the accounts in your organization. Although Compute Optimizer doesn't provide an aggregate view, you can select an account individually from the drop-down menu in the **AWS Management Console** to view recommendations per account. Compute Optimizer also helps you rightsize your EBS volumes, which we will look closely at in the next chapter.

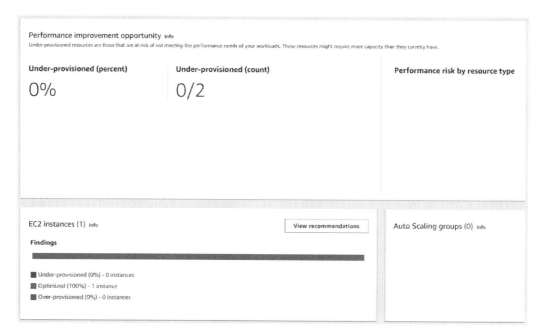

Figure 6.14 – The AWS Compute Optimizer dashboard

Compute Optimizer suggests optimizing EBS volumes using Auto Scaling groups. We will learn more about EBS volumes in *Chapter 7, Optimizing Storage,* and Auto Scaling groups in *Chapter 9, Optimizing Cloud-Native Environments.* Finally, Compute Optimizer looks at ways to optimize your **AWS Lambda** functions. Let's learn more about Lambda in the next section.

Optimizing AWS Lambda

AWS Lambda is a serverless compute service that allows you to simply write or upload code, and AWS takes care of managing the underlying infrastructure to execute your code. Compared to Amazon EC2, you don't have to worry about changing to different instance types, ensuring your instances are highly available, and securing your instances. Lambda integrates with over 200 AWS services and is great for building event-driven architectures.

To optimize Lambda, we must first understand the cost factors behind the service. The first is the execution time of your Lambda function. AWS charges your Lambda usage based on milliseconds of execution time. So, the shorter the Lambda execution time, the less you will pay.

Lambda lets you choose between several languages to execute your code. Generally, a compiled language such as C++, Rust, and Go will run faster but will take longer to initialize. Therefore, a compiled language typically works better with applications that require heavy computational complexity. Otherwise, for simple functions, choose integrated languages such as Python and Node.

You can also use **provisioned concurrency** with a compiled language to reduce its runtime. **Provisioned concurrency** is a feature that keeps functions initialized (or warmed up) to respond quickly. When you invoke a Lambda function, the request is routed to an execution environment. When the function hasn't been invoked for a while, AWS needs to create a new execution environment. This takes time. And the function's dependencies, such as having to install code and packages, can prolong the time it takes to run. This is called a *cold start*, as with having to warm up your car in cold weather. **Provisioned concurrency** seeks to reduce the cold start problem by initializing the requested number of execution environments so that they are ready to respond quickly. This ensures that the car is warmed up and the inside is nice and toasty before you start driving.

Figure 6.15 shows how you can configure provisioned concurrency in the Lambda console. To do so using the **AWS Management Console**, do the following:

1.   Select your function within the Lambda console.

2.   Select the **Configuration** tab.

3.   Select **Concurrency** on the left-side menu.

You can select several options on this page and add or edit your provisioned concurrency configurations:

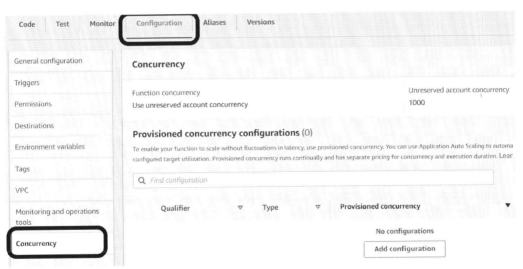

Figure 6.15 – The AWS Lambda console

What logically follows is to try and minimize the number of dependencies and libraries in your initialization code. This is a major contributor to latencies and longer execution times before you start running the code that needs to perform the task at hand.

Another cost aspect of Lambda is memory configurations. If you overprovision your Lambda function, it will bring additional costs such as those incurred by overprovisioning EC2 instances. You can set the **Memory** configuration for your Lambda function, as shown in *Figure 6.16*:

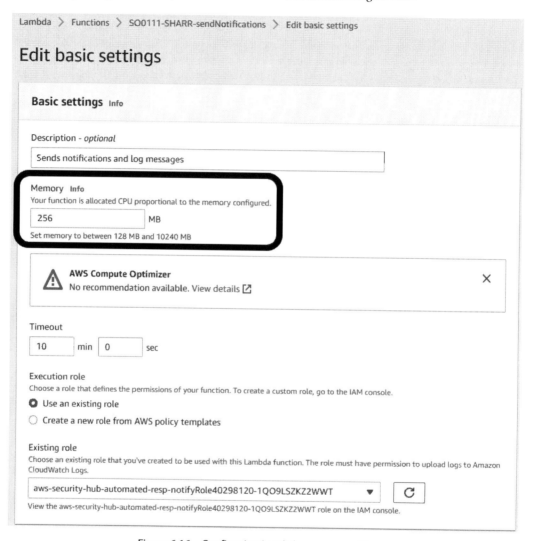

Figure 6.16 – Configuring Lambda memory settings

Don't think that overprovisioning is a poor choice. You might be tempted to automatically configure the smallest memory amount to maintain low costs, but a low memory configuration can contribute to longer execution times. The increase in memory may be negligible in terms of cost but can potentially have a greater impact on reducing your execution times. Be sure to monitor your functions and adjust them accordingly to optimize their usage. Use the Compute Optimizer tool to help you gain this visibility.

Recall that Compute SPs apply to Lambda usage as well. Not only will your EC2 instances benefit from a discounted hourly rate with Compute SPs, but your Lambda execution times will experience a lower millisecond cost if you have enough hourly commitment to cover these compute services.

We looked at ways to optimize Lambda costs in this section. Primarily, we want to reduce the execution time and configure enough memory to ensure the Lambda function runs optimally. Compute SPs and provisioned concurrency can help reduce Lambda costs as well.

Summary

Our focus in this chapter was optimizing compute services on AWS. We spent the first section of the chapter diving deep into billing mechanisms that benefit steady-state workloads. RIs and SPs are perfect for covering workloads that require compute resources to be on consistently throughout the year.

We unpacked how billing works for both options and concluded that SPs are preferable to RIs because of their flexibility and lower maintenance requirements. Because both options offer the same discount rates, there is little reason to choose RIs over SPs. Cost Explorer provides reports and recommendations to help you with your RI/SP purchasing strategy.

We also explored Spot as another option for compute services. Spot is ideal for flexible and interruptible workloads because of the deep discount AWS provides. However, we must be mindful of how we architect workloads using Spot due to the interruptible nature of Spot resources. We reviewed mechanisms to keep our workload resilient against Spot interruptions, such as the capacity-optimized allocation strategy and capacity rebalancing.

Finally, we looked at ways to right-size our compute resources through right-sizing recommendations and Compute Optimizer. We learned Lambda's mechanisms and discussed strategies to reduce its execution time to save on costs.

In the next chapter, we turn our focus toward storage. As with optimizing compute, all applications require storage to persist data. We'll find ways to optimize our storage costs on AWS.

Further reading

Have a look at the following resources:

- *Amazon EC2 Instance Types*, 2022: `https://aws.amazon.com/ec2/instance-types/`
- *Amazon EC2 On-Demand Pricing*, 2022: `https://aws.amazon.com/ec2/pricing/on-demand/`
- *EC2 Instance History*, 2015: `https://aws.amazon.com/blogs/aws/ec2-instance-history/`
- *Best practices for EC2 Spot*, 2022: `https://docs.aws.amazon.com/AWSEC2/latest/UserGuide/spot-best-practices.html`

7

Optimizing Storage

While compute focuses on the *doing of things*, storage focuses on the *keeping of things*. You need a place to store your data. Given the volume, velocity, and veracity of data, today's technology landscape commonly refers to data as the *new oil*. Enterprises are looking at ways to leverage their data as assets, monetize them, and draw meaningful insights from them. Although directly monetizing data is outside the scope of this book, we can at least optimize our stored data to make it readily available if or when you ever venture down that path.

AWS provides several ways to store your data, and we'll focus on optimizing object and block storage. We also look at optimizing databases. Some of the topics we covered in the last chapter will reappear here.

In this chapter, we're going to cover the following main topics:

- Optimizing object storage
- Optimizing databases
- Optimizing block and file storage

Technical requirements

To complete the exercises in this chapter, the requirements are the same as the previous chapters.

Optimizing object storage

We've discussed in great detail the on-demand provisioning of compute resources in the previous chapter. With all that compute capacity, whether you're using EC2 instances or Lambda functions, you need somewhere to store your data. Fortunately, storage is just as easily and readily available on AWS as compute.

Amazon Simple Storage Service (**Amazon S3**) is widely used as a storage medium on AWS. But reducing waste on storage costs with Amazon S3 is going to depend on the application, because an application used for backup and archive is going to have different needs from an e-commerce site or a streaming video service.

Reducing Amazon S3 costs boils down to three concerns:

- Where you store the data in S3

- How often you retrieve that data

- Where you move that data to

These concerns will differ based on the workload. For example, a backup workload will be less likely to have requests and retrieval requests than a video streaming service. Even for the video streaming service, access patterns will change over time, as new content will likely be requested more than older content.

We'll focus on optimizing Amazon S3 in three ways. First, we'll discuss Amazon S3 hygiene since keeping our data storage clean and manageable is critical to our optimization efforts. Then, we'll learn about the different storage classes and how you can use them to maximize savings. Lastly, we'll discuss operationalizing Amazon S3 at scale so that you can manage your storage costs even when your storage volume increases exponentially over time.

Establishing clean S3 hygiene

The first thing you need to decide is how you're going to organize the data that you store in Amazon S3. This is the same approach we took when we started. We first talked about organizing your accounts in the right multi-account structure and creating logical boundaries that reflected your business hierarchy or application domains (see *Chapter 2, Establishing the Right Account Structure*). The same goes for your data in Amazon S3. What we want to avoid is creating a kitchen sink of data that you're unable to optimize simply because you don't even know what to look for.

First, you organize your data with buckets. Buckets act as a logical container that holds objects, whether those objects are CSV files, ZIP files, MP3 files, or plain text files. You can certainly create one bucket and put everything in there. S3 will automatically scale to meet your requirements. However, it will very likely become burdensome later because you'll have to search through your entire bucket to find what you're looking for.

To minimize this risk, use **prefixes** as layers of hierarchy to organize your objects within an S3 bucket. Prefixes mimic a folder structure that you can find your data within, just as you put objects or files within a folder path. For example, if you had data representing objects in a house, a `bed` object with a prefix of `house/master/bed` would be distinct from a `bed` object with a prefix of `house/guest/bed`. Although the `bed` object may appear to be the same, the prefix allows you to not only differentiate between them but also know where to find them.

You can also associate tags with specific objects, in addition to applying tags to a bucket. We've already covered the importance of tagging in previous chapters, but it's worth reiterating its value here. Tagging not only improves your cost visibility but also allows more granular control on where you want to store objects. S3 offers several different storage classes each with a different storage price. By deciding on the appropriate storage class based on the objects' access patterns, you will reduce storage cost waste.

Now that we've set the right foundations for maintaining proper S3 hygiene, let's see how we can choose the right storage class for our data to maximize our savings potential.

Optimizing with S3 storage classes

You can choose to sacrifice durability, availability, and performance for lower storage costs. However, when you pay for a lower storage cost, you pay for a higher object retrieval cost. S3 provides a total of eight different storage classes at the time of writing, of which six are shown in *Figure 7.1*. Here we see prices for the US-EAST-2 (OHIO) Region. These percentages show the change relative to the Amazon S3 Standard storage tier. For example, Amazon S3 Glacier Instant Retrieval is 83% cheaper than Amazon S3 Standard, but 300% more expensive for retrieval requests:

	S3 Standard	S3 Standard-IA	S3 One Zone-IA	S3 Glacier Instant Retrieval	S3 Glacier Flexible Retrieval	S3 Glacier Deep Archive
Storage Costs Per GB (up to 50TB/month)	$0.023	$0.0125 (46%)	$0.01 (57%)	$0.004 (83%)	$0.0036 (84%)	$0.00099 (96%)
PUT, COPY, POST, LIST (1000) Requests	$0.005	$0.01 100%	$0.01 100%	$0.02 300%	$0.03 500%	$0.05 900%

Figure 7.1 – Amazon S3 storage class comparison

The optimal storage class will depend on an object's access pattern. As a simple example, referring to *Figure 7.2*, say you serve a 1 GB video file to clients. Storing that file in S3 Standard would cost $0.023 per month, while storing it in Glacier Instant Retrieval would cost $0.004 per month, representing an 83% savings in storage. What a dream! Let's put it in S3 Glacier Instant Retrieval to save on costs. However, it's a popular file. A million (1,000 x 1,000) clients have requested to view it. Now, it costs $20 that month to retrieve that file a thousand times, when it would have cost $5 to retrieve it from S3 Standard otherwise:

Storage Costs + Retrieval cost per 1,000 requests		
Amazon S3 Standard	1GB * $0.023 + 1,000 * $0.005	**$5.02**
Amazon S3 Glacier Instance Retrieval	1GB * $0.004 + 1,000 * $0.02	**$20.00**

Figure 7.2 – S3 cost comparison

What if you don't really know an object's access pattern, but still want to take optimize storage costs? S3 provides the *Intelligent-Tiering* storage class to run those calculations for you. Intelligent-Tiering automatically reduces your storage costs by transferring data to the most cost-effective access tier based on your access patterns. Moreover, Intelligent-Tiering has no retrieval charges. If Intelligent-Tiering detected that the video wasn't accessed for a month (a far more interesting video is trending, by the way), it would move the now-obsolete video to a lower-cost tier optimized for infrequent access. If that video became popular again and was accessed later (oh wait, it's popular again), it would automatically be moved back.

In cases where you do understand your access patterns due to recurring application processes or domain expertise, you can use *lifecycle policies* to automatically move objects to the optimal class. A textbook example is to set a lifecycle policy to move objects to colder storage tiers a said number of days after object creation. *Figure 7.3* shows an example lifecycle policy transitioning objects after 30 days since creation to Standard-IA, One Zone-IA after 60 days, and Glacier Deep Archive after 90 days.

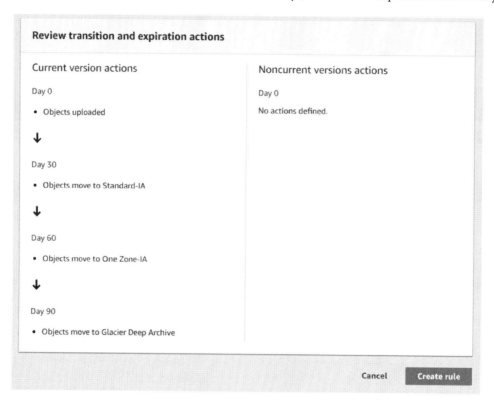

Figure 7.3 – An example of an Amazon S3 lifecycle policy

> **Important note**
> Amazon S3 Lifecycle Transition requests cost $0.01 per 1,000 requests at the time of writing. Therefore, it's always a good practice to use the AWS Pricing Calculator to estimate your costs and consider the transition cost before moving objects into any storage class.

You can use tags and prefixes for additional granularity. You may specify objects with tags and apply different lifecycle policies depending on those tags. You may also decide to apply lifecycle policies to objects contained in specific prefixes (or folders) within an S3 bucket. Or you, may choose to use a combination of both – *Figure 7.4* shows this in the Amazon S3 console view.

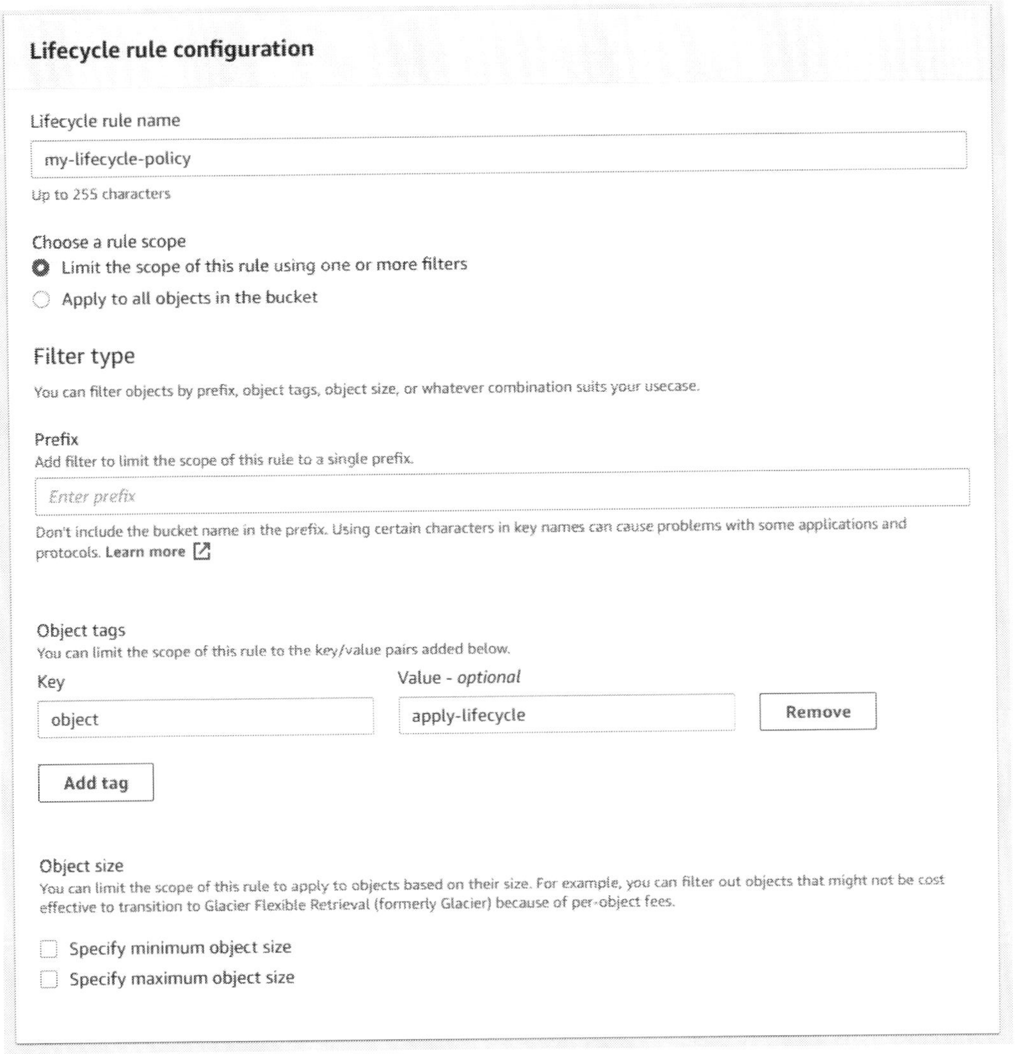

Lifecycle rule configuration

Lifecycle rule name

| my-lifecycle-policy |

Up to 255 characters

Choose a rule scope
- ● Limit the scope of this rule using one or more filters
- ○ Apply to all objects in the bucket

Filter type

You can filter objects by prefix, object tags, object size, or whatever combination suits your usecase.

Prefix
Add filter to limit the scope of this rule to a single prefix.

| Enter prefix |

Don't include the bucket name in the prefix. Using certain characters in key names can cause problems with some applications and protocols. **Learn more** [↗]

Object tags
You can limit the scope of this rule to the key/value pairs added below.

| Key | Value - *optional* | |
| object | apply-lifecycle | Remove |

Add tag

Object size
You can limit the scope of this rule to apply to objects based on their size. For example, you can filter out objects that might not be cost effective to transition to Glacier Flexible Retrieval (formerly Glacier) because of per-object fees.

- ☐ Specify minimum object size
- ☐ Specify maximum object size

Figure 7.4 – Applying lifecycle policies to objects tagged with specific object tags

VidyaReviews, a key application at VidyaGames

VidyaReviews is the core business application for VidyaGames. It is a social media platform where users share video game experiences. It was originally designed for users to share video game reviews to help other users determine whether to purchase a specific game or not. The application aggregates reviews but also allows users to follow specific profiles and popular influencers for their opinions. Users can pay a monthly premium to gain access to exclusive content and remove all digital ads from the online and mobile experience.

The application product team for VidyaReviews uses Amazon S3 to store users' video and image files. To keep things simple, the team placed all media files in the Standard storage class. However, as users grew and the amount of content uploaded and downloaded from the site increased, the team knew that this would not be a sustainable option.

The team analyzed two years of data about user access patterns. They found that once a studio releases a game on the market, demand for the game's media content on VidyaReviews usually last between one to two months. Sometimes game content demand will last three to six months, which happens for games that receive critical acclaim.

The team also found that when game studios launched a sequel to a game, demand for the previous installment of the game increases. This is likely because users want to experience or revisit a game before a highly anticipated sequel. The last finding was that demand for content can have unexpected spikes for no apparent reason. At random, demand for content for a specific game can dramatically increase even without announced sequels. A part of this can be explained because a sudden hit game within a specific genre may spark demand for other games in the same genre, or a movie release related to a game may suddenly spark demand for its content. Due to the unexpected nature of video game demand, the application team finds it difficult to generalize a pattern that they can apply to all content in S3, but they do identify two key patterns and formulate a strategy based on this.

The team decides on a two-prong strategy. Games with high aggregate reviews will have a certain tag, while games with lower aggregate reviews will have a different tag. Games with higher aggregate reviews tend to produce more content and have a higher likelihood to get a sequel in the future, whereas games with lower reviews tend to become obsolete within 30 days of their release. For games with higher aggregate reviews, the team plans to use Intelligent-Tiering. For games with lower aggregate reviews, they will implement a lifecycle policy to move the content to a colder storage tier. They will use tags to differentiate between higher and lower reviewed content.

Although they can use scrapers to analyze web content, capture trending social media topics, and use publicly available data to anticipate user demand, the team has other priorities and plans to revisit this later.

Organizing your objects in Amazon S3 will help you access them easily using separate buckets, prefixes, and tags. Save on costs by using colder storage tiers if the access patterns justify their use. You can upload them to a default colder tier or transition them to colder tiers using lifecycle policies. If you are unsure of the access patterns, you can use Intelligent-Tiering to automate the process. Next, we'll explore how to manage your data in S3 across multiple buckets and accounts.

Managing S3 at scale

Managing waste on a few S3 buckets and the objects within them is one thing, but doing this at scale with thousands of buckets can get complicated. Ideally, we've already set good practices in place so that your Cloud Center of Excellence and your teams know the purpose of those buckets and the objects within them. Having good S3 inventory hygiene reduces the headaches that come with the feeling of being overwhelmed by not knowing what you're in fact storing in S3.

Amazon Storage Lens can help with organization-wide visibility into object storage as a tool to supplement your storage hygiene. Storage Lens provides usage and activity metrics and reporting dashboards for your buckets across all your accounts within your Organization. Use Storage Lens metrics to see the access patterns for your objects so you can make data-driven choices about which storage class to choose. *Figure 7.5* shows an overview of the default **Storage Lens** dashboard in the **AWS Management Console**:

Figure 7.5 – The Storage Lens dashboard

Use the metrics in Storage Lens to your advantage. For instance, a 1 GB video is a good candidate for **multipart upload** (**MPU**) to S3. MPU allows you to upload objects to S3 in parts so that if the upload fails, you can continue uploading the other parts of the object without having to start all over again. However, when the MPU doesn't complete, the parts remain in S3 even when the task is aborted. You can see in *Figure 7.6* that there are 750 MBs of incomplete MPU. Storage Lens provides this view:

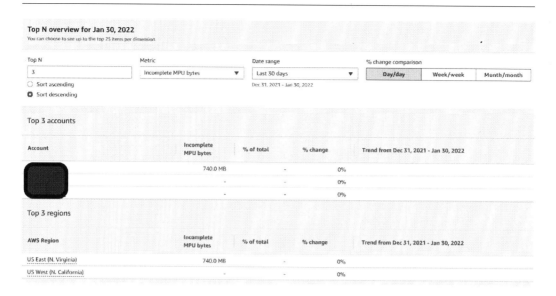

Figure 7.6 – The findings of Storage Lens

Storage Lens shows failed multi-part uploaded objects that can and should be cleaned up to reduce waste.

> **Important note**
> It is good practice to use multipart upload when your object sizes are at least 100 MB. Also, consider multipart upload over a stable high-bandwidth network to maximize the use of your networking by uploading objects in parallel.

Include Storage Lens as part of your toolkit to optimize storage across your AWS Organization. Storage Lens aggregates usage and activity metrics to the bucket and prefix level. This can help strengthen your sense of control over your AWS resources. Sometimes, overcoming the feeling of being overwhelmed by what you don't know is the first step in reducing your waste.

In this section, we covered proper Amazon S3 hygiene, choosing the right storage class, and leveraging organizational-wide visibility tools such as Storage Lens to manage your Amazon S3 storage at scale. In the next section, we'll continue our discussion on optimizing storage on AWS but focus on a different type of storage medium: the database.

Optimizing databases

We spent some time discussing RIs in the previous chapter. We concluded that compared to RIs, SPs offer less management overhead and better cost savings. Unfortunately, at the time of writing, SPs only provide discounted rates for compute services. Fortunately, though, RIs apply to database services, namely, **Amazon Relational Database Service (Amazon RDS)**, **Amazon ElastiCache**, **Amazon Redshift**, **Amazon OpenSearch Service**, and **Amazon DynamoDB**.

I won't go into the details of how each service works, although AWS documentation has plenty of information on that front (see the *Further reading* section at the end of the chapter for links). The mechanism for reserving database instances works the same as with EC2 instances. You still choose the term and payment option. You can still get recommendations in Cost Explorer for these types of reserved instances. The way AWS applies the discount works in the same way as well; if you purchased an RI, AWS would apply the discounted rate to any databases that match the configuration of the RI.

Figure 7.7 shows you several RI options for various AWS database services including Amazon RDS, ElastiCache, Redshift, and OpenSearch. You can also choose different payment options and a historical look-back period for recommendations:

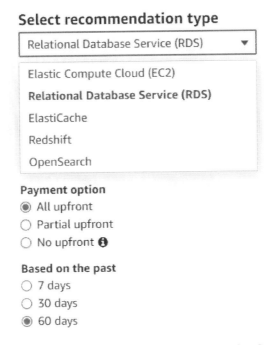

Figure 7.7 – Selecting RI recommendations for Amazon RDS in Cost Explorer

Let's now focus on how RIs work for Amazon RDS. The pricing mechanism is similar to how RIs work for Amazon EC2 instances, but there are some differences due to the nature of the service.

RDS-reserved instances

There are some RI nuances for RDS since, architecturally, databases aren't typically seen as cattle the way that servers in the cloud are. The phrase *treating servers as 'cattle'* gloomily refers to servers being easily dispensable for architects since they can quickly be replaced when running in the cloud. Databases, for better or worse, aren't as easily expendable because they can store critical data several applications may depend on.

To ensure that data is available, AWS recommends deploying an RDS instance with a multi-AZ instance configuration. *Figure 7.8* shows a logical representation of a multi-AZ RDS instance where, in fact, you have two databases running, one in **AZ 1** and the second in **AZ 2**:

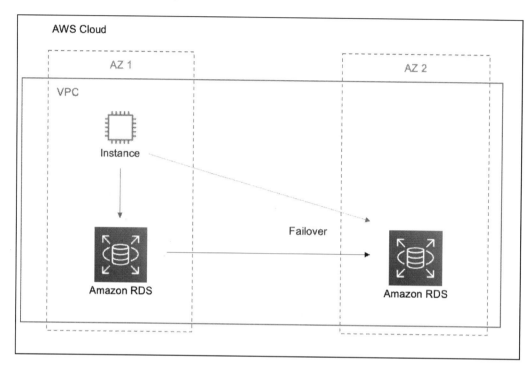

Figure 7.8 – A multi-AZ deployment of Amazon RDS

When the RDS instance in **AZ 1** fails, AWS automatically failovers to the instance in **AZ 2**, allowing an upstream instance server to continuously access data without downtime.

Because RDS is a managed service, AWS takes care of the failover by automatically switching to the standby. Hence, with this configuration you have two instances running.

> **Important note**
> Multi-AZ refers to multiple **Availability Zones** (**AZ**). In other words, RDS database instances are provisioned in more than one AZ.

If this is how you design your application, and you want to reserve the instances, then you should consider purchasing a multi-AZ deployment. If the preceding diagram matches your design and you only purchase a single-AZ reserved instance, then the discount rate will only apply to one of your

RDS instances. For example, the RDS instance in **AZ 1** will be priced at the discounted rate, while the standby in **AZ 2** will be charged the on-demand price. Therefore, purchasing a multi-AZ deployment can reduce wasteful on-demand spending if you plan to have RDS instances running on a consistent basis.

RDS RIs also provide size flexibility for most database engines. When you provision an RDS instance, you choose the engine and size of the instance, among other things. The size essentially doubles as you increase incrementally. For instance (no pun intended), an xlarge is twice the size of a large, a 2xlarge is twice the size of an xlarge, and so on (refer to our discussion on instance size flexibility in *Chapter 6, Optimizing Compute*). When you purchase an RDS-reserved instance that's enough to cover the size of a 2xlarge, you will get the discount rate if you launch either four large instances, or two xlarge instances, or one 2xlarge instance. In addition, if you launched a 4xlarge instance, half the cost will be at the on-demand rate with the other half being at the RI rate. Take advantage of the size flexibility because, where applicable, even a small reservation can cut costs even if you increase the size later.

> **Important note**
> Amazon EC2 also provides size flexibility but they only apply to Linux/Unix type instances at the time of writing. Size flexibility doesn't matter towards SPs, which should be the preferred approach.

Reserving RDS instances is an immediate way to save money since, as a billing mechanism, AWS will apply the discount on your behalf as long as the instance you launch matches the configuration of the reservation. Consider reserving multiple instances if you plan on launching several instances that have particular relevance for a HA configuration.

Using a managed service such as Amazon RDS can help optimize cost in another way, namely, to maximize the efficient use of a database. Amazon RDS supports Storage Auto Scaling, which automatically scales storage capacity in response to your workload demand. If you are running databases on Amazon EC2, you must consider the management implications of scaling out and scaling up the database when demand for storage increases or decreases. Without proper monitoring and automation, you may run into situations where you are overprovisioned to ensure the availability of your application, which can lead to cost increases. With RDS Storage Auto Scaling, AWS continuously monitors storage consumption to scale up capacity, automatically removing this management burden away from you and your teams. This improves your cost as you only pay for the storage you need when you need it. Because this feature has no additional cost, it is a benefit you can easily leverage to optimize your use of AWS database resources.

Now that we have a good understanding of optimizing Amazon RDS, let's explore how to optimize another database offering, Amazon OpenSearch Service.

Optimizing OpenSearch clusters

Amazon OpenSearch Service is a managed service for running OpenSearch clusters in the AWS Cloud. OpenSearch Service supports OpenSearch and the legacy, open source search, and analytics suite from ElasticSearch OSS.

For cost purposes, there are two main things to know about cost optimization with OpenSearch clusters. The first is reserving OpenSearch clusters. The mechanisms for reserved OpenSearch cluster instances are the same as reserved instances for Amazon RDS and Amazon EC2 instances. You still choose the payment option, the number of instances, instance type, and term length – nothing new here.

The second, more specific to OpenSearch Service, is the **UltraWarm** node storage option. Conceptually, this is similar to the colder storage classes within S3. For data stored in OpenSearch Service that you don't need as great a performance level for perhaps, and for less frequently queried or written data, UltraWarm provides a lower storage price. *Figure 7.9* shows the architecture of an Amazon OpenSearch Service cluster with both hot data and UltraWarm nodes. You can see that UltraWarm nodes are backed by Amazon S3:

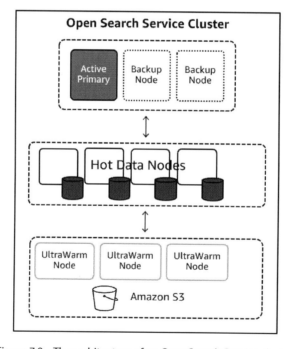

Figure 7.9 – The architecture of an OpenSearch Service cluster

While OpenSearch Service stores the hot data in EBS storage volumes, it uses S3 to store data in UltraWarm nodes. This gives you a better storage price, but still provides the durability and availability of S3. Note that UltraWarm can only store read-only indices. If you need to write to them, you must transition them to the hot nodes. An example use case would be to store your applications' log data in a search-focused data store such as OpenSearch Service. If you're planning on using OpenSearch Service to aggregate your logs, then it makes sense to store older, immutable log data in the UltraWarm tiers to reduce storage costs.

Amazon OpenSearch Service is a great place to store your applications' log data. You can respond quickly to changes in your application state and efficiently store data by moving older data to colder storage tiers to save on costs. However, you need to pick the right database for the job. We'll continue our discussion on databases by looking at a NoSQL offering from AWS, namely Amazon DynamoDB.

Optimizing DynamoDB

DynamoDB is AWS' NoSQL database. As a fully managed service, AWS takes care of the scaling, software patching, hardware provisioning, setup and configuration, and replication. When you use DynamoDB, you create database tables that store and retrieve any amount of data that scales automatically to any level of request. As a NoSQL database, DynamoDB is schemaless, meaning you don't have to define the data attributes for each column as you would in a relational database. This makes DynamoDB a great database when you need low latency and your access patterns are simple, key-value-based queries.

For optimizing DynamoDB costs, it helps to understand the different capacity modes that the service offers. You want to choose the right capacity mode based on your application's traffic patterns. The three capacity modes are provisioned, on-demand, and reserved:

1. **Provisioned mode**: When you select provisioned mode, you define the number of reads and writes requests per second. You will be billed by the hour based on your specifications. *Figure 7.10* shows setting up a DynamoDB table with **Provisioned** mode selected and **Auto scaling** turned **Off**.

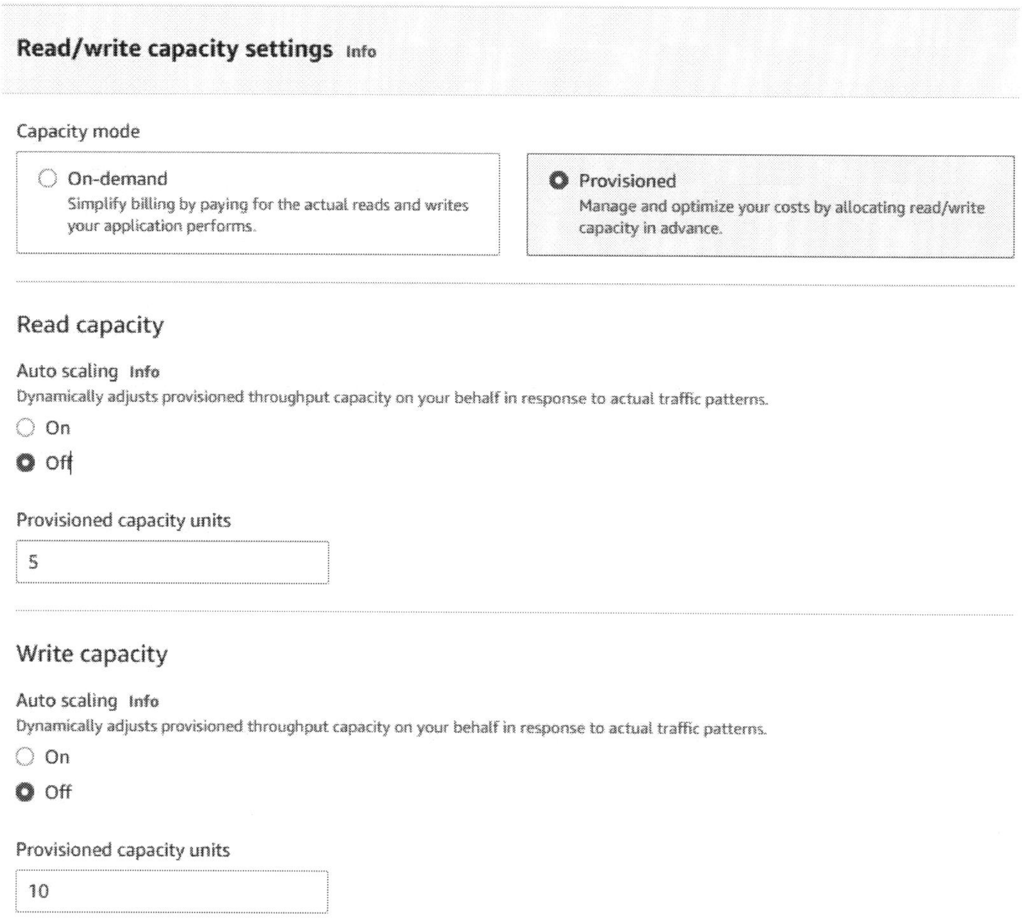

Read/write capacity settings Info

Capacity mode

○ On-demand
Simplify billing by paying for the actual reads and writes
your application performs.

● Provisioned
Manage and optimize your costs by allocating read/write
capacity in advance.

Read capacity

Auto scaling Info
Dynamically adjusts provisioned throughput capacity on your behalf in response to actual traffic patterns.

○ On
● Off

Provisioned capacity units

5

Write capacity

Auto scaling Info
Dynamically adjusts provisioned throughput capacity on your behalf in response to actual traffic patterns.

○ On
● Off

Provisioned capacity units

10

Figure 7.10 – The selected DynamoDB-provisioned mode in the
AWS Console read/write capacity settings

The DynamoDB-provisioned mode also works with auto scaling (something we'll look at more in the next chapter). Auto scaling helps you adjust your database cluster automatically. You set the minimum and maximum read/write capacity units, and a target utilization percentage. This target utilization tracks the consumed, provisioned throughput at a point in time and adjusts the provisioned throughput upward or downward in response to demand, similar to how a home thermostat maintains a target temperature for the house. Unlike a home thermostat, however, rather than setting a temperature for your DynamoDB cluster, you can set a target utilization value between 20 and 90 percent of your read/write capacity. Use provisioned mode when you have a steady state or predictable workload.

2. **On-demand mode**: The second type is on-demand. At this point, we're very familiar with how on-demand pricing works. On-demand is great for workloads that are unpredictable where you don't have to or want to predefine the throughput that you need for DynamoDB. DynamoDB will still automatically adjust to your traffic and increase or decrease the throughput accordingly. Use on-demand mode when you are testing small development, test workloads, or you have unpredictable or changing workloads that you want to test quickly.

3. **Reserved capacity mode**: Reserved capacity, the last mode, is ideal for when you can predict how much throughput you need. Reserved capacity provides you with the best discount compared to the other modes mentioned here. Although DynamoDB reservation recommendations don't appear in Cost Explorer as with the other databases, you can still reserve the capacity. You still commit to an hourly rate, and as with other RIs and SPs, you will pay the hourly rate whether you use it or not. Unlike the other reservation types, you only have the upfront payment option. *Figure 7.11* shows the reserved capacity mode in use in the AWS Console:

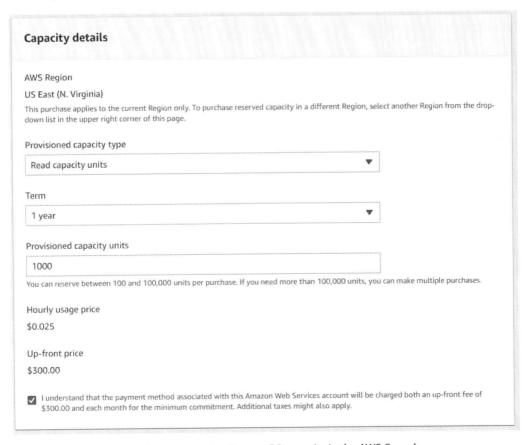

Figure 7.11 – Reserving DynamoDB capacity in the AWS Console

Purchase reservations to optimize your DynamoDB storage costs when you have predictable application traffic or can forecast capacity requirements in advance. Be mindful, though, that you pay upfront and you're committing to the minimum usage for the term, which can be either one or three years. If you're unsure of committing to the commitment term, choose provisioned mode instead because you can change between provisioned mode and on-demand mode at will.

A cost-saving feature that you can use with DynamoDB regardless of your provisioned mode is **Standard-Infrequent Access (S3 Standard-IA)**. As with Amazon S3 storage classes, if you have DynamoDB tables that are less frequently accessed, then you can use the S3 Standard-IA table class to reduce your storage costs. Because your table choice is not permanent, choose the right table class based on your requirements to optimize costs. You can update the table class easily in the Console, so don't feel as though you're locked into a certain table class.

We covered optimizing databases in this section and object storage with Amazon S3 in the section before. The last storage mediums we need to discuss for optimization are block and file storage. We will turn to these in the next section.

Optimizing block and file storage

File storage is similar to the way that a user would organize files on their personal computer. With file storage, you organize and represent data as a hierarchy of files in folders. Separately, block storage groups data into organized but evenly sized volumes. You can think of this in the same way as copy-pasting a bunch of files, images, videos, and other media files into an external hard drive. That hard drive functions as a block store. We'll explore how to optimize block and file storage next.

Optimizing EBS

For many EC2 instances that you spin up, you can associate a block storage volume to that instance. You can imagine these storage volumes as attached hard drives on your local computer; you can purchase a 1 TB hard drive, attach it to your computer, and expand your storage space. Amazon **Elastic Block Store** (**EBS**) volumes are similar in this regard but have additional bonuses, such as the ability to elastically change the volume size (increase or decrease the amount of storage at will), or take snapshots of these volumes and save your data redundantly.

> **Important note**
> Some EC2 instances only provide temporary block-level storage for your instances. These are called **instance storage** volume types. Be sure to check the instance storage configuration for your instance so you don't accidentally lose data!

As with Amazon S3, EBS provides you with several EBS volume types to meet your price and performance requirements. Generally, you categorize EBS into two volume types: **solid-state drives (SSDs)** or **hard disk drives (HDDs)**. HDD volumes have a lower storage cost than SSD, but both depend on provisioned storage. Unlike S3, where you pay for the amount stored, EBS requires you to provision the storage amount ahead. For example, you need to specifically create a volume of 40 GB. You can then use up to 40 GB of storage space on that volume, but you pay for the entire 40 GB amount even if you use less than that. But not to worry, you can elastically resize the 40 GB to 30 GB if that's all you really need.

Hence, monitoring your EBS volumes is important. The EBS volume size impacts performance. So, even if it appears that an EBS volume is overprovisioned, it may have been done on purpose. Overprovisioning is, in fact, a pattern – there are times that an EBS volume may be overprovisioned on purpose to gain the additional IOPS. For example, a team using the GP2 (for general purpose 2nd generation) volume type in EBS may initially provision 20 GB, resulting in 100 IOPS (3 IOPS/GB * 20 GB). However, if the application requires 300 IOPS, the team will resize the volume to 100 GB (3 IOPS/GB * 100 GB), even if the storage isn't fully utilized.

To make things easier, use AWS Compute Optimizer for EBS rightsizing recommendations. Monitoring your own metrics will likely be the most accurate method since you know your application needs better than anyone else (hopefully!), but Compute Optimizer provides a good starting point to have those conversations with the right teams.

Within EBS, you can choose between several EBS volume types. EBS GP2 volume types are generally recommended for most workloads. The idea behind GP2 is that the larger the capacity you provision, the higher IOPS you can expect to get. So, sometimes, you may end up provisioning more storage capacity than you need because you want the higher IOPS. However, AWS continues to launch and promote newer generation features by incentivizing them with lower costs.

At the time of writing, EBS GP3 is the most recent (latest generation) storage type to support general-purpose workloads. EBS GP3 aims to address the overprovisioning problems with GP2 that we touched upon in the previous paragraph. You can provision performance independently from storage capacities with EBS GP3 and still provide up to 20% financial savings compared to the previous generation. Consider migrating to GP3 (and subsequent newer generations in the future) if you want to get a boost in performance at a lower rate and if it's not too troublesome to change.

> **Important note**
>
> If you are planning on using AWS' auto scaling capabilities, be sure to consider your strategy for deleting EBS volumes during scale-in events. Otherwise, you will find yourself paying for a fleet of unused EBS volumes when auto scaling automatically terminates the EC2 instances, but not the EBS volumes. We'll learn more about auto scaling in *Chapter 9, Optimizing Cloud-Native Environments*.

Now that we have a better understanding of how EBS works and which type to choose, let's see how to optimize costs once you've made these decisions.

Optimizing EBS snapshots

Snapshots are an important component of EBS because they serve multiple purposes such as backup, disaster recovery, ransomware protection, and data transfer to other Regions. Snapshots are just as they sound; you take a snapshot of your EBS volume and that snapshot represents a point-in-time record of your data.

A common use case with snapshots is to create a snapshot policy to meet a business requirement. Say that your company has mandated that it should never lose more than five minutes of data at any given time – you can set a schedule to take snapshots of your application data every five minutes. Now, you can recover at any five-minute interval. However, those snapshot costs can become unruly.

AWS provides tools such as **EBS Snapshots Archive** and **EBS Recycle Bin** for Amazon EBS snapshots to ease the burden of managing them. **EBS Snapshots Archive** is a storage tier on Amazon EBS. You can save snapshot-storage-related costs by saving snapshots in the archive. You can also run a process to automatically delete snapshots that are older than a defined time range. Deleting snapshots that you don't need is exactly the type of waste reduction that we aim for. Stale EBS snapshots can accumulate over time, but **AWS Trusted Advisor** can help identify snapshots for you to clean later. Subsequently, if you happen to accidentally (or on purpose) delete a snapshot and then need to recover it, EBS **Recycle Bin** insures against accidental deletion. With **Recycle Bin**, EBS snapshots are placed in a recoverable state, and you can restore them within a certain time period before they are deleted permanently.

AWS will retain deleted snapshots for a time period that you specify. After this period, the EBS snapshots are deleted permanently. *Figure 7.12* shows an EBS **Recycle Bin** retention rule that applies to all EBS snapshots. In this example, the user specifies the retention period for 30 days. You can set the period to a maximum of 365 days.

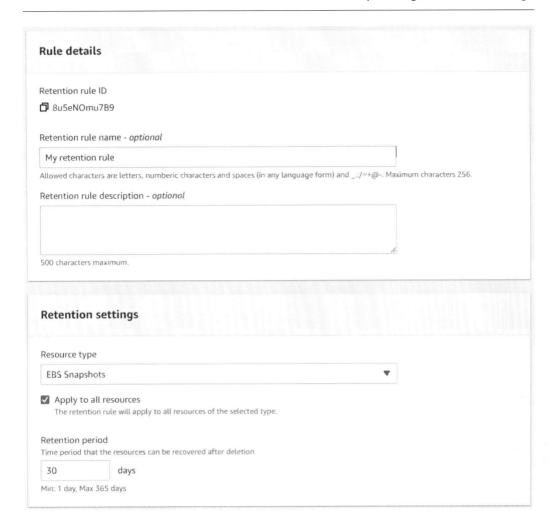

Figure 7.12 – An EBS Recycle Bin retention rule

Use **EBS Snapshots Archive** and **Recycle Bin** to apply similar policies to your snapshots as you would life-cycling your S3 objects. These may appear to be small steps that have a negligible impact on overall costs but, remember, the goal for us is to reduce waste. Any and all steps taken in this direction will positively impact your organization.

Optimizing EFS

The last type of storage type that we can optimize on AWS is file storage with **Amazon Elastic File System (EFS)**. Amazon EFS is a shared file system used with Amazon EC2 instances and on-premises servers. It provides a file system interface for file-based workloads that scales automatically depending on how much you store.

As with Amazon S3, EFS has different storage classes. The default storage class is EFS Standard, which has the highest storage cost compared to the other classes. EFS **Standard-Infrequent Access (Standard-IA)** is the cost-optimized version of EFS Standard for less accessed files. You sacrifice a bit of performance for cost – while you get single-digit millisecond latency with EFS Standard, you can expect double-digit millisecond latency with EFS Standard-IA. As long as your workload can afford this dip in performance, optimize with EFS Standard-IA.

The cheaper versions of EFS are EFS One Zone and One Zone-IA. As the name implies, EFS One Zone maintains your data within just one AZ. If it's not business-critical to maintain redundant copies of your data in EFS across multiple AZs, then consider using EFS One Zone and the cheaper EFS One Zone-IA for cost optimization reasons.

If you are unsure on which class to use, you can always use EFS Intelligent-Tiering, as a similar concept to Amazon S3's version. EFS also has lifecycle management. You can use it to move files from one class to another. I won't go into the details on these capabilities since they mirror Amazon S3's capabilities, which I outlined in earlier sections of this chapter. Know that the same strategies that you use to manage and life-cycle your S3 objects can be used for your files with Amazon EFS.

Summary

Storage is critical for any cloud-based workload. How and where you store your data will largely depend on the application and on the form of the data itself. AWS provides many storage technologies to support your workload, each with its own cost optimization strategies.

Use Amazon S3 for object storage. Once you have an idea of how you want to organize and partition your data in S3, choose the optimal storage class to lower your storage costs. You don't have to get it right the first time. You can use lifecycle policies to transition objects from one storage class to another. You can get AWS' help by using Intelligent-Tiering, which allows AWS to move objects to the optimal storage class for you. The same principles apply to file-based storage with Amazon EFS and UltraWarm storage for Amazon OpenSearch.

Use Amazon EBS for block storage of your Amazon EC2 instances, but also your on-premises servers if needed. Leverage the latest generation EBS volume types for optimal use. Archive EBS snapshots for cost savings and be sure to monitor your volume performance so that you use your available space efficiently.

Purchase RIs for your databases and cloud-based data warehouses (with Amazon Redshift) if you plan to keep these databases up and running for a long time. The discounted rate will pay off in months, which will help you get a lower price compared to the on-demand rate.

We've covered compute and storage. In the next chapter, we'll find ways to optimize the components that tie these together: networking.

Further reading

Have a look at the following resources:

- *Amazon S3 Storage Classes*, 2022: `https://aws.amazon.com/s3/storage-classes/`
- *Managing your storage lifecycle*, 2022: `https://docs.aws.amazon.com/AmazonS3/latest/userguide/object-lifecycle-mgmt.html`
- *Introducing Amazon S3 Storage Lens – Organization-wide Visibility Into Object Storage*, 2020: `https://aws.amazon.com/blogs/aws/s3-storage-lens/`
- *Reserved DB instances for Amazon RDS*, 2022: `https://docs.aws.amazon.com/AmazonRDS/latest/UserGuide/USER_WorkingWithReservedDBInstances.html`
- *Read/write capacity mode*, 2022: `https://docs.aws.amazon.com/amazondynamodb/latest/developerguide/HowItWorks.ReadWriteCapacityMode.html`
- *UltraWarm storage for Amazon OpenSearch Service*, 2022: `https://docs.aws.amazon.com/opensearch-service/latest/developerguide/ultrawarm.html`
- AWS. "*Recycle Bin*". 2022. `https://docs.aws.amazon.com/AWSEC2/latest/UserGuide/recycle-bin.html`

8
Optimizing Networking

We have data persistent with storage in the cloud. We also have compute resources to perform tasks on that data. Now, we need some form of plumbing to connect these components if they are to communicate with each other and move from one place to another. **Networking** is the plumbing that will serve these functions and is the topic at hand in this chapter. More specifically, we'll look at ways to optimize our networking workloads on AWS.

The underlying system architecture will incur different networking costs. Distributed systems, for example, which span multiple **availability zones** (**AZs**) and multiple Regions for redundancy, will have higher networking costs than a system that resides entirely in one AZ. It's hard to apply blanket network optimization strategies compared to mechanisms such as savings plans, which can potentially cover all compute usage within an AWS organization. We'll discuss ways to incorporate networking cost considerations when building systems and look closely into data transfer costs. We'll also explore AWS tools that can help reduce data transfer costs.

In this chapter, we're going to cover the following main topics:

- Understanding data transfer scenarios
- Managing data transfer costs
- Tips for minimizing data transfer costs

Technical requirements

To complete the exercises in this chapter, the requirements are the same as the previous chapters.

Understanding data transfer scenarios

Why do data transfer costs exist? Data transfer costs exist because various network boundaries exist within the AWS ecosystem and there is a cost associated with crossing those network boundaries. You might cross boundaries to get from the AWS network out to the internet, or cross boundaries to get from one AWS Region to another.

Within each AWS Region, there are at least two AZs. Each of these AZs can represent multiple data centers, and each AZ has its own infrastructure, such as power, cooling, and security. They're connected with redundant ultra-low latency connections and are physically separate from each other. These clusters of AZs constitute a Region and are set apart to protect them from issues such as power outages and natural disasters, but are still close enough to support synchronous replication scenarios for your workloads.

Now, to take advantage of AWS' global network, you can create a virtual network that spans multiple AZs and build multiple networks that span numerous Regions. You define your virtual network with Amazon **Virtual Private Cloud** (**VPC**). As we previously discussed, Amazon VPCs are Regionally scoped, logical boundaries that you define. You can deploy many AWS resources within your VPC, which acts like a virtual data center. VPCs can span multiple AZs within a set Region.

You incur data transfer costs when your applications send data that crosses AZ and Region boundaries. This often occurs within and across Amazon VPCs since many customers place their cloud applications within Amazon VPCs. It's completely fine that these data transfer occurrences take place; in fact, it's sometimes necessary when you want to architect zonal and Regionally resilient architectures. Furthermore, transferring data over networks simply costs money. You need to build using physical components such as switches, routers, cables, and other networking hardware. Then, you need to supply a networking service, whether that's broadband such as an **internet service provider** (**ISP**), mobile, satellite, or a combination thereof.

While you don't have to pay for these components specifically, you offload the maintenance and management of the network to AWS and pay indirectly via data transfer fees. AWS services have their unique data transfer pricing rates, which can also vary depending on where the sources and destinations are located and the associated AZs. Rather than unpacking each AWS service's data transfer rates, we can more broadly categorize data transfer in the following way.

Let's start with a simple scenario and add layers of complexity to understand data transfer cost implications depending on an application's architecture.

Data transfer inside an AWS AZ

Let's start with a simple example consisting of a single AZ within a single Region in *Figure 8.1*. We've deployed two VPCs in our Region, each containing two EC2 instances. The instances in the top VPC are using private IPs to communicate while the instances in the bottom VPC are using public IPs. It's possible that these instances are using **elastic IPs** (**EIPs**) as their public form of communication. The communication between the two pairs of EC2 instances within their respective VPCs is what we can call **intra-AZ data transfer** or data transfer within AZs.

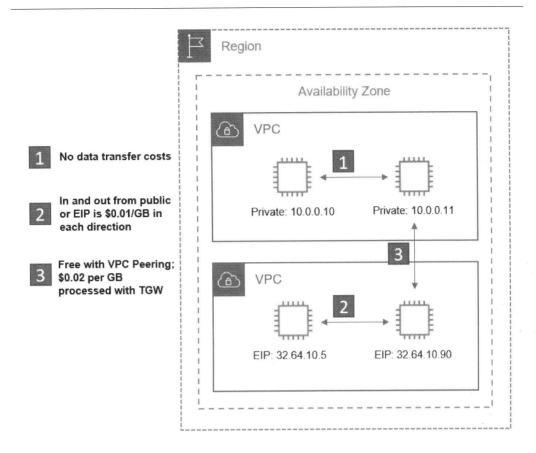

Figure 8.1 – Data transfer scenarios within an AZ in a Region

The top pair uses their private IPs, which do not incur any data transfer costs. Naturally, this is a more desirable method than communication via public IPs to minimize data transfer costs. Prioritize using private IPs for intra-AZ communication to remove data transfer waste.

The bottom pair uses EIPs. An EIP is a public IPv4 address that is reachable from the internet. They can be assigned to instances from AWS' pool of addresses, or you can assign them yourself by bringing your own IP address pool to AWS. When an instance communicates using an EIP, or any public IP address, there's a cost per **gigabyte (GB)** even when you're communicating within a single VPC in a single AZ. In the case of **2** in *Figure 8.1*, there's a $0.01 per GB charge for data transferred both *in* and *out* of the instances. In other words, transferring 1 TB of data (1,000 GB) will cost you $10 in data transfer costs.

To minimize data transfer costs in this scenario, you should prioritize using the instances' private IPs for communication. Unless you have a business-related reason for needing your instances to be reachable over the internet, it's safer and cheaper to use the private IP address. Additionally, EIPs have a per-hour cost if you associate more than one EIP to a running instance. The first EIP is free, but any subsequent ones incur hourly charges. Equally, any EIP not associated with a running instance also incurs hourly charges.

There's a nuanced difference between a public IP and an EIP. An EIP is a type of public IP. When you launch an instance, you can specify that AWS provides a public IP address for that instance from a public IPv4 address pool, assuming that the instance is placed in a part of the Amazon VPC that is reachable over the internet. However, this public IPv4 address is only associated with your instance and not your AWS account. In other words, if you stop, hibernate, or terminate your instance, your instance receives a new public IP address when it is restarted.

If you need a static public IP address and want to associate with your instance instead, then you can use an EIP that is associated with your AWS account. You can attach this EIP to whatever instance you like, for instance, a thumb drive—you attach it to an instance and that instance receives the EIP's public IP address. This helps when you need a static IPv4 address to mask a failure of an instance or software. However, be mindful of both the EIP cost itself and the data transfer costs associated when configuring your networks.

Sometimes you may have multiple VPCs and need communication to take place between them. You can use **VPC Peering** to establish this connection. They can either be peered directly or connected with an AWS **Transit Gateway** (**TGW**). In either case, there's a charge for instances communicating across the VPC boundary. Data transfer over a VPC Peering connection within an AZ is free. However, if the inter-VPC connection represented in **3** of *Figure 8.1* was made through a TGW, there is a price per GB of data processed by the TGW. This means it would cost $20 to transfer 1 TB of data using the TGW, which is double the price of data transfer using VPC Peering in the second scenario.

In such an example, it would indeed be wasteful to use a TGW for inter-VPC connectivity because using a TGW to configure a simple network between two Amazon VPCs is slight overkill. However, as you scale to thousands of VPCs, VPC-to-VPC connection becomes much easier to manage with a TGW. That's because VPC Peering connections are not transitive, meaning an A-to-B peering relationship and a B-to-C peering relationship *does not* establish a connection for A-to-C. You must explicitly configure an A-to-C peering connection if that's required for your architecture. You can imagine setting up these peering connections becomes difficult when you have tens to hundreds of Amazon VPCs.

For this simple case, using private IPs is the best way to optimize data transfer costs, but things get a bit more complicated when you need to cross the AZ boundary.

Data transfer inside an AWS Region

Let's look at a slightly more complex scenario. We're still in a single Region but now we have two AZs. Remember, a single VPC can span across all the AZs in a given Region. Each of those AZs has one or more IP subnets. In *Figure 8.2*, we have four instances in the top VPC; the instances in each AZ share a common subnet:

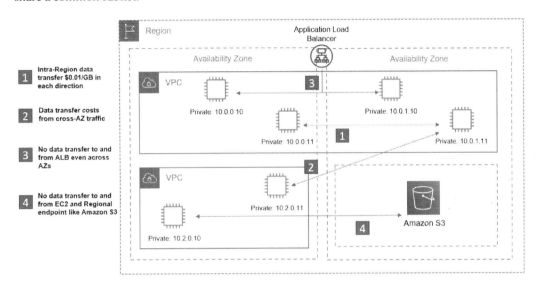

Figure 8.2 – Intra-Region data transfer scenarios

In the first case, **1**, of *Figure 8.2*, we have an EC2 instance in one AZ talking to an EC2 instance in the other AZ. They're both parts of the same AZ but they've crossed that AZ boundary. Because they cross that boundary, they incur inter-AZ data transfer usage. This would incur $10 in data transfer costs for transferring 1 TB of data, as it's considered an intra-Region data transfer and charged in both directions on a per-GB basis. Reducing your application communication across AZ boundaries is a useful technique to reduce data transfer.

In the second case, **2**, of *Figure 8.2*, an instance in the bottom VPC is communicating with an instance in a different VPC. This may be a result of VPC peering or a TGW. When you communicate between two VPCs in a Region, there's a per-GB charge in data transfer costs for crossing AZs.

In the third case, **3**, of *Figure 8.2*, we have an **application load balancer** (**ALB**). Load balancers help to share the load across multiple backend targets. Normally, communication between instances in different AZs incurs a charge. However, data transferred in and out of an ALB, in this case, or a **classic load balancer** (**CLB**) within a single Region from EC2 is free. Hence, using an ALB or CLB can minimize intra-Region data transfer costs.

Load balancers might seem like an obvious choice given that data transfer is free in this case. However, load balancers incur an hourly cost of their own. Furthermore, data transfer with load balancers *is not* free if the load balancers communicate with an instance's public address.

Finally, in the fourth case, **4**, of *Figure 8.2*, we see a service such as Amazon S3 that has a **gateway endpoint**. Gateway endpoints provide reliable connectivity to Amazon S3 and DynamoDB without requiring an internet gateway or a NAT device for your VPC. There are no data transfer charges between services with a gateway endpoint such as Amazon S3 or between EC2 instances in the same Region.

In this scenario, data transfer across AZs within a Region incurs costs. However, AWS will not charge for data transfer to and from an ALB. Nor will AWS charge for data transfer when using a Regional endpoint for services such as Amazon S3 and DynamoDB.

Now, let's look at a scenario where you don't stay within a single Region. Cross-Region traffic will be the focus of the next section.

Data transfer across AWS Regions

What happens when you are transferring data across Regions? When an EC2 instance communicates with another EC2 instance in a different Region, this becomes inter-Region communication and has an associated per-GB charge. In the case of *Figure 8.3*, there will be a $0.02 per GB charge for outbound traffic to the US-West-2 Region from US-East-1. Any communication coming back from US-West-2 to US-East-1 will be charged at $0.02 per GB as well. Note that AWS only charges for outbound traffic, thus the data transfer charges will only be assessed for the Region conducting outbound traffic.

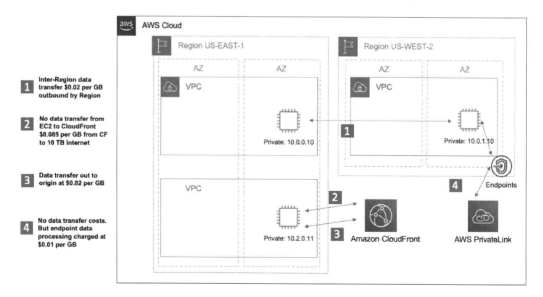

Figure 8.3 – Inter-Region data transfer scenarios

You should consider using **Amazon CloudFront** as a **content delivery network** (**CDN**) for serving content from an EC2 instance to end users in this case. A CDN accelerates your ability to serve static and dynamic content from your servers to clients across the globe. A CDN typically consists of **Points of Presence** (**PoPs**) or edge locations that are strategically placed around populated areas. These edge locations can cache content to deliver content to end users faster than having to serve a request from a server in a single location.

CloudFront works by caching data from sources such as EC2 and Amazon S3 into edge locations around the world. Edge locations are smaller data center constructs than Regions, but they are scattered globally to help AWS customers quickly deliver content to locations closer to end users.

When you deliver data from a source such as an EC2 instance to CloudFront, there is no data transfer cost (**2** of *Figure 8.3*). However, when you serve content from CloudFront to end users, there is a cost that decreases with higher volume. There are also charges for data sent from CloudFront back to an EC2 origin per GB (**3** of *Figure 8.3*).

The alternative to this would be to serve content directly from EC2. However, among the disadvantages around security, performance, and availability (not to mention, an overall poor architecture design), the data transfer costs from an EC2 instance out to the internet are greater than the costs from CloudFront.

The last element in *Figure 8.3* is a **VPC private endpoint**, which is powered by **AWS PrivateLink**. AWS PrivateLink provides connectivity between VPCs and services hosted on AWS. It uses private endpoints to connect services between different accounts and VPCs. *Figure 8.3* shows an EC2 instance in the US-West-2 Region communicating with an endpoint in the same Region. Because the endpoint is in the same Region as the EC2 instance, you would not incur data transfer costs. However, be mindful of the data processing charge for the interface endpoint, as well as the pricing per VPC endpoint at a running rate.

Things can get more complex as you traverse environments, such as moving data between the cloud and on-premises environments. Let's see how data transfer works in hybrid environments.

Data transfer from AWS to on-premises environments

There are cases where you have a hybrid setup with some resources on-premises and others in AWS, as shown in *Figure 8.4*. Naturally, you would want these systems to communicate with each other, which implies data transfer between them.

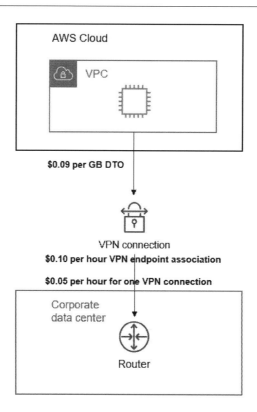

Figure 8.4 – A VPN connection between AWS and a data center

One option is to connect the systems over a VPN connection with AWS **Virtual Private Network (VPN)**. You can set up an encrypted connection between an Amazon VPC and a data center with this option. VPN connections are shared over public networks, so the bandwidth and latency can fluctuate.

You have two choices within the AWS VPN option. The first is **AWS Site-to-Site VPN**. This is just how it sounds; there's a direct connection between one site, a data center, and another, an AWS VPC environment. With AWS Site-to-Site VPN, you are charged per hour that VPN is provisioned and available. Each Site-to-Site VPN connection has two tunnels, each with a unique public IP address.

The other choice within the AWS VPN option is **AWS Client VPN**, a fully managed, elastic VPN service. You can access your AWS resources from any location using an OpenVPN-based VPN client. Pricing differs among Site-to-Site VPNs because Client VPNs charge based on the number of active client connections per hour. You are also charged for the number of subnets associated with the Client VPN per hour. Both VPN types charge standard AWS data transfer rates for all data transferred through the VPN connection.

The other option is to use **AWS Direct Connect**. Direct Connect has better performance, as it provides a dedicated link between your on-premises systems and AWS, using either 1, 10, or 100 Gbps with native AWS Dedicated Connections (although partner-hosted connections do exist at various other speeds). Because a Direct Connect connection is private and not configured over the public internet, bandwidth and latency are more stable compared to an AWS VPN. However, you can set up an AWS VPN connection quickly, while a Direct Connect connection can take much longer to set up. The Direct Connect per-hour pricing is more expensive than the VPN but the data transfer rate is lower. This is illustrated in *Figure 8.5*:

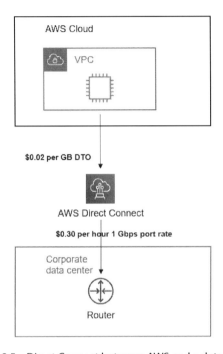

Figure 8.5 – Direct Connect between AWS and a data center

In a simple comparison between the two options, we assume we run both types for the entire year (8,760 hours). The hourly rate for having a Direct Connect connection up and running for that time is going to exceed the VPN by nearly $2,000. Where Direct Connect ends up with lower costs is when the data transfer out exceeds 24 TB. You can see the breakdown of costs between the AWS VPN and Direct Connect options in *Figure 8.6*:

AWS VPN

		Rate	Cost
8,760	Hours	$ 0.09	$ 788.40
24000	DTO (GB)	$ 0.10	$ 2,400.00
10	Connections	$ 0.05	$ 0.50
			$ 3,188.90

AWS Direct Connect

		Rate	Cost
8,760	Hours	$ 0.30	$ 2,628.00
24000	DTO GB	$ 0.02	$ 480.00
			$ 3,108.00

Figure 8.6 – A direct comparison between two hybrid connection options

We can observe a recurring pattern within the many scenarios we looked at. Optimizing for data transfer costs is commendable but can be one-sided. For instance, a VPC endpoint, or an ALB, has a running hourly rate. If you are not transferring data with those services, you are still paying for their existence. As with the example shown in *Figure 8.6*, there's a break-even point where the combined cost of a service and its associated data transfer charges equals the cost of an alternative. It's difficult to generalize a strategy because everyone's architecture and usage patterns will be unique. Use the service pricing pages and the AWS Pricing Calculator to estimate your workload's cost to decide what's best for your business. For example, you may have applications that require consistent and stable network bandwidth between an on-premises environment and an AWS cloud environment. Although VPN may be cheaper and faster to set up, Direct Connect may better meet your business requirements with long-term benefits.

There are a few general patterns to be mindful of when considering data transfer charges. If tolerable, aim to keep communication between resources within the same AZ. The trade-off with such an architecture is a higher risk of downtime in the event of an AZ failure. The same applies to inter-Region communication. There may be cases where business continuity warrants cross-Region replication or backups. However, if tolerable, keeping traffic within a Region will minimize data transfer costs, and reduce your waste if indeed it is not needed.

Equally, avoid routing traffic over the internet, as the per-GB transfer rate is the highest among the examples we've seen when routing traffic within AWS. For instance, routing traffic from EC2 out to the internet and back through the AWS network into Amazon S3 is horribly inefficient and wasteful. Instead, use VPC endpoints to keep traffic on the AWS network. We'll learn more about this server later in this chapter. But first, let's explore how to manage your data transfer costs with native AWS tooling.

Managing data transfer costs

Use Cost Explorer as a starting point to manage and visualize your data transfer costs. Just like any other resource, data transfer is part of your inventory. Arguably, it's easier to have a firm grasp of (virtually) tangible AWS resources such as EC2 instances over intangibles such as data transfer. But because Cost Explorer is free and can be used out of the box, it can help reveal data transfer costs that are seemingly intangible.

In Cost Explorer, use the suggested filters in this section to create reports that clarify your data transfer use on AWS. Apply filters at the service level, focusing on **EC2-Instances** and **EC2-ELB**, as shown in *Figure 8.7*. This reduces the amount of data we need to look at and most data transfer will also be driven by these two services:

Figure 8.7 – Service filters for two main contributors to data transfer

The other helpful filter is **Usage Type Group**. There are three usage types to focus on that correspond to the scenarios we explored in this section. Look for **EC2: Data Transfer - Inter AZ**, which covers the data transferred between two AZs in the same Region.

Then, **EC2: Data Transfer - Internet (Out)** shows the data transfer that egresses to the internet. Meanwhile, **EC2: Data Transfer - Region to Region (Out)** covers the data transfer between AWS Regions. *Figure 8.8* shows these filters in Cost Explorer:

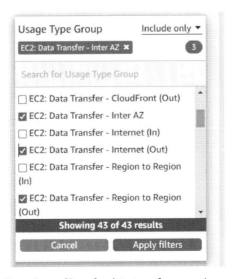

Figure 8.8 – Usage Type Group filters for data transfer scenarios contributing to costs

It is optional, but equally important, to apply the necessary filters on tags that map to your organization. Tags will provide granular visibility into certain parts of your business, whether it's by business unit, application environment, or any other dimension important to your business. Use this data to find hotspots and uncover insights into how your organization is consuming data transfer on AWS. You can use these views to see data transfer over time, grouped by Region or AZ, and get details on how the usage of data transfer maps to your organization's use of AWS.

Gaining visibility is the first step in finding data transfer usage patterns across your organization. With these reports, you can zero in on resources within accounts and/or Regions that are heavy users of data transfer, identifying where data transfer is happening. Consider using VPC Flow Logs to understand why.

VPC Flow Logs provides data about the network communication using a VPC resource such as an EC2 instance. The flow log will tell you about the source and destination of the network flow, as well as port and protocol information. This can help you find out why a given resource may be exceeding expected data transfer costs.

Amazon VPC Flow Logs is billed as you would be billed when publishing logs to Amazon CloudWatch. You are charged for data ingestion and archival of published logs but it doesn't cost you to activate the flow logs themselves. If you choose to push your logs to Amazon S3, then you will be charged for storage and retrieval, just as with any other object stored in S3.

Now, let's see how we can leverage Amazon CloudFront to lower our data transfer costs but also optimize our use of CloudFront itself.

Optimizing with Amazon CloudFront

We read in the previous section that CloudFront is a CDN that accelerates your ability to serve static and dynamic content from your server to clients across the globe. We also saw in *Chapter 6, Optimizing Compute*, that you can pay for compute resources using a reserved model. CloudFront has its own reserved model as well.

The **CloudFront Security Savings Bundle** is a flexible pricing plan that can reduce your CloudFront bill by up to 30%. As with the compute reserved model, you commit to a year term and pay a monthly usage amount. The commitment applies to all CloudFront charges, including data transfer out and request fees. The bundle also includes AWS **Web Application Firewall** (**WAF**) usage, which provides edge security for your CDN.

CloudFront quotes a given usage and estimates your monthly dollar commitment, just as Cost Explorer provides RI and SP recommendations. You can allow CloudFront to provide recommendations based on your historical or projected usage. CloudFront will estimate charges and savings based on existing data, as shown in *Figure 8.9*:

Total estimated data transfer (GB)

1000

Average object size (kb)

125

Estimated cost:

CloudFront charges

$94.23

AWS WAF charges

$12.03

Based on your estimated usage, we recommend purchasing a Savings Bundle with a monthly commitment of $65.96
This would cover $94.23 of your CloudFront usage (100%) and $6.60 of your AWS WAF usage (55%)

Before recommended purchase	After recommended purchase	Monthly Savings	Total savings
Monthly on-demand spend	Estimated monthly spend	Estimated monthly savings	Estimated 1 year savings
$106.26	$71.40	$34.86	$418.37

Figure 8.9 – CloudFront savings recommendations based on provided usage

For example, you can commit to $70 of CloudFront usage. AWS will apply a 30% discount on CloudFront. Then, AWS will provide a 10% credit of WAF, in this case, $7. During that month, your $70 monthly commitment covers $100 of CloudFront charges, including $7 of WAF credits for one year, which equates to roughly 11.6 million WAF requests. Consider the bundle if your workload requires CloudFront, and edge security, as it can help reduce your cloud waste.

Let's see how the ideas we've learned about so far come together at VidyaGames.

> **Optimizing data transfer at VidyaGames**
>
> VidyaGame's VidyaReviews application allows users to share the content of their video game experiences with other users. A key component of this shared platform is video game reviews as users will likely purchase video games depending on the aggregate score of a video game and the opinions of trusted and popular users on the platform. Users can upload their video game review content, including video reviews, written reviews, pictures, and clips to the VidyaReviews mobile and web application. The application bundles the content and stores it in Amazon S3, where a series of compute tasks compresses the files and partitions the content by user ID and upload date. Once stored in Amazon S3, a fleet of Amazon EC2 instances deliver the content per user request.
>
> Jeremy takes a closer look at the organization's data transfer costs with AWS Cost Explorer. He notices a steady increase in the **EC2: Data Transfer - Internet (Out)** costs over time and schedules a meeting with the application teams to uncover the causes for increasing data transfer out costs.
>
> By working with the application teams, Jeremy better understands the application's architecture. Amazon S3 serves as the data layer for storing the media files that constitute VidyaReview's content. The team already has a strategy to optimize storage costs using a two-pronged approach: games content with higher aggregate reviews will have a certain tag, while other games content will have a different tag. They will use these tags as attributes to apply different storage life cycle policies to optimize costs.

Amazon EC2 instances provide the web application frontend and server content in Amazon S3 to users. From Jeremy's understanding, this is fine from a data transfer perspective since the Amazon EC2 instances and Amazon S3 buckets operate within the same Region. Using the Amazon S3 Regional endpoint, data transferred to the instances does not incur data transfer costs.

Jeremy discovers the culprit behind the increasing data transfer costs. To provide a responsive and fast user experience, the VidyaReviews application team leverages a CDN service that isn't native to AWS. This third-party CDN provides content quickly to users around the world and removes the need for user requests to be directed to the Amazon EC2 instances. This CDN is critical to the application's success and is a necessary business requirement.

However, it is contributing to data transfer costs because AWS considers content transferred out from the Amazon EC2 instances to the third-party CDN as data transfer out. Specifically, this is data transferred out over the internet, which is one of the higher dollar-per-GB charges within AWS data transfer tiers.

After collaborating with the team, Jeremy learns that the team has been using the CDN for several months already. After testing and validating its technical requirements to meet the application's needs, the management approved its use without realizing the data transfer out cost implications.

Jeremy enlightens the application team that if they used the Amazon CloudFront service as the CDN, they would eliminate the data transfer out cost because data moved between origins to CloudFront incurs no charge. Given the lower technical debt of replacing the CDN versus replacing the application and storage components, the team decides to explore using CloudFront instead of their third-party CDN. If using CloudFront costs less than the total cost of ownership of the third-party CDN plus the incurred data transfer out costs, then the application team agrees with Jeremy that it may be worth the switch. The application team also requires that CloudFront's performance meets or exceeds their current solution. This will be an important factor in their migration.

We looked at how you can save on data transfer out charges with CloudFront. We also learned how you can analyze your data transfer charges with Cost Explorer. In the last section, we'll conclude our data transfer cost optimization discussion with some general tips.

Tips for minimizing data transfer costs

There are a few things to keep in mind when considering waste reduction with data transfer. The first involves data transfer out to the internet. We saw that data transfer can go directly from EC2 instances out to the internet, or that you can leverage CloudFront to serve content to your users.

Using CloudFront offers several advantages. First, while both CloudFront and traditional data transfer out are charged on a per-GB basis, you'll see cost savings by using Amazon CloudFront because CloudFront doesn't charge for **origin fetch** operations. Origin fetch is the process of retrieving content from an origin, like an EC2 instance. When the origin is an AWS service such as EC2, there is no data transfer charge between those AWS services and CloudFront. Moreover, the volume discount of data transfer out from CloudFront to the internet is greater than the rate from EC2 to the internet. So, for data transfer at scale, CloudFront will save costs in the long run.

Another thing to keep in mind is how you architect your workloads to prioritize intra-AZ traffic. Inter-AZ data transfer within a Region is charged on a per-GB basis. If you want to minimize the amount of inter-AZ data transfer, start by looking at how your applications are built within an AZ. If you build applications on AWS, it's important to use AZs to create partitions of your applications.

Partitioning involves isolating a part of your application within a single AZ, then replicating that deployment to one or more additional AZs. By doing so, you have redundant deployments of your application across multiple AZs, ensuring better reliability for your workload.

This also minimizes the amount of data transfer between different AZs. Most of the network chatter between the instances running your applications will be isolated to individual AZs. Then, you'll maintain communication through a private IP address between EC2 instances in a VPC within a single AZ and not incur any data transfer costs.

Even then, you may find occasions where communicating between two AZs is necessary. If required, use an ALB or CLB. Data transferred between EC2 instances and either an ALB or CLB is free within a given Region when using a private IP address.

For example, you may have an instance running in one AZ that needs to communicate with a fleet of instances supporting a web service in a different AZ. It might not make sense to duplicate that service fleet in the first AZ. What's more appropriate is to have a load balancer as a destination to route traffic to the intended targets. Using the ALB helps ensure that your web service stays highly available because it's fronting a fleet of servers. It also helps negate data transfer charges for requests within the Region. When data transfer between AZs is necessary, ALBs and CLBs may help defray inter-AZ data transfer charges.

Figure 8.10 provides a comparison between the various load balancer options on AWS. For ALBs and **Network Load Balancers** (**NLBs**), pricing is based on the **Load Balancer Capacity Units** (**LCU**) per hour. To calculate the cost of an ALB or NLB, you must perform four separate calculations. The maximum value of these four individual calculations determines the final cost of your load balancer. The CLB has a simpler pricing model, where cost is calculated based on the load balancer's per hour existence and per GB processed.

	Application Load Balancer	Network Load Balancer	Classic Load Balancer
	Per hour or partial hour	Per hour or partial hour	Per hour & per GB processed
Load Balaner Capacity Units (LCU)	New connection established per second	New connections or flows	
Charged only on LCU dimension with highest usage	Active connections per minute	Active connections or flows	
	GB processed for HTTP(S)	Processed bytes	
	Rules processed & request rate		

Figure 8.10 – Load balancer pricing comparison

To provide an example of an ALB cost, let's walk through performing the four necessary calculations. The first case is having 25 new connections per second. This means that if in our environment we have 500 new connections per second, then we have 20 new connection LCUs. We get this by dividing 500 by 25.

For the second calculation, an LCU contains 3,000 active connections. So, if we have 30,000 new connections, then we have 10 active connection LCUs. We get this by dividing 30,000 by 3,000.

For the third calculation, if an LCU contains 1 GB per hour for EC2 instances, and if we have 10 GB per hour of data processed, then our processed bytes for the LCU come to 10 (1 GB x 10). Lastly, an LCU contains 1,000 rule evaluations per second. And if we have 15,000 rules evaluated per second in our environment, then our rule evaluation LCU is 15.

Now that we've performed the four individual LCU calculations, we take the maximum value of 20 LCUs and use that to estimate our cost. At the time of writing, an LCU is priced at $0.008 LUC price per hour. Thus, 20 LCUs x $0.008 LUC price per hour x an estimated 730 hours per month gives us an estimated charge of $116.80 per month for operating our ALB.

One last thing to note is to remove any EIPs that are sitting idle unassociated with any EC2 instances. Recall that the first EIPs attached to instances are free but any sitting around will incur waste. Even though a single EIP is charged at $0.01 per hour, assuming you have two EIPs across fifty accounts, you can accumulate upwards of $8,000 per year of wasteful expenditure. This is where inventory management and tagging can help you identify unused resources.

Summary

In this chapter, we unpacked the different manifestations of data transfer on AWS. We learned about the data transfer flow within an AZ, within a Region, across AZs, and across Regions. We also looked at hybrid architectures and the implications they have for data transfer.

We used Cost Explorer to understand and visualize our data transfer costs. Tools such as Cost Explorer can help interpret the sometimes mysterious data transfer charges by identifying where these charges occur. We also mentioned how VPC Flow Logs can uncover the *why* behind data transfer through the logs it provides.

Lastly, we saw how AWS services such as CloudFront and load balancers can minimize data transfer charges. Application architecture can also minimize data transfer charges by prioritizing network communication within an AZ.

We'll conclude our discussion on cost optimization tactics in the next chapter, in which we'll explore ways to optimize the machine learning and analytics domains. We'll also dive deeper into the cloud's elasticity and how autoscaling is a critical architecture component within cost optimization.

Further reading

Have a look at the following resources:

- AWS – *How CloudFront delivers content*, 2022: `https://docs.aws.amazon.com/ AmazonCloudFront/latest/DeveloperGuide/HowCloudFrontWorks.html`

- AWS – *Gateway VPC endpoint*, 2022: `https://docs.aws.amazon.com/vpc/latest/ privatelink/vpce-gateway.html`

- AWS – *VPC endpoint*, 2022: `https://docs.aws.amazon.com/vpc/latest/ privatelink/vpc-endpoints.html`

- AWS – *Tunnel options for your Site-to-Site VPN connection*, 2022: `https://docs.aws. amazon.com/vpn/latest/s2svpn/VPNTunnels.html`

- AWS – *AWS Direct Connect pricing*, 2022: `https://aws.amazon.com/directconnect/ pricing/?nc=sn&loc=3`

9

Optimizing Cloud-Native Environments

Compute, networking, and storage form the bulk of **Amazon Web Services** (**AWS**) cost and usage. We've covered the services that are most common in these categories, such as Amazon **Elastic Compute Cloud** (**EC2**), Amazon **Simple Storage Service** (**S3**), AWS's various database services, and Amazon **Virtual Private Cloud** (**VPC**). However, given that AWS' complete portfolio exceeds 200 services, we've only scratched the surface.

This chapter covers optimization opportunities that result from the induced demand of cloud-native environments; what I mean by this is the demand for AWS services that are more easily obtained in the cloud than from on-premises systems. For example, automatically horizontally scaling a fleet of servers is more easily done in the cloud than on-premises because if you were to horizontally scale your on-premises servers, you would first need to buy the maximum number of servers to meet your peak capacity, whereas, in a cloud environment, you simply scale when you need to and expect the cloud provider to supply your demand for servers. Also, for an on-premises **machine learning** (**ML**) workload, you need to purchase and maintain the maximum number of servers to run distributed training jobs, but in the cloud, you simply utilize the distributed training cluster through an **application programming interface** (**API**) call and once training is complete, you stop paying for (expensive) servers for ML training. We define cloud-native environments in this way and use this chapter to identify ways to optimize costs.

Although it would require more than one chapter to cover every service, we'll look at a few and generalize optimization best practices from what we've seen thus far. We start with **AWS Auto Scaling**, which covers not only EC2 instances but containers and databases as well. Then, we'll see the role optimization plays in an **end-to-end** (**E2E**) analytics workflow including ML. Finally, we'll glance at a few more services and generalize based on these patterns.

In this chapter, we're going to cover the following main topics:

- Maximizing efficiency with AWS Auto Scaling

- Optimizing analytics

- Optimizing ML

Technical requirements

To complete the exercises in this chapter, the requirements are the same as what we've been using in the previous chapters.

Maximizing efficiency with AWS Auto Scaling

We'll begin by understanding **auto scaling**, which is the embodiment of elasticity in the cloud. After we define auto scaling, we'll learn how you can leverage different auto-scaling policies and strategies to meet your workload requirements. Implementing auto scaling will be key in your cloud waste reduction efforts because it's the closest thing to not paying for resources you don't need. Let's define what it is by looking at a simple example.

What is auto scaling?

Large social gatherings such as weddings, banquets, or even the Thanksgiving holiday celebrated in the **United States** (**US**) justify more than enough food to satisfy the esteemed guests. Normally, when preparing food for ourselves, we primarily provision enough food to satisfy hunger at a given moment.

Before the cloud, provisioning **information technology** (**IT**) resources reflected more of the social gathering approach to preparing food. You had to provide enough compute and storage power to satisfy peak demand. Otherwise, you'd risk your application not being available when clients demanded it the most. The following screenshot shows this approach, with the line representing the target provisioned amount to accommodate the highest demands in traffic:

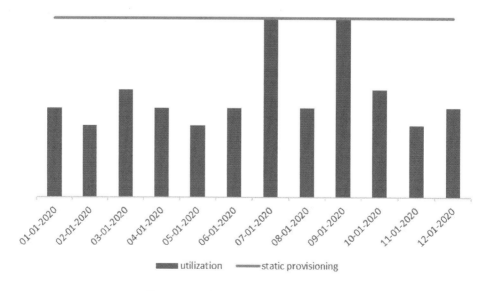

Figure 9.1 – Static provisioning for peak

The distance between the static, flat line and the top of the bar graph represents waste. We have 2 days of maximized utilization efficiency but inefficient usage (that is, waste) for the remainder of the days.

The elasticity of the cloud allows you to reduce this waste by provisioning resources you need when you need them. AWS uses the term *auto scaling* to represent the elastic provisioning of resources on demand to meet your system requirements. With elasticity, you achieve the efficiency that's represented in the following screenshot. The difference between the provisioned line amount and the usage amount is lesser than the usage pattern in *Figure 9.1* and shows better efficiency and less waste:

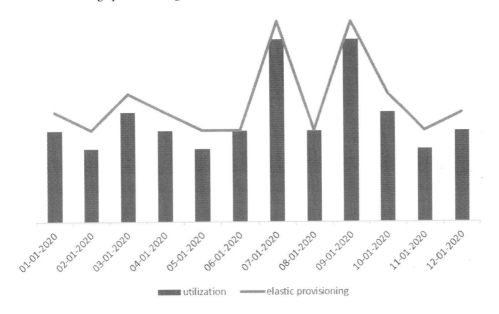

Figure 9.2 – Elastic provisioning matching supply with demand

AWS Auto Scaling is a service that helps you optimize your applications by supplying the resources you need, depending on your applications' demands. The resources with AWS Auto Scaling can be EC2 instances, EC2 spot fleets, containers with **Elastic Container Service** (**ECS**), NoSQL databases such as DynamoDB, and AWS' proprietary relational database service, Amazon Aurora. You define when you need these resources provisioned by a scaling policy.

Now that we've defined auto scaling, let's see how AWS applies auto scaling to Amazon EC2 in various forms.

AWS Auto Scaling versus Amazon EC2 Auto Scaling

You can leverage resource-specific managed scaling such as **Amazon EC2 Auto Scaling** or **AWS Auto Scaling** to dynamically provision resources when needed. Both help to reduce waste because you only need (and pay) for those resources when your applications require them. Whereas resource-specific managed scaling applies only to said resources such as Amazon EC2, AWS Auto Scaling provides managed scaling for multiple resources across multiple services.

Let's compare the two by looking at Amazon EC2 as a service. Amazon EC2 Auto Scaling optimizes your resource use by providing your application with the appropriate number of servers it needs to handle the required load. The service replaces unhealthy instances automatically, terminates instances when unneeded, and launches more (scales out) when required. You define how the service adds or removes instances by the policy.

You control scaling in one of two ways, as follows:

1. The first is with **manual scaling**. You can scale manually, which involves monitoring your application and changing the configuration as needed. As a user, you can go into your Amazon EC2 auto-scaling fleet and make manual adjustments based on changes in demand in your environment.

2. The other option is **automatic scaling**, which uses several AWS-provided scaling mechanisms through auto scaling. As humans, although we generally have good intentions, we are error-prone and tend to get bored of repetitive tasks. Auto scaling makes much more sense. The two types of automatic scaling are scheduled scaling and dynamic auto scaling. We'll look at these two next:

   - For predictive workloads, **scheduled scaling** can avoid delays due to extended startup times for EC2 instances. With scheduled scaling, we can evaluate historical runtimes to identify recurring scaling events such as scaling up at the beginning of the work week and scaling down as the work week ends. We can also take in individual events such as new product releases, new marketing campaigns, or special holiday deals that may drive an increase in traffic to our AWS environment. Amazon EC2 Auto Scaling takes care of launching and terminating resources based on our scaling policy's predefined schedules.

   - For unpredictable workloads, **dynamic auto scaling** fits the bill. Within dynamic auto scaling, there are three types, as outlined here:

     - **Simple scaling** is the most elementary dynamic auto scaling type. With simple scaling, you must set a CloudWatch alarm to monitor a certain metric—say, **central processing unit** (**CPU**) utilization. If you set a policy such that when CPU utilization breaches a threshold of 80%, AWS is to add 20% more capacity, then auto scaling will perform this action when the application meets this condition. This is a very straightforward approach and doesn't consider health checks or cooldowns. In other words, if an event occurred to launch 20% more capacity, the auto-scaling mechanism must wait for health checks on the new instances to complete and the cooldown on the scaling event to expire before it considers adding or removing instances. This might pose a problem, particularly when you experience sudden increases in load—you might not be able to afford to wait for these expiration times but need the environments to change rapidly.

- **Step scaling** is another policy that gives you more granular control. Rather than a blanket policy such as simple scaling, instead, you define different scaling events at different thresholds. In the preceding example, we said to provision 20% more capacity when CPU utilization is at 80%. With step scaling, you can use more granular metrics such as 10% more capacity when CPU utilization is between 60% and 70%, and 30% more capacity when CPU utilization is above 70%. Additionally, step scaling continues to respond to alarms even when a scaling activity or a health check is taking place. This makes step scaling more responsive than simple scaling.

- If we are to continue using CPU utilization as the defined scaling metric, then **target tracking** is the most convenient scaling policy that requires the least management. This is because, for step and simple scaling, you still have to create CloudWatch metrics and associate them with the policies, but for target tracking, Amazon EC2 Auto Scaling creates and manages CloudWatch alarms for you. With target tracking, you simply provide the desired application state, just like how you set your home thermostat to the desired temperature. Once set, the heating or cooling system will intermittently turn on/off to maintain that temperature. Similarly, a target tracking policy set at an aggregate average CPU utilization of 40% will ensure you have the optimal resources to maintain that target metric.

You can use Amazon EC2 Auto Scaling to manually or automatically scale your servers to meet your demand. Save your auto-scaling configurations in the form of **launch templates**. Launch templates make it easier for you to manage how your workloads automatically scale because you define the method in advance. In other words, launch templates are the *what* for when auto scaling occurs. Doing this drives efficiency and reduces waste because you only use the compute resources you need when you need them rather than overbuying to meet unexpected or expected demand.

CPU is a common metric when implementing auto scaling, but it's not the only metric you can use. Many customers use memory, disk space, and network latency as metrics to trigger when an auto-scaling event should occur. You can even use your own custom metrics based on your workload requirements. For example, if you have a web application and want to use request-response error rates as the metric to scale more EC2 instances, then you can use a custom metric that counts for error rates and have Amazon EC2 Auto Scaling deploy more servers when your threshold has been breached.

Now, let's see how AWS Auto Scaling relates to Amazon EC2 Auto Scaling.

When to use AWS Auto Scaling

Although the preceding example is specific to Amazon EC2, other services such as Amazon ECS, Amazon Aurora, and DynamoDB also have their own specific auto-scaling policies, which is why AWS Auto Scaling attempts to aggregate these disparate services into a unified interface where you can manage their scaling policies in one place.

AWS Auto Scaling supports only target-tracking scaling policies at the time of writing. Use AWS Auto Scaling if you intend to use target tracking because it is easier to manage and can also be used to set auto-scaling policies for other AWS services. Say you had a workload consisting of an auto-scaled group of EC2 instances, an Aurora cluster as a database, a spot fleet for batch processing, and were utilizing a target tracking metric. In that case, it would be more cumbersome to have to manage scaling for each service individually than managing them in one place through the AWS Auto Scaling service.

Predictive scaling leverages the capabilities of both AWS Auto Scaling and EC2 Auto Scaling, providing the ability to use ML models to analyze traffic over the past 14 days. Based on this historic data, predictive scaling identifies scheduled events for the next 2 days and then repeats the cycle every day to update your scheduled events based on the latest information available.

AWS Auto Scaling may simplify your auto-scaling needs across your AWS environment, but Amazon EC2 Auto Scaling gives you more control over your Amazon EC2 resources. Note that you don't necessarily need choose one or the other. You may choose AWS Auto Scaling for certain workloads that encompass various services, but when the need arises, you may use Amazon EC2 Auto Scaling to specify scaling policies for your Amazon EC2 fleet. Let's move on to optimize other areas of our AWS environment—namely, within the analytics domain.

Optimizing analytics

If *data is the new gold*, we want to ensure we're mining it without incurring waste. Data analytics and ML are discussion topics that deserve their own books but, in this section, we'll summarize cost-optimization considerations when running these types of workloads. Broadly, we can categorize the steps involved as data ingestion, data exploration, model training, and model deployment.

We already know about Amazon S3 as an object store that functions nicely as a data lake. With data in S3, we can use a managed service such as **Amazon Athena** to run **Structured Query Language (SQL)** queries directly on our data in Amazon S3. Athena is serverless, meaning you don't have to manage any infrastructure to run SQL queries on your data. Additionally, it scales automatically and parallelizes queries on large datasets without you having to specify configurations. It also requires no maintenance because the underlying servers powering Athena are managed by AWS. You pay for the query you run on Athena, thus optimizing data storage and minimizing query execution, which ensures lower costs.

Amazon Redshift is a data warehousing service on AWS that allows you to run complex analytic queries at a **petabyte (PB)** scale. These queries run on distributed and parallelized nodes. Unlike traditional relational databases, Redshift stores data in columns that are optimized for analytical applications, whereas it's often the case to query based on aggregate summary statistics on columns. We'll see an example of this in the next section.

For ML, **Amazon SageMaker** is a service that provides an ML platform for building, training, deploying, and monitoring ML models. SageMaker comes with a host of features that range from labeling data to monitoring a complete ML pipeline. With Amazon SageMaker, data scientists can launch ML-specific notebook instances (indicated by an `ml.` prefix) to prepare data, build ML models, and deploy them at scale. We'll cover how to optimize ML compute using SageMaker in the next section.

Optimizing data ingestion and preparation

Data analytics starts with having data; you can't get insights from data if you don't have any, and you need a place to store that data. We've already discussed Amazon S3 Intelligent-Tiering in *Chapter 7, Optimizing Storage,* as an easy way to optimize storage costs by allowing AWS to manage the optimal storage class on our behalf.

We can also save on costs through the format in which we store our data. With Amazon S3, you are charged by the amount of storage, hence if we can find ways to minimize that storage amount, we can reduce our storage costs. Storing only the data that you need is always good to have in mind. It's easy to create a data swamp out of a lake because you just never know if, and when, you'll need a dataset. But instead of blindly putting all your data in Amazon S3 Standard or Intelligent-Tiering, try to understand your data's access patterns, future needs, and business value. We may always intend to *clean up* our data afterward, but the more we put it off, the more data accumulates and the harder it becomes to comb through data to find what we actually need.

For data that you do need, use compression to save on storage space and pay less. Parquet is a popular columnar format for large-scale analytics workloads and can be used to save on storage costs but also save on query performance if you end up using AWS services such as Amazon Athena or Amazon Redshift. Values of a similar type such as string, data, and integer can be compressed and stored together, and because column values are stored together on disk, the query performance is more efficient.

The following screenshot shows a representation of columnar-based storage of a table. If you were to run a query on total views for `Active` users, you'd only need to query the `ViewCount` and `UserStatus` columns in a columnar store such as Redshift. This is much more efficient than having to query each row and read columns that you don't need, as you would do in a traditional relational database:

Videold	Userld	ViewCount	UserStatus
1	1111	50	Active
2	1112	120	Active
3	1113	600	Active
4	1114	20	InActive

Block 1	1, 2, 3, 4
Block 2	1111, 1112, 1113, 1114
Block 3	50, 120, 600, 20
Block 4	Active, Active, Active, InActive

Figure 9.3 – Table with columnar-based storage

When using Athena, consider using a shared Amazon S3 location for query results. When setting up Athena, you must specify a location in S3 to store query results. By choosing a shared location, you can reuse cached query results, improve query performance, and save on data transfer costs. With Athena, you pay for the time it takes for the query to run. Hence, by minimizing the query execution time, you will be spending less. This is generally a good pattern, especially if you're planning on using Athena to run ad hoc queries on your organization's **Cost and Usage Reports** (**CUR**) data.

The following screenshot shows where you can manage these settings in the Amazon Athena console. Here, we specify the query result location (and optionally choose to encrypt) within the **Query editor** page.

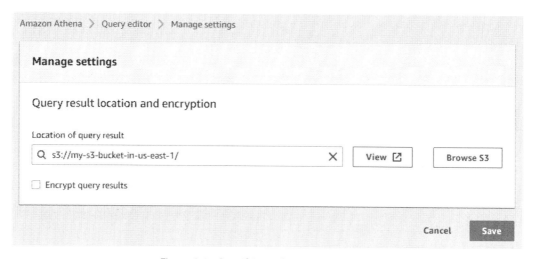

Figure 9.4 – Specifying Athena query results

We looked at Amazon Athena as an example service to run ad hoc queries. Another option is to use Amazon Redshift if you plan to run more complex joins and read workloads with long-running query times. Unlike Athena, you don't pay per query with Redshift. Instead, you provision a cluster that is purpose-built for data warehousing-type workloads. You can also purchase Redshift RIs to save on costs for running steady-state, consistent Redshift clusters. Because we understand RI mechanics, let's instead focus on optimizing the performance and cost of Redshift in how we use and operate the cluster.

You can leverage a feature of Amazon Redshift called **concurrency scaling**. This offers the ability to support scalable concurrent users and queries. When you enable concurrency scaling, Amazon Redshift automatically adds additional cluster capacity to specifically process read queries. When a Redshift cluster with concurrency scaling meets specific requirements such as Region location, node type, and node amount, queries can be routed to a concurrency-scaling cluster. You route queries to concurrency-scaling clusters by enabling a **Workload Manager** (**WLM**) queue.

Although you're charged for concurrency-scaling clusters, you're only charged for the time they're in use. The concept here is similar to the auto-scaling discussion we had in the previous section. Consider provisioning a large Redshift cluster to meet high-performance requirements even if peak performance only occurs during a small percentage of the cluster's lifetime. Usually, larger clusters equate to larger costs. If instead, you were able to leverage the dynamism of the cloud such as the concurrency-scaling feature of Redshift, you could meet your performance requirements, and only pay for it when needed.

In the following diagram, we see an example of concurrency scaling on Redshift in action. When a user initiates a query with concurrency scaling, the leader node of the main Redshift cluster receives the request and determines whether it fits the requirements for the concurrency-scaling queue. Redshift then sends the request to add the cluster depicted on the right side of the diagram. These two clusters constitute your concurrency cluster. As more queries arrive, they are sent to the concurrency-scaling cluster for processing. Optionally, we have Amazon S3, which stores the cluster's snapshots, enabling the new concurrency cluster access by way of a caching layer. Finally, the results are delivered to the user through the response:

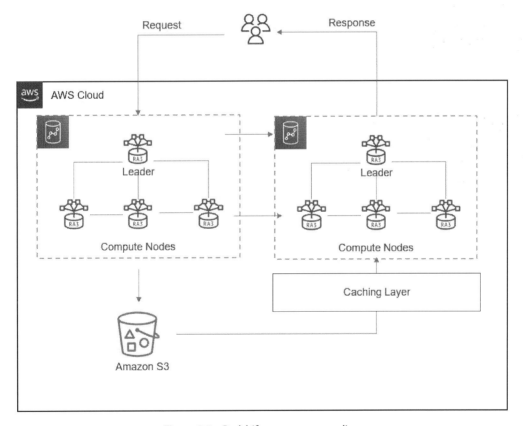

Figure 9.5 – Redshift concurrency scaling

Amazon Redshift also offers elastic resize options to resize your cluster quickly by adding nodes when your workload increases and removing nodes when demand decreases. This gives you some flexibility and comfort in knowing that you do not need to make the right decision upfront. You can iterate on your cluster's configuration as your needs change. Elastic resizing automatically redistributes data to new nodes quickly when you resize using the same node type. Elastic resize can also change node types, whereby a snapshot is created and copied to a new node-type cluster.

An additional option for resizing your Redshift cluster is to use **Amazon Redshift Spectrum**. This feature of Redshift allows you to scale your data lake without needing to load data into the Redshift cluster. You can directly query data in Amazon S3 and join the data in S3 with Redshift. This saves you from having to duplicate storage costs in both services.

Lastly, because Amazon Redshift allows you to pause and later resume a cluster, be mindful of when a cluster is needed by teams. Although you can purchase RIs to save on cluster costs, if an always-on philosophy isn't required for a workload, then save on costs by turning off the cluster. A practical exercise is to turn it off during weekends and holidays when you know teams or applications won't need to be accessing your cluster. When a cluster is paused, on-demand billing is suspended, helping you to reduce waste.

We learned how you can optimize costs with Athena and Redshift in this section. Storing data efficiently by compressing it and leveraging columnar storage tools such as Redshift are ways to reduce the operational costs of using analytics services. We looked at some of Redshift's features, focusing on elasticity to use and scale the service when you need to. In the next section, we'll shift to the related but separate topic of ML. Because ML is often done after data preparation and data analysis, it logically fits as the next step in our data pipeline.

Optimizing ML

To uncover how we can optimize our ML costs, we must first understand which tasks constitute an ML workflow. We'll look at the various steps involved in a typical ML process. Then, we'll apply optimization methods to those specific steps using the various capabilities in AWS. We'll focus on how you can optimize your model-training costs and model-deployment costs with Amazon SageMaker.

Understanding an ML workflow

An ML workflow typically requires data exploration and then **feature engineering** (FE) to transfer data to a format that can be used by an ML algorithm. The algorithm reads the data to find patterns and *learns* in a sense to generalize patterns so that it can predict outcomes on new, or unknown, data. This is often referred to as *model training*—you're applying some mathematical algorithm that may be known and used popularly or something you created yourself to data that is proprietary to you or your organization. The application of an algorithm to your data creates an ML model. Then, you can apply this model to make predictions on new data. Amazon SageMaker is a fully managed platform that allows you to do just this.

SageMaker has tons of features that provide you with a unified platform to complete all tasks involved in an E2E ML workflow. This includes things such as data cleansing and preparation. Before you build an ML model, you need to format the data to remove unnecessary columns, remove missing values, change text columns to numeric values, and even add columns to define your *features*. Usually, you want to document all your steps into code to facilitate automation of these tasks in the form of a processing script so that you can run these data processing steps automatically and at scale.

You can use **SageMaker Processing** jobs to execute a processing script. Running these scripts can help you optimize because you only pay for the processing job for the duration of the task. An alternative could be to conduct your processing jobs in an Amazon EC2 instance if wanting to keep things in a cloud environment. However, this would require you to install all the necessary software on a fleet of instances for **high availability** (**HA**) and parallel processing, patch the instances, secure them, and right-size them, among other things. Rather than managing all this yourself, SageMaker Processing takes care of the resource provisioning, and data and artifact transfer, and terminates the resources once your job completes. Thus, you only pay for the resources used for the processing job while it runs. At the same time, you only need to use a relatively small SageMaker notebook instance to test and orchestrate your processing jobs.

Leveraging a fully managed service such as SageMaker helps you avoid unnecessary costs when it comes to managing and paying for compute resources for your ML workload. In line with our discussion from the beginning of this chapter, SageMaker helps you take advantage of AWS' elasticity by having SageMaker manage your ML tasks' infrastructure and paying for them only for the duration of the tasks' runtime.

> **Important note**
> You may, however, choose to manage the infrastructure yourself if you find that you obtain a competitive advantage by doing so. Some companies have robust data science teams that have the knowledge and experience to manage their own ML infrastructure. They may even have the expertise to optimize that infrastructure at various levels such as code optimization, Savings Plans, and the use of **open source software** (**OSS**). If indeed you find better cost savings by managing your own ML workloads, then SageMaker may not be the right choice for you. However, we'll continue the rest of this section assuming you chose SageMaker as your ML platform.

Let's now move to the next step of the ML workflow and learn how to optimize our model-training tasks.

Optimizing model training and tuning

Because SageMaker decouples the ML development from task execution, you can easily adopt a pay-as-you-go model. For example, you can spin up a small, cheaper `ml.t2.small` instance to work on ML development tasks such as testing code, setting up configuration files, and defining your ML pipeline. You attach a SageMaker execution role to that instance with the required permissions to access datasets and then run the SageMaker Python SDK commands to run processing scripts, initiate training jobs, and deploy model endpoints.

At this point, you're only paying for that `ml.t2.small` instance. You don't necessarily want to train and deploy models on that instance because you'll likely face **out-of-memory (OOM)** exceptions or other errors because of the computational- and memory-intensive requirements of model training. Rather than running resource-intensive training jobs on your `ml.t2.small` instance, you can elect to run training jobs on a separate, **graphics processing unit (GPU)**-based instance to optimize performance. SageMaker will spin up the resource required for your training job, and then spin down the instances when the job is complete. This allows you to only pay for the required resources when you need them, thereby reducing waste related to ML workloads.

At the same time, you don't have to provision an expensive, GPU-based instance if you simply need it for data exploration and testing. SageMaker allows you to decouple training or processing jobs from experimentation. For example, the next code snippet shows a model-training job specifying that the training should be done on a single `ml.m4.4xlarge` instance. Even though the notebook instance used to instantiate and execute this code may be on an `ml.t2.small` instance, you gain the benefit of paying for the more expensive `ml.m4.4xlarge` instance only while the training job runs, while paying for a cheaper `ml.t2.small` instance for exploration. SageMaker will manage the training on your behalf and terminate it when the training job is complete, so you only pay for it while it runs.

In the following code snippet, we are calling the SageMaker estimator to train our model. We specify the container image we'd like to use, then the execution role that has permission to access the training data. Then, we specify the instance type and count to tell SageMaker which type of instance and how many of these instances to use for this training job:

```
model = sagemaker.estimator.Estimator(
container,
role,
train_instance_count=1,
train_instance_type='ml.m4.4xlarge,
sagemaker_session=sess)
```

That begs the following questions: *What if my training jobs run a very long time? How can I ensure I'm not wasting valuable training time?* **SageMaker Debugger** helps profile these job runs and provides recommendations to fix bottlenecks that may prolong unnecessarily long training jobs. Debugger can suggest things such as using a small instance based on lower GPU utilization or stopping training jobs early if subsequent training iterations are not improving the desired model metrics.

For example, training a **deep learning (DL)** model on a **neural network (NN)** usually involves adjusting weights on each training run (epoch) and observing the resulting model metrics. The network adjusts weights to see if those changes positively impact the model. However, there may come a point where adjusting the weights does not yield better results. If you are continuously running model-tuning jobs, but for every iteration it's not improving your model, then it is wasteful to have those resources running. It's better to *early stop* jobs to reduce unnecessary iterations. Early stopping can help reduce SageMaker training times, which correlate with your efforts to reduce waste.

You also have the option to use spot instances for training jobs, which may be appropriate for training jobs that can tolerate interruptions, or when using algorithms that support checkpointing (refer to *Chapter 6, Optimizing Compute,* for details on spot). You can specify the use of spot instances within the estimator by using the following code:

```
use_spot_instance=True.
Model = sagemaker.estimator.Estimator(
container,
role,
train_instance_count=1,
train_instance_type='ml.m4.4xlarge,
use_spot_instance=True,
max_wait = 120,
sagemaker_session=sess)
```

Because a spot instance may terminate before the training job completes, using the max_wait parameter will tell SageMaker to wait a certain number of seconds (in this case, 120 seconds) for new spot instances to replace terminated ones. Once the max_wait time passes, the job completes. If using checkpoints, the training job will commence from the latest checkpoint when the spot instances were terminated.

Another cost-reducing strategy is in the way we specify how data is made ready by SageMaker during training. By default, files are read using File mode, which copies all data to an instance when a training job starts. The alternative is to use Pipe mode, which loads data like a stream. Note that these modes do not appear on the screen as options to select; you must specify these as parameters.

Using File mode for large files (above 10 **gigabytes (GB)**) prevents a long pause at the start of a training job just to get the file loaded into SageMaker. Instead, by using Pipe mode, data will be streamed in parallel from S3 directly into a training run. This provides higher **input/output (I/O)** and allows the training job to start early and end faster, and ultimately reduces training-job costs. We can specify the use of Pipe mode through the input_mode configuration, as illustrated in the following code snippet:

```
model = sagemaker.estimator.Estimator(
container,
role,
train_instance_count=1,
train_instance_type='ml.m4.4xlarge,
input_mode='Pipe'…)
```

We looked at several ways to reduce your training costs on Amazon SageMaker. Leverage spot instances if you can tolerate interruption to pay for spare compute as a discount versus paying for on-demand instances for training. Additionally, consider using the `Pipe` input mode to ensure the training job ends sooner. Also, leverage built-in features such as SageMaker Debugger to help you identify ways to optimize your training configuration. Because you only pay for the resources for the duration of your training and tuning jobs, use these tools to ensure those jobs don't take longer than necessary. Let's move on to the next step of an ML workflow: the deployment phase.

Optimizing model deployment

Once you have a trained model, you can deploy them to **SageMaker endpoints**. These endpoints can be persistent for real-time online inference. Many customers create **Hypertext Transfer Protocol Secure (HTTPS)** endpoints that allow users and applications to request real-time inference for low-latency use cases. SageMaker will manage these endpoints on your behalf, including automatically scaling them on your behalf to meet demand. However, you will be paying for these endpoints on an hourly basis, depending on the instance type you choose for the endpoint. As you can imagine, the more endpoints you have running, the more your costs will increase.

Endpoints are long-running resources that are easy to leave running even if you may not have use for them. Let's imagine you deploy a real-time ML model using a blue/green deployment. You have two identical model endpoints and, once ready, you cut over from the blue environment to the green environment. The green environment now serves 100% of inference requests through your endpoint while the blue environment sits idle. To remove unused SageMaker endpoints, we can apply the same discipline we used to remove stale **Elastic Block Store (EBS)** volumes, as discussed in *Chapter 7, Optimizing Storage*. CloudWatch alerts can help notify you when a SageMaker endpoint is not receiving invocation requests. For example, use the `Invocations` metric to get the total number of requests sent to a model endpoint using `Sum` statistics. If you see zero invocations consistently, it may be a good time to delete the endpoint.

There may be more than one EC2 instance up and running behind a SageMaker endpoint serving predictions using SageMaker hosting services. Therefore, the more endpoints you have, the more costs you will incur. Although SageMaker Savings Plans can help offset the costs, it's also wise to minimize the number of endpoints to remove unnecessary costs.

If you have similar models that can serve predictions through a shared serving endpoint, consider using **SageMaker multi-model endpoints** to avoid paying for additional endpoints. Multi-model endpoints are a scalable and cost-efficient solution to deploying several models while minimizing the cost of paying for endpoints. These models share a container that can host multiple models. This not only reduces cost, but also the administrative requirement of you having to manage multiple models across multiple endpoints.

For example, you may have a model that predicts home prices for a geographic region in the US. Home prices vary based on location. You may have a model that serves distinct predictions for homes in New York versus homes in Texas and other locations. You can place all these models under a single endpoint and invoke a location-specific model based on the request.

Multi-model endpoints are useful when similar models can be served without needing to access all the models at the same time. You can invoke a specific model by specifying the target model name as a parameter in the prediction request, as shown in the next diagram.

Here, we see a multi-model endpoint with two models, `model_1` and `model_2`. SageMaker automatically serves the model based on the `TargetModel` parameter specified in the `invoke_endpoint` method. SageMaker will route the inference request to the instance behind the endpoint and will download the model from the Amazon S3 bucket that holds the model artifacts:

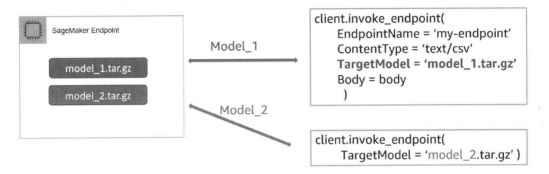

Figure 9.6 – SageMaker multi-model endpoint

Although SageMaker provides a variety of instance types for processing, model training, and deployment, sometimes you may not be able to find quite the right size. GPU instances are appropriate for model training on large datasets, but they can typically be oversized for smaller-batch inference requests.

By attaching an **Elastic Inference Accelerator** (**EIA**), you can boost your instance with a GPU-based add-on. This provides you the flexibility to choose a base CPU instance and dynamically add GPUs with the EIA until you find the right specification you require for your inference needs. This helps you optimize your base resources such as CPU and **random-access memory** (**RAM**) while keeping GPUs lower but having the flexibility to add GPUs when needed, all while saving costs. The following code snippet shows you how to add an `ml.eia2.medium` instance to an `ml.m4.xlarge` instance when deploying a SageMaker model:

```
predictor = model.deploy(
initial_instance_count=1,
instance_type='ml.m4.xlarge',
accelerator_type='ml.eia2.medium')
```

SageMaker also offers Savings Plans such as EC2 Instance and Compute Savings Plans. We unpacked a lot of how Savings Plans work in *Chapter 6*, *Optimizing Compute*, and their mechanisms are similar in how they are applied to SageMaker usage. You still specify a term length and payment option (no upfront, partial upfront, or all upfront). However, unlike EC2 Savings Plans, SageMaker Saving

Plans only have one discount rate, meaning you cannot choose between instance-specific Savings Plans (such as EC2 Instance Savings Plans) and Compute Savings Plans.

The following screenshot shows how to select a SageMaker Savings Plan in Cost Explorer. You simply select a term (1 or 3 years), an hourly commitment, and a payment option:

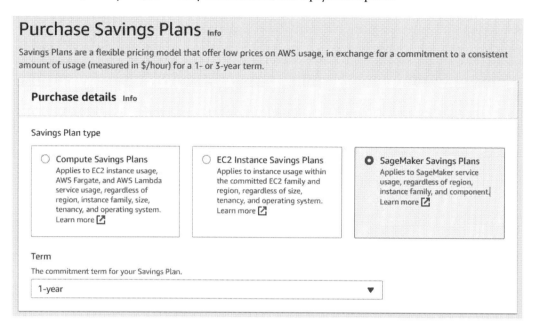

Figure 9.7 – SageMaker Savings Plans

SageMaker Savings Plans apply to all eligible Regions and SageMaker components. Whether you use SageMaker Processing, training, hosting, or just a notebook instance for testing, the Savings Plan commitment will apply to these components to help you save as an organization. And as with EC2 Savings Plans, if your usage of SageMaker exceeds your Savings Plan commitment, that usage will be charged the on-demand rate.

We covered optimization considerations for deploying ML models using Amazon SageMaker. We learned about SageMaker endpoint hygiene to ensure we're not paying for persistent endpoints unnecessarily. We also learned about multi-model endpoints to reduce the cost of paying for multiple endpoints. Finally, we learned about the applicability of SageMaker Savings Plans to cover our ML workloads.

Summary

In this chapter, we covered topics that went beyond compute, storage, and networking. We saw how to apply cost-optimization methods for more advanced cloud-native environments including analytics and ML.

We unpacked AWS elasticity and what that means for architecting our workload. Take advantage of auto-scaling tools on AWS. These tools themselves are free. You only pay for the resources provisioned by scale-out activities and benefit by not paying for terminated resources from scale-in events. You learned about the various scaling policies and the difference between AWS Auto Scaling and Amazon EC2 Auto Scaling.

We then explored the realm of analytics. We found ways to optimize costs using compression, setting up the right data structure, and Redshift concurrency-scaling and workload management features.

Lastly, we learned about the various steps in a typical ML workload. We looked at ways to optimize data processing jobs using a managed service such as Amazon SageMaker. We also looked at optimization strategies for training and tuning jobs by leveraging spot instances, SageMaker Debugger, and file input modes. Then, we found optimization opportunities in model deployment using multi-model endpoints, elastic inference, and SageMaker Savings Plans.

We covered many topics in this section, focusing on the tactical work to optimize your cloud environments. In the next and final part of the book, we'll learn about operationalizing these tasks in ways to optimize at scale as your organization grows. We'll also focus on the people aspect of cost optimization and the importance of people, processes, and communication so that cost optimization doesn't become a one-time activity but a continuous discipline that yields long-term results for your organization.

Further reading

For more information, refer to the following links:

- *AWS Auto Scaling*, 2022: `https://aws.amazon.com/autoscaling/`
- *Amazon EC2 Auto Scaling*, 2022: `https://aws.amazon.com/ec2/autoscaling/`
- *Predictive scaling for Amazon EC2 Auto Scaling*, 2022: `https://docs.aws.amazon.com/autoscaling/ec2/userguide/ec2-auto-scaling-predictive-scaling.html`
- *Athena compression support*, 2022: `https://docs.aws.amazon.com/athena/latest/ug/compression-formats.html`
- *Working with concurrency scaling*, 2022: `https://docs.aws.amazon.com/redshift/latest/dg/concurrency-scaling.html`
- *Implementing workload management*, 2022: `https://docs.aws.amazon.com/redshift/latest/dg/cm-c-implementing-workload-management.html`
- *Host multiple models in one container behind one endpoint*, 2022: `https://docs.aws.amazon.com/sagemaker/latest/dg/multi-model-endpoints.html`

- *Monitor Amazon SageMaker with Amazon CloudWatch*, 2022: `https://docs.aws.amazon.com/sagemaker/latest/dg/monitoring-cloudwatch.html#cloudwatch-metrics-endpoint-invocation`

- *Processing*, 2022: `https://sagemaker.readthedocs.io/en/stable/api/training/processing.html#module-sagemaker.processing`

Part 3: Operationalizing FinOps

The objective of *Part 3* is to put everything we've learned in the previous chapters into practice on a larger scale. We've identified ways to pick the right pricing model, to rightsize, to autoscale, to set budgets, and so much more. This last section of the book helps you to operationalize these practices so that they are not one-off projects, and to incorporate them into your day-to-day operations for long-term success.

This part of the book comprises the following chapters:

- *Chapter 10, Data-Driven Fin-Ops*
- *Chapter 11, Driving FinOps Autonomously*
- *Chapter 12, Management Functions*

10
Data-Driven FinOps

So far, you've learned about the various AWS tools and services you can use to monitor, plan, and optimize your AWS resources. You can use these tools to a certain extent, but tools alone cannot provide your organization with sustainable FinOps practices. You also need to involve the right people and the right processes to realize the long-term benefits of FinOps.

In these final chapters, you'll learn how to apply FinOps practices at scale across your organization while going beyond the core IT functionalities such as compute, networking, and storage. We will start by looking at how you can apply these AWS tools and services centrally. In the previous chapters, we discussed the importance of having a central team, or a **Cloud Center of Excellence** (**CCoE**). A CCoE is just an example of a centralized team that can drive FinOps best practices across your organization. CCoE certainly does not have to be the name you choose for your organization, but naming conventions aside, a centralized team's function is critical for enabling teams to adopt FinOps and embed cost-saving practices within their daily operations.

In this chapter, we're going to cover the following main topics:

- Establishing a centralized function
- Creating an effective metrics strategy
- Defining the right metrics
- Leveraging the CUR

Establishing a centralized function

I've advocated throughout this book that FinOps isn't just for a single team or a single line of business but requires a cross-team, collaborative effort. No one team can or should be responsible for managing an entire, large enterprise's cloud spending. Although certain teams may have more responsibilities than others in terms of managing cloud spending, and the scope of these responsibilities may have a broader impact than others, the success of FinOps depends on everyone's involvement. For example, in a small, startup environment, embracing an *all-hands-on-deck* type of philosophy will benefit those that want to adopt a FinOps mindset, regardless of the size and maturity of your business.

Reducing waste by embedding FinOps practices within your organization involves reacting to real-time events and matching supply to demand in a dynamic environment while embracing the variable nature of IT spending in the cloud. It's precisely this reason why you need to have a balance between centralized and decentralized functions – too much decentralization leads to competing goals among teams while too much centralization leads to teams not being able to produce. This is where a centralized team can help. They can define goals that contribute to the overall success of the business while providing the framework that teams can operate within. They can also have visibility into the costs of all teams and steer teams in the right direction when costs seem to be getting out of control.

Let's look at what a centralized FinOps function looks like by justifying the reasons for establishing one.

Reasons for a centralized FinOps function

There are several reasons why you should consider having a central FinOps team.

Teams have competing priorities that often conflict with cost optimization. Cost optimization has never been a leading priority for application developers, nor is it likely that it will become a priority in the future. It's true that, generally, developers love optimizing, but most businesses operate with performance and agility in mind. Pushing products out to market quickly ahead of competitors is usually the driving force over reducing spending in a high-growth environment.

Moreover, before the cloud, developers had to build on the hardware the organization provided based on a regular IT resource refresh cycle. Application developers never had to worry about costs because IT resources were already budgeted and planned for. They only needed to build based on what was given to them. This removed the need for developers to be cost-conscious in how they built since the boundary within which to operate largely depended on allocated budgets, as well as the performance ceilings of the provisioned hardware. However, given the dynamism of the cloud, developers cannot afford the luxury of being completely ignorant of cost. The cost boundaries are much tighter than what they were previously, and it's helpful to have guidance from a central FinOps team to advise on how to operate within these new boundaries.

Furthermore, developers are expected to produce quickly in today's ever-changing market. To stay competitive, companies are leveraging the cloud for the on-demand provisioning of IT resources and focusing on differentiators for their business domain instead of occupying themselves with the undifferentiated heavy lifting of managing IT infrastructure. Developers are primarily concerned with agile deployments and quick releases. Cost is not something that is at the forefront of developers' minds. It may not even be something that they have the bandwidth to consider.

Managing costs is itself a full-time job, not just a one-time activity. Many companies dedicate resources to improving processes within business functions. For example, process improvement is the business practice of identifying, analyzing, and improving business processes that can decrease inefficiencies within operations. These functions provide business value because process improvement can decrease costs, which directly impacts a company's revenue. Cloud FinOps is no different. Due to the dynamic nature of the cloud, monitoring, analyzing, and identifying cloud spending warrants dedicated resources to continually find ways to decrease costs.

Your organization may choose to leverage multiple public cloud vendors, depending on your business strategy. In this case, having a centralized FinOps team that understands the cost implications of going multi-cloud, as well as the pricing mechanisms that different public cloud providers offer, will be beneficial to your broader organization. Application developers and architects are generally not well suited to holding private pricing agreements between cloud providers. This task is something a centralized team can own. They have the domain knowledge and the deep financial expertise to understand what financial impact long-term agreements with a cloud provider can have on the broader organization. This is a topic we'll cover in greater detail in *Chapter 12, Driving FinOps Collaboratively*.

Technology iterates at a rapid pace and having a team to own change management helps your organization adapt. AWS constantly releases new services and new capabilities within existing services. Oftentimes, pricing adjustments accompany these changes. A centralized team needs to be aware not only of these technological changes but also of the pricing implications of those changes to the business. Technology teams may very much be aware of new service offerings from public cloud providers because newer generation resources tend to have better price-to-performance ratios. But technology teams may not have the bandwidth to run the cost analyses to change to newer generation services. It's valuable to have a team to run and analyze these reports to see the overall impact on the business.

Technology is changing and will continue to change. This means that as organizations have had to shift their way of thinking about IT from procurement to on-demand provisioning, chances are they will have to continue to shift to new ways of thinking as industries and technologies change. Change management is often something companies struggle with because change management is something *individuals* themselves struggle with. Having a centralized team to develop change management strategies and execute their plans can help the organization adjust to new settings as they come.

Now that we've discussed the reasons for having centralized FinOps teams, we'll identify the right personas to make up a centralized FinOps function.

Personas for a centralized FinOps function

A successful FinOps practice depends on a cross-functional team. This encourages collaboration between teams that perhaps would have little to no reason to engage otherwise. Because teams have different priorities, it's important to find a common ground. Ultimately, teams are looking to achieve the same goal – that is, they are looking to grow the business. They are simply trying to reach this goal in their own way. Thus, a centralized, cross-functional FinOps team looks to empower teams to reach this goal efficiently in ways that don't impede other teams' efforts.

Most organizations already have the personnel required to start building a centralized FinOps team. These are personas that span the business, technology, and finance domains within a business. You can always start with the talent that you have, and then fill the necessary gaps as you scale:

- **Executives**: Executives provide the high-level support and visibility a central FinOps team needs to be successful. Grassroots efforts without executive alignment are admirable but unsustainable. Business strategy can change from a variety of factors, which usually originate from the executive level. However, having an executive such as a CFO, CTO, CIO, or VP of Infrastructure to drive cloud cost accountability and ensure the FinOps objectives align with the broader business empowers a FinOps team's operations.

Executives can also provide objective business metrics that provide measurable goals for FinOps practices. These **key performance metrics** (**KPIs**) can be goals such as reducing cloud spending by 10% but maintaining the same number of **daily active users** (**DAUs**) or increasing the **Reserved Instance** (**RI**) and **Savings Plans** (**SP**) coverage rates while maintaining the same level of availability for an application. These are metrics that can be attributed to broader business goals. Having executive sponsorship to identify these goals and track progress toward these goals will validate FinOps practices and show the value that FinOps can have for the organization.

- **Engineering lead**: Most AWS usage will originate from the engineering and operations teams because these teams will be building products and services on AWS. Team members can include software development engineers, DevOps engineers, cloud architects, platform engineers, and even **machine learning** (**ML**) engineers.

Cost is one of many metrics within their building space. And oftentimes, it is a metric that contradicts other metrics such as high availability and performance. Typically, if you want to build a highly available system, you need to ensure redundancy of the system, which implies higher costs. Thus, having the engineering perspective allows the cross-functional team to consider other factors that ensure business continuity.

Personas from the technology side also possess the technical skills often needed to build automation and operationalize FinOps tasks. This could be something such as building a data pipeline workflow to ingest cost and usage data and aggregating them in one place. This also requires implementing the right security guardrails to provide folks with the right level of data access to view and download reports.

- **Product owner**: Product owners are folks within the organization that want to bring the products built by engineers to market. They also have responsibilities that entail analyzing business trends, historical product data, and measuring the performance of launched products. These include product managers, business analysts, and business operations managers.

Product owners bring a unique perspective as they can help develop business KPIs. Whereas engineering leads may introduce operational metrics from an infrastructure perspective such as revenue per infrastructure cost or cost per deployed AWS service, product owners provide unit cost metrics. These perspectives show the business how much revenue a product is generating based on the amount of cloud spending or decreasing gross margins over time. Because product owners are generally more in-tune with broader market trends than engineering teams, it is valuable to have both perspectives in a cross-functional team.

- **FinOps practitioner**: A FinOps practitioner's primary goals are to educate and enable FinOps best practices across the organization. FinOps practitioners have a deeper knowledge of cloud economics. They understand the different pricing models, regardless of the cloud provider. They can decipher a cloud bill, which can be saturated with cloud-specific jargon, and can translate cloud bill service spending into a language that makes sense to the business. They are also able to interpret and analyze the bill to find areas of improvement, such as reducing waste.

FinOps practitioners understand both the business and technical requirements of business products and apply the right pricing models and cost optimization strategies to meet those requirements. For example, they understand and communicate the cost implications of rightsizing servers. Rather than blindly following the rightsizing recommendations in Cost Explorer, a FinOps practitioner can interpret those recommendations, collaborate with the engineering teams, and see if it makes business sense to right-size certain instances. FinOps practitioners are also the cost optimization champions within an organization driving operational and cultural changes to help teams adopt a FinOps mindset as they operate in the cloud.

FinOps practitioners usually have some overlap with business analysts. Business analysts know how to work with and manipulate data using several business productivity tools such as Microsoft Excel and run simple **structured query language (SQL)** queries. These skills help analyze cost and usage data when using the tools natively available on AWS, or when using the tools built by the technologies personas that enable self-service cost and usage data discovery.

- **Finance persona**: Finance personas have deep experience in managing IT budgets, forecasting, accounting, and procurement. However, they are not only limited in scope to IT. Finance personas must manage the spending for the entire enterprise, so they have a broader view of cost and usage. This involves things both inside and outside of AWS spending.

  They will have had many years of experience in planning IT spending for an enterprise and will be familiar with traditional IT accounting practices. They know how to account for cost and usage and thus can allocate those to business metrics. They understand historical billing and forecasting and thus are essential collaborators with FinOps practitioners. Depending on the size of your organization, you may need to include other personas in a centralized cross-functional team, such as folks from the procurement side, or an IT finance manager.

Generally, we can bucket personas into these four broad categories: an executive sponsor and folks from the technology, business, and finance side. With these personas in mind, let's take a closer look at a critical function that this centralized team will own that will be the foundation for all FinOps efforts – that is, creating an effective *metrics strategy* for your organization.

Creating an effective metrics strategy

In *Part 2* of this book, we covered many optimization topics that encompass compute, storage, networking, and more. But the question remains: *are we really saving?* You won't be able to validate the answer to this question without quantitative evidence. This is where a metrics strategy can help. A metric strategy not only defines the metrics your organization uses to measure FinOps success, but also defines how to use those metrics, where they come from, and who owns those metrics. In other words, it involves metrics governance as well.

The purpose of a metrics strategy for FinOps is to help your organization answer questions such as the following:

- How do we know how much we're saving on our AWS cost and usage?

- What metrics or KPIs should we use?

- How can we tell our KPIs are useful?

- How many KPIs should we track?

Companies often struggle to gauge the impact of FinOps measures on financial statements such as balance sheets and income statements because the old methods of accounting for IT resources do not apply. The variable nature of the cloud creates a dynamic spending environment that is difficult to account for if there are no strong channels of communication among teams and business units. And if your organization is experiencing a period of growth, it becomes even more challenging to know if you're optimizing your AWS usage.

It's crucial to address these challenges with a well-defined governance strategy for metrics. We will define what metric strategy governance is and see what it looks like in practice in the next section.

What is metrics strategy governance?

Before we define what we mean by this phrase, let's see what a business might look like when it *doesn't* have governance in a metrics strategy.

> **A non-existent metrics strategy**
>
> Jeremy learns of the various reports Alexander must sift through when working within the office of the CFO. Alexander has a read-only view of AWS Cost Explorer on the management account. Alexander also has access to third-party tools that aggregate cost and usage data across all the business's AWS accounts and bring a unified dashboard for cost and usage reporting. Alexander uses several pre-built views to see cost and usage activity by accounts, teams, and business-critical application names.
>
> Alexander shows these reports to Jeremy and shares that he mainly uses five reports when looking at and reporting AWS spending to the CFO. In the user interface, Jeremy notices that there are multiple folders and many views within those folders that have been created by various users. These reports have similar but different naming conventions such as *spend per revenue ratio, total spend per revenue, forecast variance: monthly, commitment rate,* and other views with variable levels of clarity; some reports make intuitive sense while others are completely cryptic.
>
> Jeremy asks Alexander how he determines which report to use since many of them have similar names but slightly different values. Alexander says that he uses the reports that were vetted by the finance teams and that have a clear owner he can contact when he has questions.
>
> Jeremy realizes that for the business to successfully use cost and usage data, the business must govern the way teams report this data.

Without governance, you run the risk of anybody in the organization creating a report in production and defining a metric however they like. As these occurrences compound, your organization becomes mired in reports and metrics that do not provide any meaningful value. This makes it more difficult to understand the source of truth.

Therefore, metrics strategy governance is an organization-wide policy that defines what metric to use, how to define that metric, and who owns the metric. This ultimately leads to a metric providing business value to your organization. In short, if it doesn't bring any business value, there is a good chance it's unnecessary.

If you want to know if you have poor governance in your metric strategy, you can ask yourself the following questions:

- Who created this metric?
- What is this metric's source of truth?
- How did you create this metric?
- What is the goal for this metric?
- How do we measure success concerning this metric?

Documenting these answers for each metric ensures that the metric is indeed useful to your business. Documenting also helps you keep track of changes as your business needs change so that you can see the evolution of your metrics over time. You will be able to track different versions of metrics, when they changed, who changes them, and the causes for the changes. Documentation provides metadata about your cost and usage data. Metadata and data cataloging is essential for any company looking to be a data-driven organization. If businesses are trying to uncover insights from their data by establishing a sound data governance strategy for their operational, sales, and marketing data, then the business can apply the same vigor toward their cost and usage data to draw the same insights.

For example, let's take a generic but useful metric such as **IT Spend/Revenue**, which explains why spending on it accounts for the growth of the organization over time by having revenue in the denominator. To apply governance, identify who created this metric and how they define *spending*. It could be what the accounting system says, a subset of cost, or some other method.

This helps you identify the source of truth for those inputs that can help anyone within the organization to recreate the metric. This also helps build consistency with other departments as they may have different numbers or purposes for creating a metric. If each team documents how they created the metric and for what purpose, then this will avoid confusion when interpreting these metrics and applying them when measuring cost savings. Teams can use different metrics for different audiences. Implementing governance ensures the business uses metrics for the right purpose.

Enterprises are keen to apply data governance to their enterprise data. Data governance helps with building a common understanding of data, improving the quality of data, having well-defined processes for the use of that data, operating within legal restrictions of that data, and more. You can apply the same discipline to your cost and usage data to build a data-driven practice toward FinOps.

There are many data governance frameworks out there, but they apply differently to the various data types. In the next section, I'll propose a data governance framework for your cost and usage data. This framework will help you create your own cost and usage metrics that are meaningful to your organization.

Applying a metric governance framework

Organizations will have their own ways of applying metrics governance. Many factors will influence how companies do this, such as the size of the organization, method of communication, the organization of teams, and the maturity of their cloud journey. However, we can generalize the application of metrics governance through a framework.

Companies that have successful metrics governances operate within the bounds of this framework, which is composed of an approval process, standardization mechanism, monitoring and reporting cadences, and a central governance team. Let's take a closer look at each component:

1. It's common to start with an *approval process*, which requires that all the metrics are reviewed to ensure they are clear and relevant to a business function. In this case, the business function is optimizing the use of cloud resources by either eliminating unnecessary spending or using what is needed efficiently.

    Without an established approval process, you run the risk of metrics sprawl. When teams can create, share, and report on their metrics, then your business will eventually get duplicate metrics, metrics that have the same intended meaning but are spelled differently, and other data quality issues.

    An approval process ensures you have good metric hygiene. You don't want to be in a situation where you not only lose control of knowing what resources you have within your AWS environment, but also lose control of the metrics that you're trying to use to manage those resources. A central FinOps practice can define the metrics that the business will use and manage the metadata around those metrics.

2. Next, businesses should define a mechanism to control or identify which metrics can and should be *standardized*. One thing I've seen customers do is create a tiered hierarchy of metrics. The metrics that should be standardized and used in production are tier-1 metrics. These are metrics that teams present on executive reports and are shared among all teams. Tier-2 metrics are shared within specific teams because they only apply to specific contexts. A simple example would be the number of active rightsizing recommendations. This metric is of less concern to executive teams than it is to the technology and FinOps teams. A more useful metric for executives would be the actual amount saved because of rightsizing compute. Tier-3 metrics are metrics that are not yet used in production because they need to be refined or because they don't provide business value at a point in time.

Standardizing how metrics will be moved between tiers or when they will be promoted to production helps maintain metric hygiene. With good hygiene, you can use the metrics that are most meaningful in reports to be shared with the appropriate stakeholders. Without this mechanism, teams might create duplicate reports, alter existing reports, and likely not delete unneeded reports. This helps cut down on unnecessary replication of reporting that plagues so many organizations to the point that most people end up ignoring the reports due to the abundance of noise.

3. Finally, businesses should define a *monitoring and reporting cadence*. This ensures that the use of reports and metrics is reviewed at regular intervals. Without a review, certain metrics and reports can become stale and meaningless over time. As business needs change, so will the metrics needed to define the success of the requirements to address those changes. This also helps teams identify which metrics should be retired or promoted to production.

These efforts help businesses define, manage, and approve metrics that will be used to inform their FinOps practices. Without a clear process, cost and usage metrics will have little meaning and won't provide teams with the data that they need to act. Defining and promoting a metric governance framework for all teams to follow within a business is a function of a centralized FinOps team. The personas within a central FinOps team will have the business, technical, and financial expertise to do this successfully, assuming the team is diverse and made up of the personas listed in the previous section.

Let's take a closer look at what each persona might do when applying a metrics strategy within an organization.

Metrics strategy persona responsibilities

The three personas to operate on the metrics strategy are the finance, tech, and FinOps personas, as shown in the following diagram:

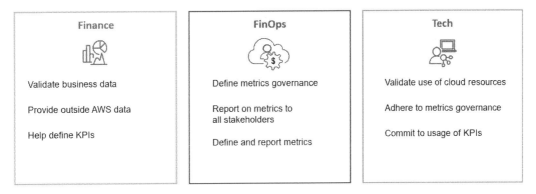

Figure 10.1 – FinOps personas for the metrics strategy

Let's take a look at these personas in more detail:

- The *finance persona* is essential to validating KPIs because they are not necessarily tied to just AWS spending. Enterprises will invest in other items beyond AWS such as research and development, marketing, and people development. Having experience in defining KPIs for other domains beyond IT, the finance persona brings valuable experience and insight to a centralized team to ensure the KPIs with cloud spending will be of value to your business.

- While the finance persona brings breadth, the *technology (tech) persona* brings depth into the IT domain. Specifically, the tech persona validates and makes cloud usage data from AWS available. A finance persona won't be able to interpret the billing items on an AWS bill as well as a tech persona whose daily activities require paying attention to AWS usage. The tech persona can define the metrics within the domain context of FinOps.

- The two personas mentioned previously will feed the *FinOps persona* their input. The FinOps persona will lead the process of defining a dashboard, roadmap, or reporting framework with the required metrics. The FinOps persona is ultimately responsible for delivering those metrics promptly to all stakeholders.

All three personas are involved in the metrics approval process. Each brings their domain knowledge to decide on what metrics are meaningful and bring value to the relevant stakeholders. Once they've been approved, they can move toward standardizing how the organization will produce the metric, in addition to identifying the owner and the process of creating the metric. Then, based on stakeholders' needs, they decide on the monitoring and reporting cadence, as well as when and how readers will receive reports.

They own the governance of these metrics. They may not own all the metrics themselves, but they act as the gatekeepers for defining how a metric will be used, how it will be shared or presented across the business, and who owns the metric.

With these governance practices in mind, we can move on to creating sound cloud metrics for your business.

Defining the right metrics

Creating cloud metrics that are meaningful to your organization may not be meaningful at all to another organization. Like the metrics governance framework, the metrics themselves are contextual and specific in scope to every organization. So, rather than suggesting specific metrics, I'll provide a framework you can use to define metrics for your business. With this framework, you can pose five questions, in no particular order, to justify the existence and use of a metric. You can refer to these questions as a kind of litmus test.

Five considerations for metrics development

The first question you want to ask is if this metric is *substantive*. In other words, does the use and reporting of this metric lead to action? This question essentially justifies the metric's significance in bringing business value. You want to ensure that the metric makes a difference to your organization.

A common metric that's used by many organizations in this regard is the **overall spend-to-revenue ratio**. This is a ratio that measures the total cloud spend to the total application revenue.

At face value, this metric might not say much, or it may provide too generic of a view. But, remember, we've assumed that we've put strong metrics governance in place first. Under this assumption, we've established good governance and can define the source of truth for this metric's input. By doing so, people can rely on the metric and use it as a common language. The metric's generic applicability also means it takes into account all the cloud spending in an organization and adjusts for growth over time.

The second question to ask is if the metric is *dynamic*. There's quite a mismatch if you use a static metric to report on the dynamic use of the cloud. Although there are cases to justify static usages such as RI or SP, most of your cloud usage will be dynamic. Indeed, static usage measures are a specific component of the broader dynamic compute usage of cloud resources and, generally, variable usage provides more information than static usage.

Metrics that don't ever change can't convey any useful information to your organization. The correct way to approach metrics is to add dynamism to make them more useful. An example is the **untagged spend rate** metric, which represents the percentage of AWS spending that isn't associated with a cost allocation tag. This metric only makes sense when you have a robust tagging governance strategy across your organization. An untagged spending rate that corresponds to a spiky period of high usage can be very informative. If this pattern is seasonally reoccurring, then you have enough data to warrant making changes to your service levels.

A helpful gauge to see if your metric is dynamic is if folks within your organization pass over the metric and simply ignore its existence. This is like walking by a warning sign that you see every day that cautions you of a slippery floor. Most days, there's no water on the floor, but someone simply forgot to remove the sign. If you get into the habit of seeing that sign and expecting no presence of water, then the sign loses its value. Similarly, if a metric is simply there and glossed over, then it also loses its value and should be discarded. You want metrics that capture readers' attention because it means something to them and the business.

The third question to ask is if the metric is easily understandable. This qualifies the *clarity* of the metric. In other words, if the metric is confusing or incomprehensible, it brings no value to your organization and could cause more headaches. One way to think about the metric is to see if it can be reproduced and calculated using elementary school-level math. If not, try to use a simpler way to convey the information and the intended meaning of the metric. There are times when the nomenclature of the metric itself may not be able to encapsulate the intended meaning of the metric, but an associated description of the metric should be able to clarify its meaning.

Let's take the **workload spending-to-transaction ratio** as an example. By itself, the metric may cause confusion, but you may have metadata that points to the metric, describing it as the ratio of workload-specific cloud spend to an identified demand driver such as the number of transactions or API calls in the same period. This metric may address a specific technical topic, but it's not overly complicated in that you can explain it within 30 seconds of reading it.

The fourth question helps determine whether the metric itself is *actionable*. Metrics that don't lead to cost optimization efforts are interesting but not as valuable as metrics that lead to organizational change. If the metric you see cannot define an action, then you should question its use.

An example metric could be something such as compute rightsizing recommendations. If a metric from rightsizing recommendations shows the estimated monthly savings from rightsizing resources or terminating idle ones, then it provides specific actions that teams can take to realize those savings. Not all metrics will be this straightforward. Some metrics might lead to two or three additional metrics before you get to an action item, but all metrics should lead to an actionable insight pointing teams toward optimization.

The last question to ask is, if you were to remove the metric, would anyone miss it? This qualifies the *scarcity* of the metric. This quality helps you scale down the number of metrics useful to your organization. The pattern we are trying to avoid is drowning your organization in metrics; to avoid having too much metric *noise* that folks lose interest and trust in your metrics.

The number of metrics should be inversely proportional to the number of people in your group or organization. For example, for a group or organization of fewer than five people, you want to keep a maximum of 20 metrics. This is for folks that are operating metrics on a day-to-day basis. This is also to discourage metric sprawl but consider it only as a guideline. Conversely, for a group or organization that contains over 30 people, you want to limit your metrics to around five. This especially applies to presenting metrics in a conference room setting. Presenting five of the more important metrics will facilitate a more focused discussion than if you were to present 20 metrics. The main idea is to apply proper metrics governance to ensure that your business maintains metrics hygiene, such as having proper AWS resource use hygiene.

Let's take a closer look at the sample metrics you can use as a starting point.

Cloud metric examples

The following is a list of sample cloud metrics that have successfully helped customers control their cloud spending on AWS. I have provided definitions and interpretations of the metrics to inspire you to adopt or tailor them to fit your business needs:

- **Bill trend rate**: This is a starting metric that shows AWS spend trends over time that can also help you identify unexpected behavior. You can use AWS Cost Explorer to see the total AWS cloud spend over a specified period. You can use this to see daily, weekly, monthly, and annual spending, or any period in between.

- **Untagged spend rate**: This is a ratio of AWS spend that does not correspond to any cost allocation tag. This helps ensure that every dollar spent on AWS aligns with a business purpose. You should aim to maximize the number of resources with a cost allocation tag. Setting a business goal such as keeping the untagged spending rate below 1% ensures that you minimize waste. You can use AWS Tag Editor and AWS Cost Explorer to apply and view tagged resources, respectively. A similar metric to this can be untagged resources that set a count of AWS resources without a cost allocation tag.

- **Unallocated spend rate**: This metric shows the percentage of total AWS spend that has not been allocated to a business unit, product line, owner, or any other required tag key. This provides you with collective accountability and governs your showback/chargeback of AWS spending. This also encourages teams to maintain good hygiene as you can gamify this system to show a leaderboard of teams with the highest tagging rate. Teams will be incentivized to rank highest on the leaderboard when this type of visibility is available to the whole organization.

- **Compute rightsizing opportunities**: This metric shows the estimated monthly savings from rightsizing underutilized resources and from terminating idle ones. This metric ensures that teams are only using what they need. AWS provides these recommendations out-of-the-box through AWS Cost Explorer, so it requires little overhead to get started. You can ensure teams follow rightsizing recommendations during monthly reviews, and that they are evaluated by tech teams. A centralized FinOps function would lead in coordinating these meetings and facilitating discussion.

- **Commitments utilization and coverage rates**: These are the percentage of utilization of each active RI and SP commitment. Separately, the commitment rate shows the percentage of all eligible on-demand spend not covered by an active RI/SP commitment. You want to maximize the utilization rate since any below 100% utilization would mean you're not using what you've already paid for. AWS Cost Explorer's utilization report can help track this metric. On the other hand, a 100% coverage rate may not be ideal since you don't necessarily want all your compute usage to be at the SP rate, especially if you have spiky or unpredictable workloads. As outlined in *Chapter 6*, *Optimizing Compute*, aiming for a coverage rate between 60% to 80% is reasonable. Then, using spot instances for spiky, fault-tolerant workloads maximizing savings, ensure that your business uses RI/SPs for steady-state workloads.

- **Non-production spend**: This is a metric that shows the ratio of non-production AWS resources such as Amazon EC2 and RDS to the total applicable 24/7 spending. In other words, non-critical AWS resources such as those in the testing, staging, and dev environments can and should be scheduled to run only during office hours.

- **Modernization key**: This is more of a tagging strategy to tag resources based on their active generation. AWS frequently releases new generations of instances. For example, the m1.xlarge instance is the first generation while the m5.xlarge is the fifth generation. Newer generations tend to have lower costs and better performance. So, simply upgrading your resources to the newer generation with all else being equal can help you realize cost savings. By tagging resources to help you identify which generation is being used, you can compare those resources to the most recent generation of products that are being offered by AWS. Being aware of AWS' latest generation announcement is an important component of this, which can be led and communicated by the central FinOps function.

- **Forecast variance**: This metric measures the percentage of the change between the actuals and forecasted values when budgeting. This can be done for your desired time frame (monthly, daily, and so on). Forecasts help set the right expectations across teams. A metric such as forecast variance helps avoid bill shock, or unwanted situations when actual costs exceed budgeted amounts.

- **Bill shock frequency**: If you're at the stage where your AWS cost and usage are relatively stable, you may want to count the frequency of times when actuals exceed set thresholds. You should feel in control of your AWS spending and, ideally, avoid any surprises. You can set this frequency as a metric and recalibrate it based on the observed behavior. You can leverage AWS Cost Anomaly Detection to help reports on these cases.

- **Overall spend-to-revenue ratio**: This shows whether your growth in the cloud is correlated to profits for the organization. This metric is a good starting point but should only be temporary. The metric is easily affected by external factors such as free tier offerings, marketing campaigns, and proof-of-concept usage, so consider using it as an initial estimate that provides a *back-of-the-envelope* calculation to see costs-to-revenue.

- **Workload spending-to-transaction ratio**: This is a refined version of the overall spend-to-revenue ratio. This requires finding a suitable demand driver with a strong correlation to workload-specific cloud spending. If you're in the hospitality business, this could be a workload spending-to-hotel reservations ratio. If you're in the AdTech space, this could be a workload spending-to-ad clicks ratio. Adding specificity ensures you have the best possible demand driver that is unique to your business.

These are example metrics that are meant to get you thinking about metrics that might be useful within your business. Be sure to not just rely on these metrics alone. Metrics without a business goal are just interesting tidbits of information. You want to align these metrics to specified goals. For example, you may have non-production spend metrics that show that 50% of usage occurs during the weekend. Based on this metric, the FinOps team works with the engineering teams to identify a realistic goal and expectation for non-production usage. Through collaboration, they may identify that less than 5% is feasible and achievable. With this goal, teams can move toward achieving a non-production usage rate of 5%.

We've covered a lot of ground in identifying the personas for a centralized FinOps function, and their responsibility in creating, governing, and managing cloud spend metrics that bring value and insight to the organization. Due to their scope, a centralized function is better equipped to do this at an organizational scale rather than in individual teams.

So, once we've defined our metrics, the question then becomes, how do we track these metrics? How do we visualize and report on these metrics to drive cost-optimizing change? The best way to do this natively in AWS is to use the AWS CUR. We'll take a closer look at this in the next section.

Leveraging the CUR

In *Chapter 3*, *Managing Inventory*, we looked at how to use AWS Cost Explorer to quickly and easily track and monitor AWS cost and usage data. When accessing AWS Cost Explorer from the payer account, you have visibility into your AWS cost and usage across all AWS accounts in your organization. It's easy to get started understanding your cost and usage data with AWS Cost Explorer because it is free to activate at a click of a button.

However, there are some limitations of Cost Explorer:

- It only provides data for the past 12 months. You will not be able to access cost and usage data for your AWS resources after a 12-month lookback period.

- Second, there are limitations around how granularly you are able to view your data. For example, Cost Explorer's user interface only provides aggregate, group by views on a single dimension – you won't be able to group by both AWS account ID and service type in one view.

- Third, it may not contain all the information you need to meet certain analysis requirements, such as seeing at what hourly rate AWS charged your usage, or the **stock keeping unit** (**SKU**) for the consumed resource.

- Lastly, Cost Explorer's UI doesn't provide the level of flexibility you need to track your defined metrics. It can display your defined tags after you activate them but you won't be able to create any custom metrics using the UI. Therefore, the better approach is to use the AWS CUR.

The AWS CUR is an alternative dataset that provides visibility into your AWS spending data. The CUR provides a more comprehensive view of your cost and usage compared to Cost Explorer. When you create a CUR report, you select the Amazon S3 bucket where you wish to designate AWS to send your cost and usage data. The following screenshot shows a setup where I specified the S3 bucket and report path prefix at an hourly time granularity with data integration with the Amazon Athena service. AWS automatically compresses the data in Parquet format:

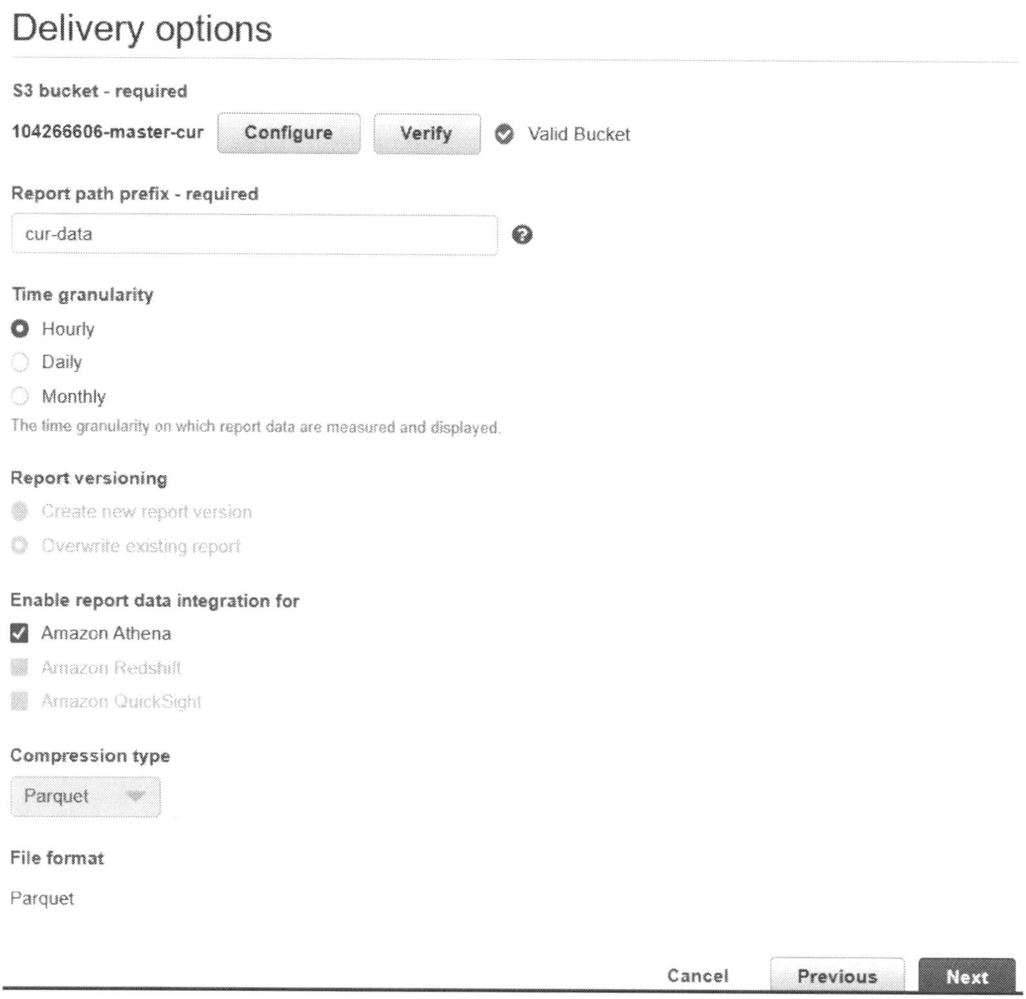

Delivery options

S3 bucket - required

104266606-master-cur   [Configure]   [Verify]   ✓ Valid Bucket

Report path prefix - required

| cur-data | ❓

Time granularity

◉ Hourly
○ Daily
○ Monthly

The time granularity on which report data are measured and displayed.

Report versioning

◉ Create new report version
○ Overwrite existing report

Enable report data integration for

☑ Amazon Athena
☐ Amazon Redshift
☐ Amazon QuickSight

Compression type

[Parquet ▾]

File format

Parquet

Cancel   [Previous]   [Next]

Figure 10.2 – Setting up the AWS CUR

Once you configure the CUR, it can take up to 24 hours for AWS to deliver the first report to your S3 bucket. AWS will deliver data at least once per day. Thus, although the CUR doesn't provide data in real time, it will at least provide an hourly point-in-time report of your cost and usage. Whenever your CUR data is available in your S3 bucket, you have a lot of flexibility in how you can query, visualize, and share that data to meet your business needs. The following screenshot shows how you can directly query the CUR data with S3 Select:

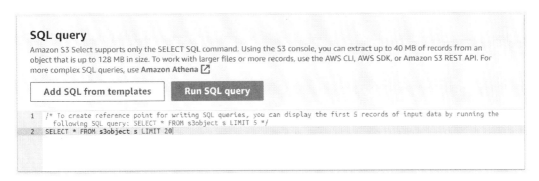

SQL query

Amazon S3 Select supports only the SELECT SQL command. Using the S3 console, you can extract up to 40 MB of records from an object that is up to 128 MB in size. To work with larger files or more records, use the AWS CLI, AWS SDK, or Amazon S3 REST API. For more complex SQL queries, use **Amazon Athena** [⤢]

| Add SQL from templates | Run SQL query |

```
1  /* To create reference point for writing SQL queries, you can display the first 5 records of input data by running the
      following SQL query: SELECT * FROM s3object s LIMIT 5 */
2  SELECT * FROM s3object s LIMIT 20
```

Figure 10.3 – Querying CUR with S3 Select

The following screenshot shows the results of that query directly beneath where you enter the query command. S3 Select provides an easy way to query your data in Amazon S3 without having to move it to another data store. The query simply returns the first 20 line items from this sample account's CUR. The results are Saving Plans monthly fees for a variety of Compute Savings Plans types. If you run this query on your own CUR, then the results will differ since each AWS account has a unique usage pattern. You can see the results of the query highlighted in the following screenshot:

Status
⊘ Successfully returned 20 records in 440 ms
Bytes returned: 21970 B

Raw   Formatted

						< 1 >
SavingsPlanRecurringFee	2022-05-01T08:00:00.000Z	2022-05-01T09:00:00.000Z	ComputeSavingsPlans	ComputeSP:3yrNoUpfront	1.0	0.0
SavingsPlanRecurringFee	2022-05-01T17:00:00.000Z	2022-05-01T18:00:00.000Z	ComputeSavingsPlans	ComputeSP:3yrAllUpfront	1.0	0.0
SavingsPlanRecurringFee	2022-05-01T22:00:00.000Z	2022-05-01T23:00:00.000Z	ComputeSavingsPlans	ComputeSP:3yrPartialUpfront	1.0	0.0
SavingsPlanRecurringFee	2022-05-01T22:00:00.000Z	2022-05-01T23:00:00.000Z	ComputeSavingsPlans	ComputeSP:3yrNoUpfront	1.0	0.0
SavingsPlanRecurringFee	2022-05-02T04:00:00.000Z	2022-05-02T05:00:00.000Z	ComputeSavingsPlans	ComputeSP:3yrPartialUpfront	1.0	0.0
SavingsPlanRecurringFee	2022-05-02T22:00:00.000Z	2022-05-02T23:00:00.000Z	ComputeSavingsPlans	ComputeSP:3yrPartialUpfront	1.0	0.0
SavingsPlanRecurringFee	2022-05-02T22:00:00.000Z	2022-05-02T23:00:00.000Z	ComputeSavingsPlans	ComputeSP:3yrNoUpfront	1.0	0.0
SavingsPlanRecurringFee	2022-05-03T16:00:00.000Z	2022-05-03T17:00:00.000Z	ComputeSavingsPlans	ComputeSP:3yrAllUpfront	1.0	0.0

Figure 10.4 – S3 Select query results

With Amazon S3 Select, you can run simple SQL queries directly on your CUR data to filter the contents of the Parquet file AWS delivers to your specified S3 bucket. You can run a simple query and download the results. This is useful for ad hoc analyses but does not scale well to meet our long-term FinOps goals. We must turn to other methods, but the foundation is set in activating our CUR so that we have our cost and usage data.

Let's look at the CUR more closely and see how we can integrate other services with our data.

Accessing the CUR in Amazon S3

AWS automatically partitions your CUR data by year and then by month. When you select the S3 bucket that holds your CUR data, you'll notice `aws-programmatic-test-object`, which AWS places there to verify that it can deliver reports to your designated bucket:

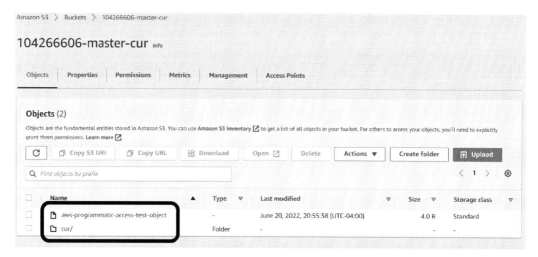

Figure 10.5 – Verifying that AWS can deliver CUR data

You can select the CUR prefix and then navigate to the prefix that you specified when you configured your CUR reports. In the following screenshot, you can see that my prefix is **masterCUR/** and that AWS automatically partitioned my data first by year:

Figure 10.6 – Partitioned CUR data

Drilling down even further into each year prefix, you'll find that the CUR data is then partitioned by month. We can use this to our advantage; we can use SQL to filter data to access only the data we need for a specific time, or we can set up an automated process to create new databases and tables for newly delivered files. To do the latter, we'll use **AWS Glue**, which we will turn to next.

Integrating AWS Glue with the CUR

AWS Glue is a serverless **extract, transform, load** (ETL) service that allows you to categorize, transform, and transport your data from one data source to another. Glue is serverless, meaning that there is no need for you to manage, secure, or maintain any underlying infrastructure. You can think of an AWS Glue job as a compute service that simply executes your data transformation logic. You pay for the time it takes for the job to complete, and then AWS automatically deprovisions the compute capacity, abstracting the infrastructure management away from your operations.

Within AWS Glue, you can use a **Glue Crawler** to populate an AWS Glue data catalog with tables. The crawler automatically examines your data sources, identifies the schema, and writes the metadata to a data catalog. The crawler is also serverless, freeing you from the undifferentiated work of managing any hardware or software to maintain your crawler. We can use this to our advantage to schedule a Glue crawler to automatically scan CUR data for new months and populate a data catalog. Then, we can reference this data catalog when we run ad hoc or regular queries with Athena.

In the AWS Management Console, you can initiate a Glue crawler by adding a crawler to the Glue console. Follow these steps:

1. Give your crawler a name:

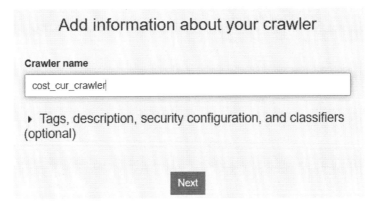

Figure 10.7 – Creating a Glue crawler

2. Choose S3 as the data store.

3.   Point to where your CUR data is in Amazon S3:

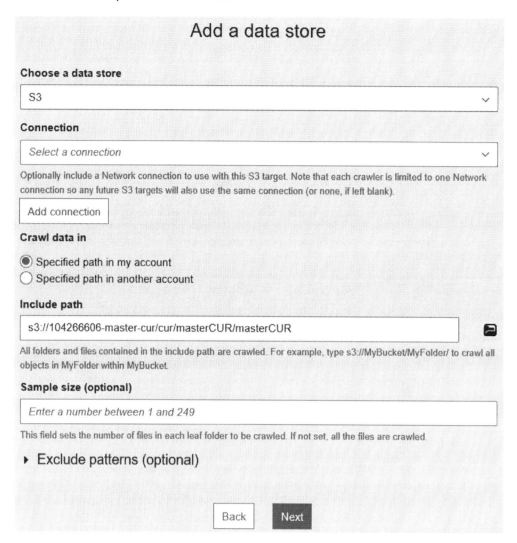

Figure 10.8 – Selecting a data store in Glue

4.   Provide the Glue crawler with the appropriate IAM permissions to access the S3 data store.

5.   Specify a frequency for how often you want the crawler to run. In this case, we will use a daily frequency of 20:00 UTC:

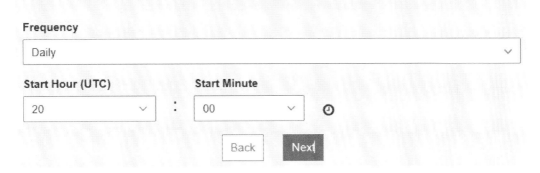

Figure 10.9 – Creating a crawler schedule

6. Select the database where you will store the crawler's output:

Figure 10.10 – Designating the crawler output

7.   Once your crawler runs, you'll find the output within AWS Glue Data Catalog. You can select the created database and see the table properties, as shown in the following screenshot. We have 381,393 records for this particular job run:

Figure 10.11 – Glue crawler output

Now that we have our metadata stored and accessible in a central data catalog, we can use Amazon Athena to query our data and create contextualized reports for the appropriate audience. We'll see how we can do that next.

Querying CUR with Amazon Athena

In the Amazon Athena console, we can query our CUR data with the query editor. Our data source is in the AWS data catalog, and you specify the database that you created from the Glue crawler job in the previous section. You'll find that the table is available because the Glue crawler output has been saved to the Glue data catalog. Athena easily integrates with the Glue data catalog so that you can quickly query data with little effort.

The following screenshot shows a simple query that shows the first 10 rows, as well as all the columns:

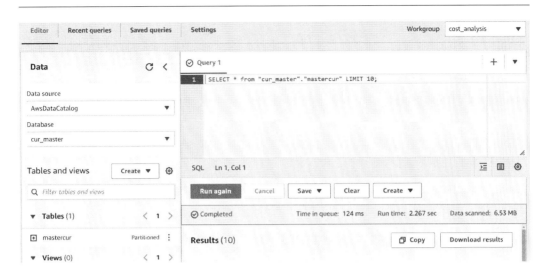

Figure 10.12 – Querying CUR with Athena

Business analysts and data professionals comfortable with SQL will feel at home using Athena to slice and dice data. This provides your teams with more flexibility in viewing cost and usage data and creating reports than the views Cost Explorer provides out of the box. At a cost of a little more setup, you gain more customizability to analyze cost data.

Here are some example queries that can help you get started. You can add a WHERE clause to specify a date range, but given the highly contextual nature of the date, I've removed them from this sample query:

- Find the top 10 costs by account ID:

```
SELECT "line_item_usage_account_id", round(sum("line_
item_unblended_cost"),2) as cost from"<your_
database>"."<your_table>"
 GROUP BY "line_item_usage_account_id"
 ORDER BY cost desc
 LIMIT 10;
```

- Find the top 10 costs by product code:

```
SELECT "line_item_product_code", round(sum("line_item_
unblended_cost"),2) as cost from"<your_database>"."<your_
table>"
 GROUP BY "line_item_product_code"
 ORDER BY cost desc
 LIMIT 10;
```

- Find the top EC2 OnDemand Costs:

```
SELECT "line_item_product_code", "line_item_line_item_
description", round(sum("line_item_unblended_cost"),2) as
cost from"<your_database>"."<your_table>"
 WHERE "line_item_product_code" like '%AmazonEC2%' and
"line_item_usage_type" like '%BoxUsage%'
 GROUP BY "line_item_product_code", "line_item_line_item_
description"
 ORDER BY cost desc
 LIMIT 10;
```

- Find the top 20 costs by line item description and the Tag team (note that TAG must exist and be configured as a billing tag because these won't show up in the reports by default):

```
SELECT "bill_payer_account_id", "product_product_
name", "line_item_usage_type", "line_item_line_
item_description", resource_tags_user_team,
round(sum(line_item_unblended_cost),2) as cost
FROM"<your_database>"."<your_table>"
 WHERE length("resource_tags_user_team") >0
 GROUP BY "resource_tags_user_team", "bill_payer_account_
id", "product_product_name", "line_item_usage_type",
"line_item_line_item_description"
 ORDER BY cost desc
 LIMIT 20
```

There are many other types of queries you can run. You can also save queries to set up repeatable processes, save and share views, and even materialize those views into other data stores to create a broader ecosystem of cost and usage data for your organization. The following screenshot shows sample saved queries within Athena:

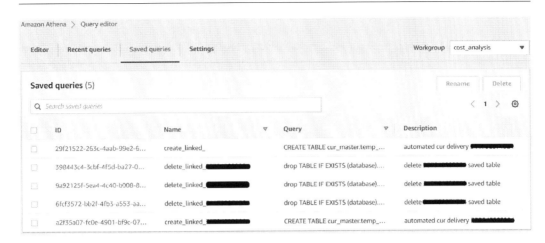

Figure 10.13 – Accessing saved Athena queries

As a centralized FinOps team that wants to provide cost and usage for other teams and other AWS accounts, you can run recurring Athena queries each time new CUR data is delivered to an S3 bucket. Then, you can filter out the information for the sub-accounts, or distinct teams, and write the output to target S3 locations for the teams to access.

By facilitating the sharing of cost and usage data across your organizations, teams have better visibility into their AWS spending. This visibility not only helps report on teams' cost performance but also creates accountability to ensure teams are operating within budget.

The transformative ability of Athena will allow you to create metrics and integrate them into your CUR reports. You can use standard SQL to aggregate data, calculate custom fields, and create views that reflect the metrics that are important to your business. This can be done using SQL, but we'll focus on how we can manipulate our data visually next.

Now that we can query our data using SQL, let's turn to how we can visualize our cost and usage data using Amazon QuickSight by referencing the table available in Athena.

Visualizing CUR data with Amazon QuickSight

You can use QuickSight to create visuals, share them among colleagues, and even embed them within applications. For our purposes, QuickSight will help create reports and dashboards for teams and leadership to understand how the business is spending on AWS resources. For FinOps teams, QuickSight can be used to uncover insights about cost and usage data and to find areas to optimize.

Once you get set up using QuickSight, you must create a new dataset. You can choose from several different data sources both within your AWS environment and external data and storage providers. In our case, we'll select Athena as the dataset source since our CUR has already been cataloged and available through Athena. As shown in the following screenshot, we will select the database and table we want to use for visualization:

Figure 10.14 – Athena as the source for QuickSight

QuickSight allows you to import your dataset to **SPICE** for quicker analytics. SPICE is QuickSight's super-fast, parallel, in-memory calculation engine. It is an in-memory engine that allows for very fast query capabilities. You have a limit on the amount of data you can store in memory using SPICE before you have to pay for additional storage. You can select **visualize** to start using QuickSight.

My intent here isn't to provide a detailed walkthrough of how to use QuickSight. There are many publicly available resources you can access to get a better grasp of QuickSight. Rather, I intend to show you that QuickSight can be a tool that you can use to produce the visual analyses and dashboarding abilities you need to generate meaningful insights from your data. Data-driven insights that shape behavior and help you move toward your optimization goals are critical to any FinOps practice. Therefore, whether you use Cost Explorer, QuickSight, an external or partner product, or a combination of all these, creating visualizations will be an important part of your FinOps toolkit.

The following screenshot shows a horizontal bar chart of spending by AWS account ID and product name. A filter ensures that only costs exceeding 50 dollars are displayed on the graph to ignore inconsequential spending. This highlights the top spending by account and product:

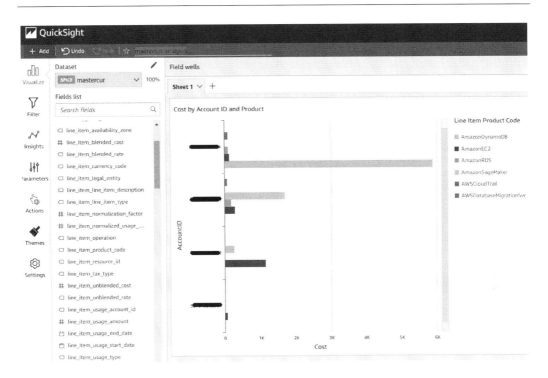

Figure 10.15 – Visualizing spending in QuickSight

Dashboards like the one shown in the preceding screenshot can be distributed to the necessary team members. QuickSight provides three ways to do this:

1. You can share the dashboard with specific users or groups. As a QuickSight administrator, you can manage various users within QuickSight. You can also enable access for all users within an AWS account. So, if you're using an AWS account designed for FinOps reporting purposes, all users within the account would have read permissions on your dashboards, so long as they are shared with them.

2. Alternatively, you can email the report on a schedule. You simply set the schedule and input other information such as a title, subject, and body text if desired. Select the recipients, and QuickSight will distribute them to your user list on the schedule you specify. The following screenshot shows an example of this in the QuickSight console:

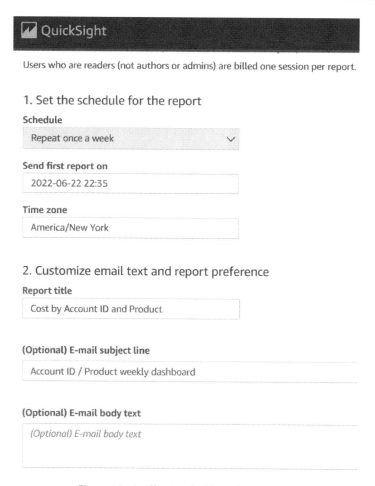

Figure 10.16 – Sharing dashboards via email

If you don't want to inundate folks with emailed reports, you can share the view as a link. Only people with dashboard permissions can access the link.

3. Lastly, if you are building an application that your FinOps function can use to aggregate cost and usage, then you can embed these QuickSight dashboards within your application using the QuickSight embedded analytics function. Although it requires the Enterprise Edition of QuickSight, it frees users from having to log directly into QuickSight to access reports. Instead, you can bring QuickSight to your end users if they are already using another tool or application to run their job functions.

Creating metrics with QuickSight

Creating visuals using just the raw data in the CUR is only the first step. You can create calculated fields with QuickSight to align your reports with your defined metrics, as we learned at the beginning of this chapter. We'll use an example calculated field to see how we can create custom metrics for use with our dashboards.

Let's say we want to show usage for every hour by purchase type. In other words, we want to capture metrics on what payment options Amazon EC2 teams are using for their workloads. If our organization metric was to optimize usage by leveraging 60% as reserved instance pricing and 20% as spot pricing, then we can use a calculated field to capture this information. Measuring the purchase type will help you optimize cost since the alternative would be to use 100% on-demand instances, which are the most expensive. By leveraging our types of payment options for Amazon EC2, you'll experience immediate savings, and capturing this type of metric will ensure teams are using the most appropriate payment option when it comes to paying for compute.

You can add a calculated field by selecting the + **Add** button in QuickSight and then selecting **Add calculated field**:

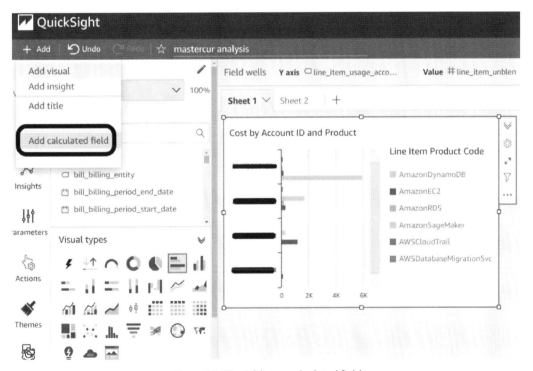

Figure 10.17 – Adding a calculated field

When you add a calculated field, you have the option to use built-in functions such as the average, sum, median, and count, as well as logic statements (if, greater than, less than, and so on) to manipulate your cost and usage data in ways that are meaningful to your business. Alternatively, you can apply formulas to obtain the desired metric. For example, the following formula sets **PaymentOption** to Spot if lineitem/usagetype is SpotUsage. Otherwise, if product/usagetype is BoxUsage, then **PaymentOption** will be pricing/term; otherwise, it will be other:

```
ifelse(split({line_item_usage_type},':',1) =
'SpotUsage','Spot',ifelse(right(split({product_
usagetype},':',1), 8) = 'BoxUsage',{pricing_term},'other'))
```

You can input the formula directly into the box, as shown in the following screenshot, and then click on **Save** to create the calculated field:

Figure 10.18 – Creating a calculated field

With this calculated field, you can apply necessary filters to categorize spot versus on-demand versus reserved instance use. The following screenshot shows a custom filter list applied to include (or exclude) records that contain specific values. We will apply this filter to see only the three payment options for Amazon EC2:

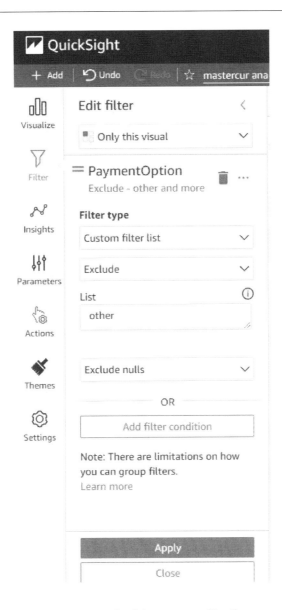

Figure 10.19 – Applying a custom filter list

The result is the chart shown in the following screenshot. We apply the filter to show a line graph differentiating by payment option:

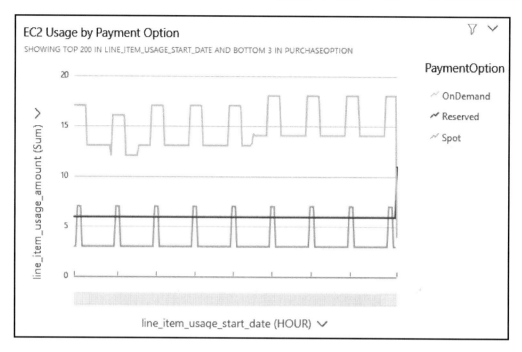

Figure 10.20 – Visualizing payment option usage for EC2

Here, we can see the hourly usage for the three Amazon EC2 payment options. Based on this visual, we can see which purchase options teams are using to deploy Amazon EC2 resources.

In this section, you learned how to use Amazon QuickSight as a data visualization tool to create reports of your CUR. This provides greater flexibility than Cost Explorer as you have more options to slice and dice, as well as present your data to your users. You also have more flexibility by being able to embed these dashboards into existing applications. You now have a good grasp of using a variety of native AWS tools such as Glue, Athena, and QuickSight to draw more insights from your comprehensive CUR data.

Summary

In this chapter, you discovered the importance of establishing a centralized FinOps function. You looked at the reasons for doing so and the types of personas to include to make up such a function. Then, you learned about a key responsibility for these cross-functional teams, which is to create an effective metrics strategy.

Then, you learned that an effective metrics strategy comes with a solid foundation in metrics governance. You want to be able to trust the metric data that you will be using to drive your FinOps efforts. You looked at the requirements and processes needed to build the right metrics governance strategy.

After that, you learned how to create the right metrics for your business and looked at some examples in the process. These metrics will provide the data you need, which will eventually turn into actionable insights.

Lastly, you used more advanced analytics tools to track and visualize your cost and usage data, as well as your custom metrics. You learned how to integrate the comprehensive CUR data with other AWS services such as Glue, Athena, and QuickSight. You also learned how to use Athena to create custom metrics that you can use to track your cost optimization performance across your organization, and how you can use QuickSight to visualize those results.

In the next chapter, we will look at some more advanced techniques that involve using these tools and see how we can empower teams to own cost savings themselves.

Further reading

To learn more about the topics that were covered in this chapter, take a look at the following resources:

- AWS. 2022. *How the Cost and Usage Report Works*: `https://docs.aws.amazon.com/cur/latest/userguide/how-cur-works.html`

- AWS. 2022. *What is AWS Glue?*: `https://docs.aws.amazon.com/glue/latest/dg/what-is-glue.html`

- AWS. 2022. *How workgroups work*: `https://docs.aws.amazon.com/athena/latest/ug/user-created-workgroups.html`

- AWS. 2022. *Setting up for Amazon QuickSight*: `https://docs.aws.amazon.com/quicksight/latest/user/setting-up.html`

- AWS. 2022. *Embedding overview*: `https://docs.aws.amazon.com/quicksight/latest/user/embedding-overview.html`

- AWS. 2022. *Adding text filters*: `https://docs.aws.amazon.com/quicksight/latest/user/add-a-text-filter-data-prep.html`

Driving FinOps Autonomously

In the previous chapter, we laid the groundwork for creating and governing the right metrics for our FinOps purposes. We need data to track how well we are moving toward our FinOps goals. We used a framework to define how we will capture and manage that data through meaningful metrics. We also looked at doing this through a cross-functional, centralized team made up of various personas within our organization. We also took an introductory glance at using several AWS analytical tools to query and visualize our cost and usage data.

In this chapter, we'll learn about more advanced techniques for leveraging these tools to help you drive FinOps for your organization. We'll broaden our use of AWS services to incorporate messaging, application integration, and **machine learning** (**ML**) to make our FinOps efforts more robust.

In this chapter, we're going to cover the following main topics:

- Creating a self-service FinOps portal
- Forecasting spending using ML-driven insights
- Forecasting cost and usage with Amazon Forecast
- Automating cost optimization within operations
- Integrating Trusted Advisor with other AWS services

Creating a self-service FinOps portal

We have covered much ground in using many AWS services to build the visibility you need to enable your FinOps practice. First, we looked at AWS **Cost and Usage Reports** (**CUR**) as the dataset to fuel our cost visibility. Then, we looked at AWS Glue to crawl our data and catalog our metadata. After, we looked at Athena as a tool to query our data, and QuickSight to visualize it. Putting all these pieces together does take time, and can take longer to build the processes you need to operationalize these into a FinOps practice. Wouldn't it be nice to be able to deploy all these resources at once and start with a baseline template that you can use to iterate as your FinOps practice matures?

This is where AWS' **Enterprise Dashboard** solutions can come in to help remove the complexities in building these solutions and streamline the process of making these dashboards available. AWS provides a series of out-of-the-box dashboard templates that you can use to gain insight into your cost and usage, as well as enabling your FinOps team to better understand the cost landscape of AWS environments to find opportunities to optimize.

The ability to quickly deploy these solutions requires us to better understand AWS' **infrastructure as code (IaC)** offering. That is what we'll look at next before we dive deeper into the dashboards.

Understanding AWS CloudFormation

AWS CloudFormation is an IaC service that helps you define and model your AWS resources. You define what AWS resources you want to use in a template. Then, you use that template and instruct AWS to provision the resources you defined in the template for deployment. In this way, CloudFormation is a declarative IaC tool. Using CloudFormation helps you provision resources quickly. An alternative way to provision AWS resources is to do so through the AWS Management Console via a series of point-and-click actions. This method has its advantages as users can see what resources and configurations they will use through a user interface. However, it takes time to select all the options. Additionally, doing this at scale is less efficient when you have repetitive processes.

Codifying your steps by declaring the AWS resources you want to provision through code is a much more efficient, scalable, and secure way to deploy AWS resources. Not only can you reuse the same template to deploy resources in different accounts and AWS Regions, but you can version control your templates to streamline operations as well.

There are a few reasons why deploying your AWS resources using an IaC service such as CloudFormation can help control your AWS spending:

- It helps you stay within budget. Since the AWS resources that will be deployed through CloudFormation are predefined, you can expect your costs to be as planned. For example, if you know you will be deploying 10 specific instance types to support a particular workload, you'll know how much you'll be spending per hour, assuming you've already researched to find out how much each of those instances will cost per hour. The CloudFormation template will have already specified those 10 instances, so you'll know what you'll be paying after deployment. On the contrary, if you expect teams to deploy resources without a controlled IaC template such as CloudFormation, then your costs will be more unexpected.

- On a related note, CloudFormation simplifies your infrastructure management, so you only deploy the resources you need. Assuming teams have clearly defined the workload needs and outlined the required resources, CloudFormation will help teams adhere to deploying only those resources they need, reducing the risks of unnecessary resources that contribute to costs.

Using the CloudFormation services doesn't cost anything. You only pay for the resources CloudFormation deploys, as declared by your template. In that sense, CloudFormation doesn't provide any direct cost savings over any other method of provisioning resources, but it is helpful to understand how CloudFormation works as we move into the next section of deploying Enterprise Dashboards through CloudFormation.

Getting to know AWS' Enterprise Dashboards

AWS provides out-of-the-box solutions that your organization can use to manage cloud costs. These solutions use the AWS services we covered in the previous chapter to build dashboards that help you view and analyze your AWS cloud spending. For example, with these dashboards, you can create chargeback and showback reports to see how teams are performing when managing their cloud costs, view how teams are using Savings Plans and reserved instances, track spot instance usage, and track unit metrics based on your defined tags.

You can use the steps outlined in this section to create a Cloud Cost Intelligence Dashboard framework. You can choose to do this at the AWS Organization level to view costs across your organization. You can also provide this framework for individual teams to implement within their AWS accounts. Teams can leverage this self-service approach to create their own cost and usage portals and see how they are performing concerning organizational standards. It also reduces the need for teams to configure each required AWS resource separately. Teams can use CloudFormation to deploy the solution in a self-service manner, removing the need for members to have in-depth technical knowledge or understanding of AWS services.

These dashboards begin with AWS CUR as the most comprehensive set of cost and usage data available for AWS accounts. Starting with this data source, you can aggregate your costs across all AWS accounts within your AWS Organization, or separate your costs by accounts and/or cost allocation tags and cost categories.

Now, let's see how we can integrate these services to build the metrics visibility we need to scale our FinOps efforts.

Setting up the dashboards

Regarding the prerequisites, you will need to enable the following services:

- Set up AWS CUR for your account
- Get started with using Amazon Athena by setting a query location in Amazon S3
- Enable Amazon QuickSight

Please refer to the previous chapter to get these set up.

Once you have set up CUR and AWS sends the CUR data to your designated Amazon S3 bucket, you will have access to the `crawler-cfn.yml` file within the Amazon S3 bucket. The following screenshot shows this file within Amazon S3:

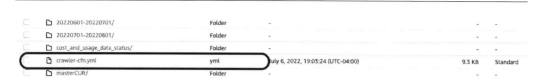

Figure 11.1 – Accessing the crawler-cfn.yml file

You can typically find this file within the file path, which follows the `<your-S3-bucket-name>/cur/<your-cur-report-name>/crawler-cfn.yml` pattern.

You will reference this file in the next section when you deploy a CloudFormation stack. When you access the AWS CloudFormation page in the AWS Management Console, you can choose to upload a template file or reference a file by providing the Amazon S3 URL. The following screenshot shows the option to upload a template file for deploying the stack:

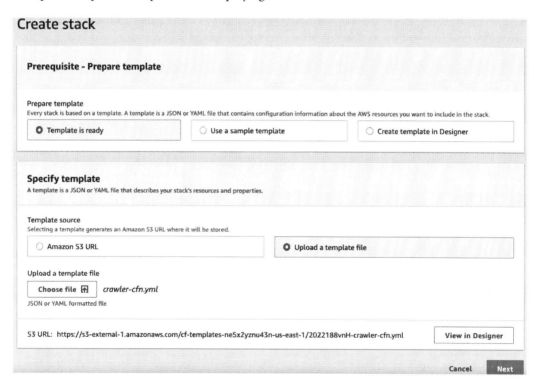

Figure 11.2 – Uploading a CloudFormation template

Important note

You will notice that the template that was uploaded to CloudFormation was in YML format. You can also provide the template in JSON format.

Next, you can add tags, configure rollback configurations, set up notifications, and more to set up advanced options.

On the final page before deployment, you can review your options and acknowledge that CloudFormation will create resources on your behalf, as shown in the following screenshot. Sometimes, CloudFormation templates create roles through AWS IAM resources, which make changes to your AWS environment. These roles are required to perform specific tasks and so long as you are aware of what the template intends to do with your environment, you will not see any unnecessary or unexpected changes. Keep in mind that the CloudFormation service itself does not incur costs. However, the resources that are deployed by CloudFormation may incur costs, such as if you deploy an Amazon EC2 instance through CloudFormation. In that case, you will be charged normal Amazon EC2 hourly rates. Thus, CloudFormation wants to ensure that you intend to deploy the template and all its subsequent actions for resource provisioning:

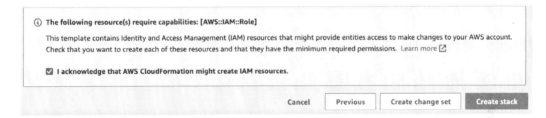

Figure 11.3 – Acknowledging CloudFormation resources

Once you create the stack, CloudFormation will deploy the resources as defined by your template. In this case, CloudFormation creates several IAM roles that provide certain AWS services with the necessary permissions to invoke and access other AWS resources. Services such as AWS Lambda assume these roles and can run tasks such as initiating an AWS Glue crawler job and sending event notifications. The CloudFormation template also creates an AWS Glue table to catalog your cost and usage data. The following screenshot shows CloudFormation's progress as it deploys these resources:

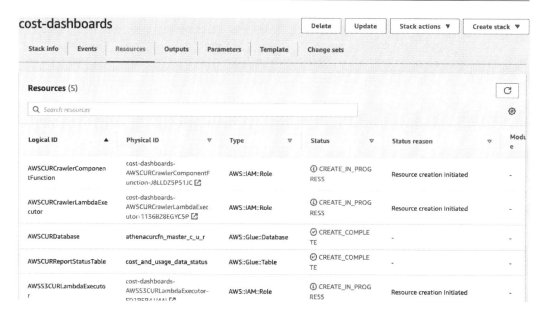

Figure 11.4 – CloudFormation provisioning resources

Once CloudFormation provisions these resources, you have everything that you need to create the dashboards necessary to report on your cost and usage data. Using CloudFormation, we've automated the steps of setting up the resources we need for our teams to implement these solutions on their own. In this way, teams can leverage this self-service mechanism to set up these dashboards within their accounts if necessary.

The last step is to set up the dashboards themselves in QuickSight. We already have the data integration between CUR and Amazon Athena. We did this when we activated CUR. We also learned how to create dashboards in the previous chapter using QuickSight.

Fortunately, AWS provides a command-line tool that helps us quickly and easily set up these dashboards with a few commands. All we need to do is to install the **Cloud Intelligence Dashboard** (**CID**) Python automation package and then deploy the dashboards. You can do these steps by running the CID-cmd deploy command on your local shell or in AWS CloudShell on the Management Console.

> **What is CloudShell?**
>
> AWS provides CloudShell, which allows you to interact with your AWS environment and resources in a browser-based shell. When you use CloudShell, you are already authenticated with the credentials you used to log into the AWS Management Console. This provides an easy way to use shell commands to interact with your AWS account.

The following screenshot shows deploying the CUDOS dashboard in CloudShell. You can use the commands shown here to deploy the solution:

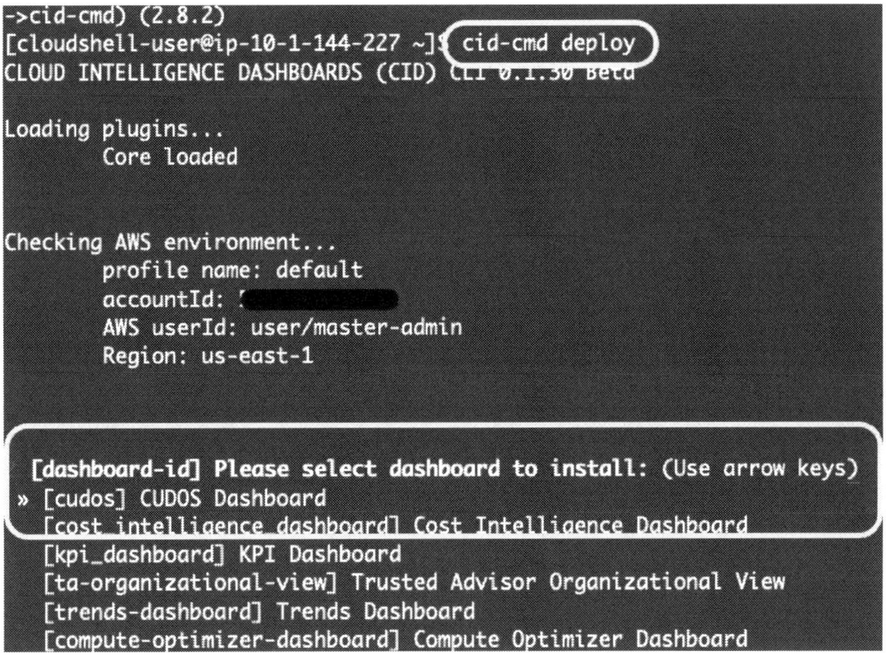

```
->cid-cmd) (2.8.2)
[cloudshell-user@ip-10-1-144-227 ~]$ cid-cmd deploy
CLOUD INTELLIGENCE DASHBOARDS (CID) CLI 0.1.30 Beta

Loading plugins...
        Core loaded


Checking AWS environment...
        profile name: default
        accountId: ███████████
        AWS userId: user/master-admin
        Region: us-east-1



  [dashboard-id] Please select dashboard to install: (Use arrow keys)
» [cudos] CUDOS Dashboard
  [cost intelligence dashboard] Cost Intelligence Dashboard
  [kpi_dashboard] KPI Dashboard
  [ta-organizational-view] Trusted Advisor Organizational View
  [trends-dashboard] Trends Dashboard
  [compute-optimizer-dashboard] Compute Optimizer Dashboard
```

Figure 11.5 – AWS CloudShell

The CID-cmd deploy command allows you to choose among several Enterprise Dashboard types. CUDOS Dashboard is a CID that provides a foundation for your cost management and optimization reporting tools. This is an interactive, customizable, and interactive dashboard that uses Amazon QuickSight to help you gain visibility into your cost and usage.

Next, let's see this dashboard in action.

Using the Cloud Intelligence Dashboard

AWS provides a demo dashboard for your reference. We'll use this dashboard throughout this section as it helps set a shared baseline. Since this dashboard is customizable, using the demo version will ensure there are no differences between users.

The **Billing Summary** dashboard (*Figure 11.6*) provides a snapshot of the cost and usage of your actual cloud spending. This provides teams and executives with visibility into historical and forecasted spending and how they are trending over time for both invoiced and amortized costs. This summary page is a great first step to checking the overall cloud spending. Then, you can drill down into specific cost and usage patterns:

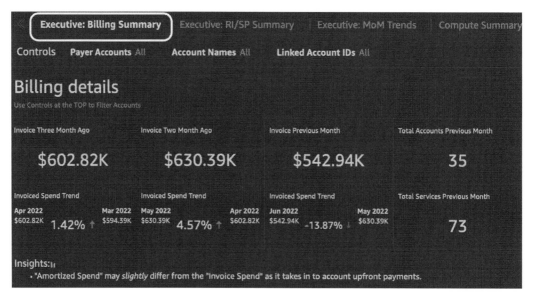

Figure 11.6 – Billing Summary dashboard

For example, the **Billing Summary** dashboard provides a visual for **Invoiced Spend Trend**. This chart provides an overall view of invoiced spending for the whole AWS Organization (*Figure 11.7*). AWS categorizes invoiced spending by usage, reserved instance fees, Savings Plans fees, and others. Although the default view is aggregated for all AWS accounts, you can select the visual and control to view spending by account ID or account name. Furthermore, since these visuals are ultimately available in Amazon QuickSight, you can customize the dashboard to view cost and usage by some other dimension such as team or cost center:

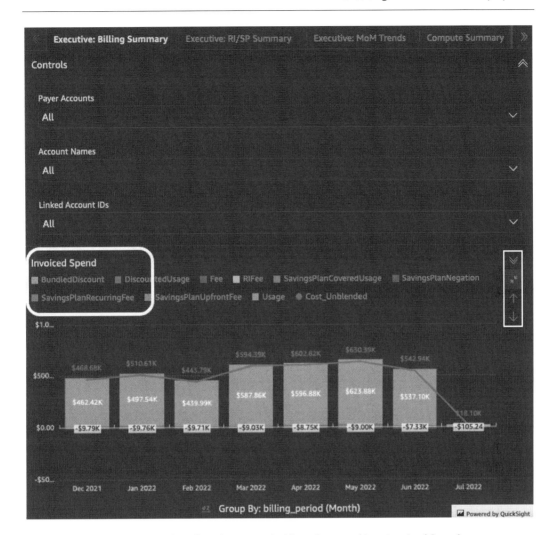

Figure 11.7 – The Billing Summary dashboard zoomed into Invoiced Spend

The CUDOS dashboard provides two other executive-level views – the **RI/SP Summary** view and the month-over-month or **MoM Trends** view. The **MoM Trends** view (*Figure 11.8*) informs you of usage trends over a set period. You can see how teams' usage of specific AWS products changes over months as well as the spend usage patterns for particular accounts within your organization:

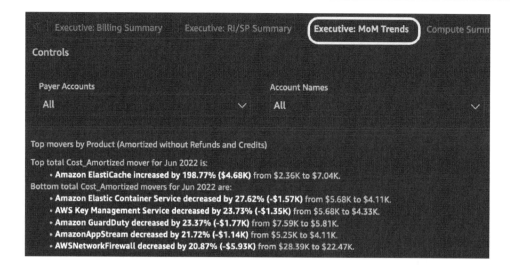

Figure 11.8 – The MoM Trends view

The **RI/SP Summary** view (*Figure 11.9*) combines your reserved instance and Savings Plans purchases in one place. For a given month, you can see how much of your commitments you've leveraged to experience savings. You'll see what teams benefited from these savings in addition to the applications if you've been tagging your resource use properly with application tags:

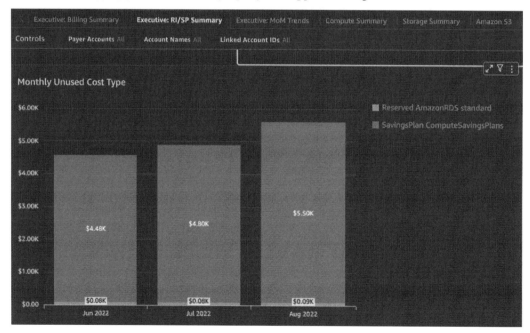

Figure 11.9 – The RI/SP Summary view

You can also view amortized spending by purchase to see how well you are leveraging the on-demand, steady-state, and spot prices across your AWS accounts. By default, the view applies to all AWS accounts within your enterprise. You can filter by specific AWS accounts, or apply any custom filters via the QuickSight interface. The bottom views show potential future savings by highlighting the hourly Amazon EC2 costs by pricing model to show where your current coverage rate is at. The preceding screenshot shows the Compute Savings Plans' eligible savings to highlight areas of opportunity to optimize.

The dashboard provides focused visibility into your compute and storage costs. The following screenshot shows the **Compute Summary** view, where the dashboard breaks down your compute spend by purchase option. You can see how well your enterprise has adopted Spot and Savings Plans to optimize your compute spend. The default view also provides visibility into compute spending by AWS account ID, EC2 instance type, and even AWS Lambda usage:

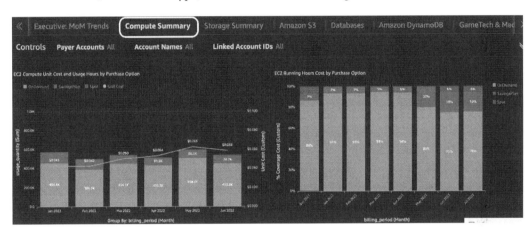

Figure 11.10 – Compute Summary view

The **Compute Summary** view contains other widgets to help you find opportunities to optimize. For example, it provides recommendations to upgrade to newer-generation instance families to take advantage of lower costs. It also presents insights toward purchasing additional Savings Plans for optimization.

In addition to compute optimizations, the dashboard provides a storage optimization view for both Amazon S3 and database solutions on AWS. The following screenshot highlights the storage optimization views for both use cases:

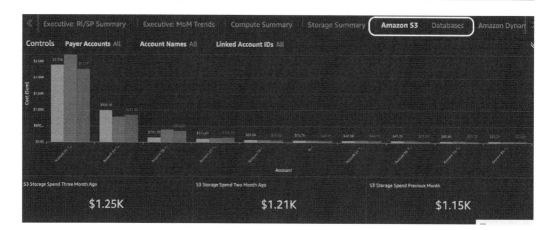

Figure 11.11 – Storage optimization views

The views for Amazon S3 break down your storage cost by storage tiers. You can use this information to see how teams are leveraging the various storage tiers to take advantage of lower storage costs. The view also aggregates S3 storage usage, similar to how Amazon S3 Storage Lens aggregates storage costs across your organization (see *Chapter 7, Optimizing Storage*).

For databases, the view provides insight into database reserved instances use to ensure you're optimizing usage for databases, especially if their workload patterns are steady-state. There are alerts for idle databases, which will further reduce your storage costs since these will help you deprovision resources to prevent you from paying for unneeded resources. And, like compute, the view shows you opportunities to leverage the latest (and cheapest) generation of databases to optimize.

For network optimization, the dashboard has a **Data Transfer Summary** view that aggregates networking costs, as discussed in *Chapter 8, Optimizing Networking*. The following screenshot shows the different visuals available under the **Data Transfer Summary** view:

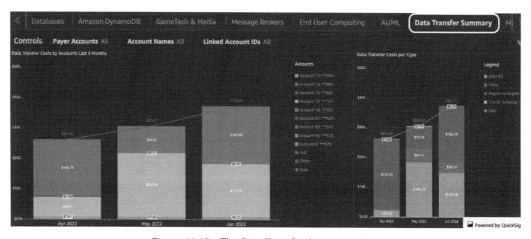

Figure 11.12 – The Data Transfer Summary view

You'll see data transfer costs by account and by type, which will help you zero in on which accounts and applications are contributing most to your networking costs. You'll also find recommendations for reducing data transfer costs as the view presents opportunities to optimize by inspecting idle load balancers and NAT gateways.

> **What are NAT gateways?**
>
> NAT gateways help you improve your security posture by allowing network connectivity out to the public internet within private subnets. Typically, you need resources to be placed in public subnets to obtain public internet access, but sometimes, you only want to egress traffic out to the internet from your secure Amazon VPC. NAT gateways make this possible.

Customers often struggle to demystify their data transfer costs. The **Data Transfer Summary** view helps you understand how data transfer costs are accumulated within your organization. Some visuals show your data transfer usage ranked by highest to lowest for each region, AWS account, and resource. These are provided out of the box so that you can easily access this information. Understanding where your highest data transfer usage is within the enterprise is the first step in finding ways to optimize that usage.

The **AI/ML Summary** view contains visuals and recommendations for the topics we covered in *Chapter 9, Optimizing Cloud-Native Environments*. First, it provides recommendations to optimize AI/ML-based workloads. It suggests using Spot for SageMaker training jobs, which can reduce your training costs by up to 90%. It suggests auto-detecting idle notebook instances to turn them off on a schedule to remove waste. This ensures these data science workstations are only incurring costs when data scientists are using them. It suggests auto-scaling for your model endpoints to adjust the scaling policy based on CloudWatch metrics so that your model endpoint deployments are optimized. Naturally, it recommends using SageMaker Savings Plans to reduce costs for folks within your organizations that regularly use SageMaker.

The following screenshot shows charts within the **AI/ML** view, which differentiates costs by instance type and usage type. The chart by instance type can help you identify instances that may be over-provisioned. One of SageMaker's benefits is that you can decouple data science exploration and script development from the training and inference steps. In other words, you have the flexibility to develop training scripts and code your ML workflows on a relatively smaller (and cheaper) ML instance type but use more powerful CPU- or GPU-based instances for model training and deployment. You're not tied to using a faster or more expensive instance type because you can leverage the elasticity of the cloud to use the compute resources you need on demand. If you identify that many data scientists are using more expensive instance types than they need, you can lower costs by right-sizing their development environments:

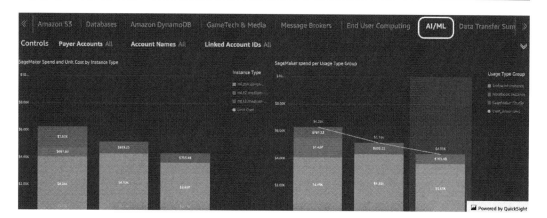

Figure 11.13 – The AI/ML view

You can also differentiate between the SageMaker usage types to break down what the costs are between model development, training, and inference. Generally, inference is going to cost more when you are using ML-based workloads at scale. This is because inference has a longer lifespan than training or development. You want to have a useful ML model running for years providing valuable inference opportunities. The training time to build that model will likely not have taken years to develop. You can use this data to see the cost ratio between model development and training to model endpoints and optimize your processes for both.

In this section, we looked at native AWS solutions for cost visibility and analysis using your cost and usage data. We looked at how you can easily build cost and usage dashboards for folks across your enterprise to give them the visibility they need on your AWS spending. We also learned about using CloudFormation to deploy resources quickly and efficiently through code. Everything we discussed involved looking at our cost and usage in the past to see what we can improve in the future.

Next, we will shift our time horizon to look to the future by seeing how we can leverage some native AWS tools to forecast our AWS spending using ML-driven insights.

Forecasting spending using ML-driven insights

An integral part of managing costs and spending is planning what your costs will be in the future. Thoughtful planning has the advantage of you getting ahead of yourself and making sure your AWS spending is within budget. We saw a bit of this in *Chapter 4, Planning and Metrics Tracking*, where we learned about budgeting and cost anomaly detection using **AWS Budgets** and **AWS Cost Explorer**, respectively. We'll expand more into the forecasting side of things in this section.

Forecasting is the process of predicting or estimating your AWS spending based on past and present data. But it can also be based on new organizational initiatives and the workloads they entail to help launch a product or service for your enterprise. If you can plan your costs ahead of time and communicate these estimated but expected charges to the appropriate stakeholders, then you're less likely to be surprised by a sudden spike in charges and questioned by leadership.

However, because these are just estimates, the actual values may deviate significantly from your expectations. These are called prediction intervals. If a prediction interval is high, the forecast will most likely have a wider range. Let's say you expect your next month's total AWS spending to be $100. An 80% prediction interval might say that 80% of the time, the actual AWS spend will be somewhere between $90 to $110. In other words, 20% of the time, your actual AWS spending will not be between $90 to $110.

Cost Explorer has a native forecasting function built into its user interface and provides an 80% prediction interval for forecasts. You can use this forecast to explore what your AWS costs will be based on your historical usage. You can see Cost Explorer's forecasting in the following screenshot. Based on the daily costs, Cost Explorer provides an 80% prediction interval for the next 18 days:

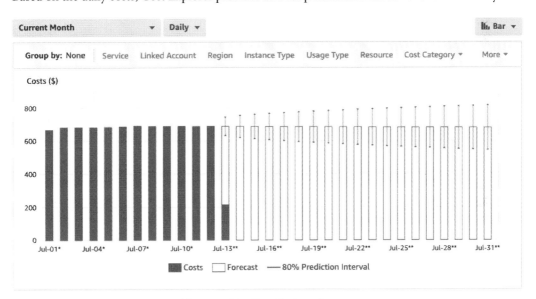

Figure 11.14 – Cost Explorer forecast

You can observe that the prediction intervals increase farther away from the current and past data. This is because the range of the prediction interval is dependent on your historical spend volatility. If you have more consistent usage (for example, steady-state workloads), Cost Explorer will show narrower prediction ranges.

Cost Explorer's limitation is that it cannot provide forecasts when your charts are grouped by a selected dimension. For example, you will not be able to see forecasts by account ID or AWS service name. These forecasts are only available in an aggregate view. You can, however, see forecasts for individual accounts if you access an individual account's Cost Explorer. However, this view is unavailable at the payer or management account level.

Also, Cost Explorer only provides data for the last 12 months. That is, your historical cost and usage, as well as the forecasts, are only based on the past trailing 12 months. If you've been working with AWS for 2 years already, the first year of cost and usage data is not included in Cost Explorer's features. If having the complete cost and usage historical data is important, then AWS CUR is a better alternative, assuming you activated CUR when you first started with AWS.

Let's assume you do have cost and usage data for your entire AWS journey, and that you want to develop forecasts based on your full cost and usage data. What can you do? You can leverage **Amazon Forecast**, an ML service that delivers highly accurate time-series forecasts. We'll turn our attention to this next.

Forecasting cost and usage with Amazon Forecast

Amazon Forecast is best suited for time-series data. Time-series data is data collected over a period that shows changes over time. This is well suited for CUR data since AWS collects your cost and usage data with a daily time interval. Amazon Forecast expects your data to have a timestamp field that aligns with the CUR schema since the cost and usage line-item column has this format already.

> **Important note**
>
> Amazon Forecast has costs associated with its usage. Strongly consider whether using an **artificial intelligence** (**AI**)-based service is worth the investment since ML-related costs tend to be more expensive than storage, compute, and networking hourly costs. I present this solution as an option but it may not be suitable for everyone.

To get started, access the Amazon Forecast console page and create a dataset group. This is the first step since you need to define what your time-series data will be for forecasting. Provide a name for the dataset group, as shown in the following screenshot:

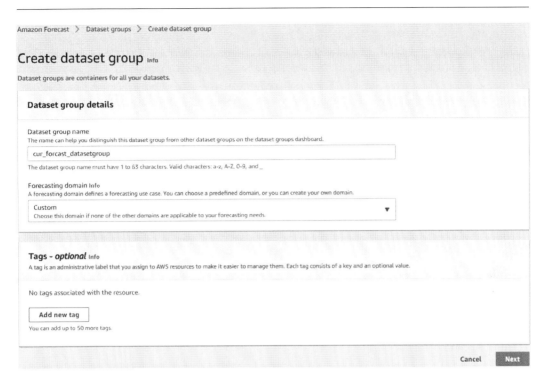

Figure 11.15 – Creating an Amazon Forecast dataset group

You need to create a target time-series dataset by specifying the dataset name and data frequency. In the following screenshot, we are selecting a 1-day frequency since CUR was activated daily:

Figure 11.16 – Dataset name and frequency

You can also define the data schema to help Amazon Forecast become aware of our data types. The timestamp format is required. The following screenshot shows it set in the *yyyy-MM-dd* format. You can add other attribute names such as account ID, AWS service name, or even application tags. This allows you to specify if your forecasts reflect a certain dimension. Recall from the previous section that Cost Explorer is unable to forecast using a group-by view. To overcome this limitation, you can specify different attribute names as dimensions for your Amazon Forecast predictions to provide a more customized view:

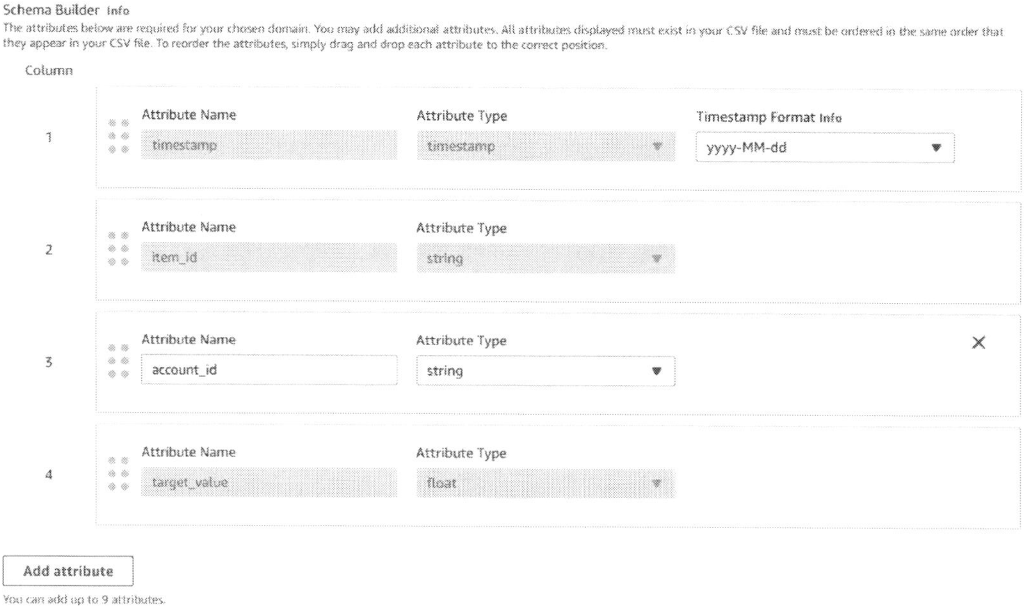

Figure 11.17 – Dataset schema and attributes

After you go through the steps and import the dataset group, Forecast will create the dataset group and alert you when the import is active. The next step is to train a predictor with your data.

You provide your predictor a name and specify a forecast horizon. This number tells Amazon Forecast how far into the future to predict your data at the specified forecast frequency. You can also choose an algorithm for your time-series forecast. If you are unsure, choose the AutoML option when creating a predictor and let Forecast select the optimal algorithm for your datasets, which automatically trains a model, provides accuracy metrics, and generates forecasts. You can also add a forecast dimension of `account_id`. This will allow Forecast to predict cost by account ID. If you'd like to be able to forecast on other dimensions, you can add them here. The following screenshot documents these steps:

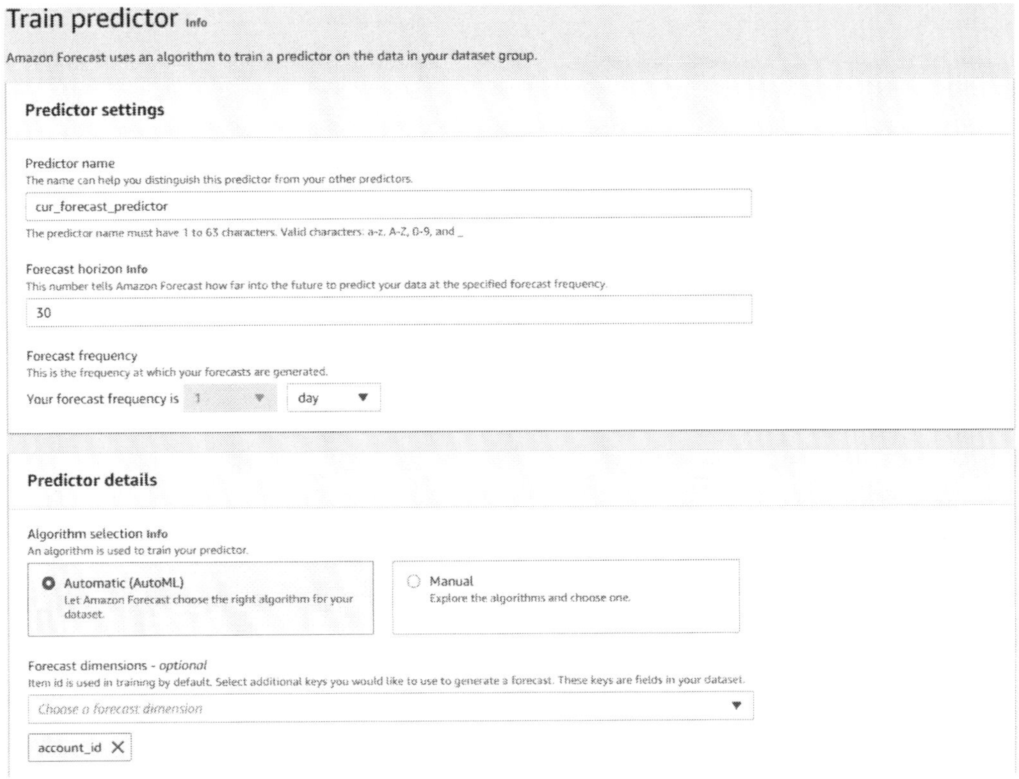

Figure 11.18 – Training an Amazon Forecast predictor

Amazon Forecast will begin training the optimal ML model on your dataset. This could take up to an hour to complete. You can check on the training status under **Predictors**. You can generate a forecast once the predictor training shows as **Active**.

When you generate a prediction, you must give the prediction a name. But first, you must choose the predictor that we created in the previous section. Then, you can enter up to five quantile values and specify the forecast type. Once you're ready, you can request Amazon Forecast to create a new forecast, as shown in the following screenshot:

Figure 11.19 – Creating a forecast

The forecast will display as *Active* when complete. You can create a forecast lookup by specifying the generated forecast, the start/end date, and the service name. The following screenshot shows this as an example where I request a forecast for my Amazon RDS spending:

Figure 11.20 – Generating predictions

Amazon Forecast returns various prediction interval bounds, as shown in the following screenshot. Depending on your use case, you may choose narrower or broader intervals:

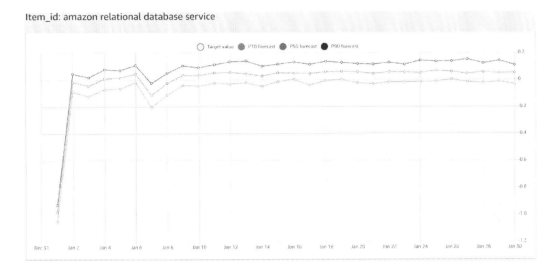

Figure 11.21 – Creating predictions for Amazon RDS cost

Amazon Forecast provides a way for you to create ML-based predictions without having to build complex ML workflows. You can simply point to your CUR data, specify the types of predictions for the dimensions you want, and then have AWS manage the model training and building to get the results you need.

In this section, we looked at how AWS provides native tools to easily visualize your cost and usage data. We also saw how services such as Cost Explorer and Forecast can help track your AWS spending into the future with ML-based forecasts. In the final section, you will leverage AWS Trusted Advisor to monitor your costs and optimization opportunities regularly.

Automating cost optimization within operations

AWS Trusted Advisor is a management tool that provides visibility into your AWS accounts to see how well they are adhering to best practices across five categories – cost optimization, performance, security, fault tolerance, and service limits. We will stay within the bounds of cost optimization since that is the focus of our discussion.

> **Important note**
>
> Trusted Advisor requires you to engage in Business- or Enterprise-level support, the latter of which can cost you $15,000 (USD) per month. However, for some organizations, the benefits of having elevated support and response times may outweigh these financial costs. Be sure to gauge what the right level of support is for your organization.

Trusted Advisor provides recommendations for ways to help reduce costs for your AWS accounts. These can be recommendations to delete unused and idle resources or to use reserved capacity. The following screenshot shows the **Cost optimization** dashboard view of Trusted Advisor with action and investigation recommendations, in addition to problem detection:

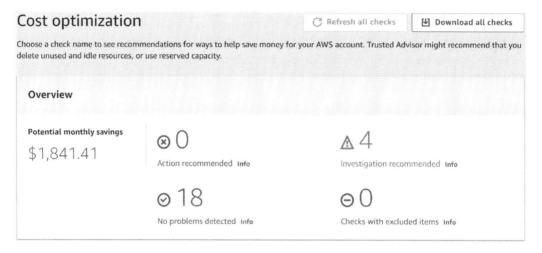

Figure 11.22 – Trusted Advisor Cost optimization dashboard

You can use Trusted Advisor to inform you about the numerous cost optimization strategies we covered in *Part 2* of this book. For example, Trusted Advisor will recommend that you reserve additional Amazon EC2 instances or purchase additional Savings Plans to increase your coverage of discounted rates for steady-state workloads based on your usage history (see *Chapter 6, Optimizing Compute*). Trust Advisor will also recommend reserving database instances such as Amazon RDS or Amazon Redshift, or decreasing the size of Amazon EBS when it detects over-provisioned volumes (see *Chapter 7, Optimizing Storage*). But Trusted Advisor can also provide insights into topics that we haven't covered, such as deleting Amazon Comprehend's under-utilized endpoints or checking for Amazon Route 53 latency record sets that are configured inefficiently.

> **Amazon Comprehend and Amazon Route 53**
>
> Amazon Comprehend is an AI service that allows you to use **natural language processing (NLP)** on text documents to extract keywords, phrases, topics, and sentiments without having to manage your ML infrastructure. A Comprehend endpoint provides real-time inference abilities for NLP workloads.
>
> Amazon Route 53 is a **Domain Name System (DNS)** web service that you can use to route users to both internal and external applications.

You can see a sample of the various checks that Trusted Advisor provides in the following screenshot:

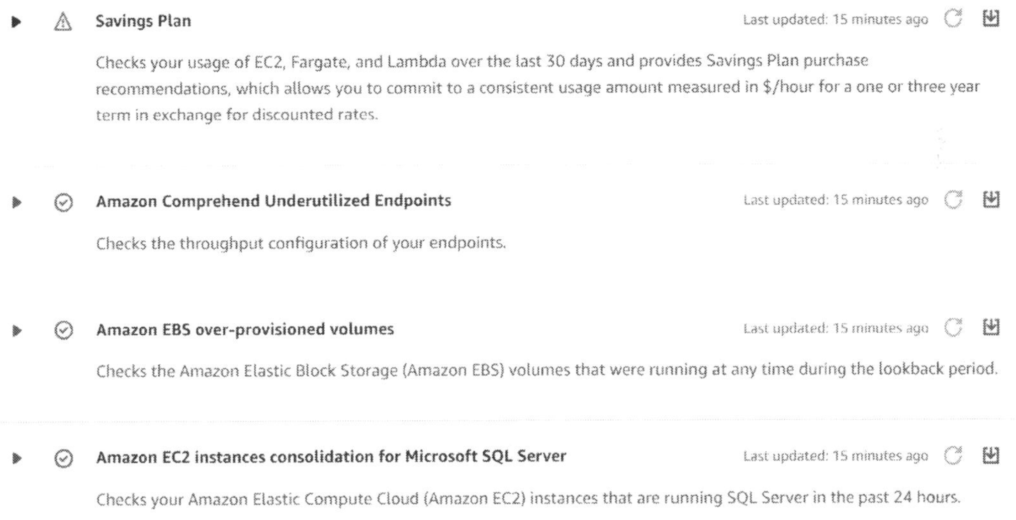

▶   ⚠   **Savings Plan**   Last updated: 15 minutes ago   ⟳   ⬇

   Checks your usage of EC2, Fargate, and Lambda over the last 30 days and provides Savings Plan purchase recommendations, which allows you to commit to a consistent usage amount measured in $/hour for a one or three year term in exchange for discounted rates.

▶   ⊘   **Amazon Comprehend Underutilized Endpoints**   Last updated: 15 minutes ago   ⟳   ⬇

   Checks the throughput configuration of your endpoints.

▶   ⊘   **Amazon EBS over-provisioned volumes**   Last updated: 15 minutes ago   ⟳   ⬇

   Checks the Amazon Elastic Block Storage (Amazon EBS) volumes that were running at any time during the lookback period.

▶   ⊘   **Amazon EC2 instances consolidation for Microsoft SQL Server**   Last updated: 15 minutes ago   ⟳   ⬇

   Checks your Amazon Elastic Compute Cloud (Amazon EC2) instances that are running SQL Server in the past 24 hours.

Figure 11.23 – Trusted Advisor cost optimization checks

Trusted Advisor can help you get a high-level overview of cost implications for individual accounts and accounts across your entire AWS organization. This tool is well suited for centralized FinOps teams because, especially for large organizations, it's difficult for a centralized FinOps team to have resource-level granularity within each account. It's easier to manage costs by starting broadly using checks such as the ones Trusted Advisor provides, and then diving deeper into the specifics once you have identified a critical finding.

Trusted Advisor helps report on and directs you to cost optimization recommendations. However, you can also integrate it with other services such as AWS **Systems Manager (SM)**. With SM, you can build and customize operations dashboards that provide an aggregated view of **operations data (OpsData)** for your AWS resources across your accounts and regions. You can integrate Trusted Advisor with the SM Explorer view to report on AWS Compute Optimizer, for example, to see where you can improve your efficiency in using Amazon EC2 instances. We'll look at how to do this in the next section.

Integrating Trusted Advisor with other AWS services

Trusted Advisor is one of many tools that you can use to monitor costs across your accounts. At the beginning of this chapter, we established that tools alone aren't enough to leverage the long-term benefits of cost optimization. You need people and processes as well. In this case, the people involved are folks that constitute a centralized FinOps team. The process that we'll outline here involves integrating Trusted Advisor with SM to provide a comprehensive view of cost optimization checks across your AWS Organization.

The first thing you'll want to do is enable **SM Explorer**. You can create a customizable operations dashboard using SM Explorer to report on information about your AWS resources. This is helpful for a centralized FinOps function that requires a pan-account resource view to find opportunities to optimize. Although SM Explorer isn't limited to only viewing cost-related components of your cloud infrastructure, we'll see how we can use it to specifically focus on a cost view.

You can access SM Explorer through the AWS Management Console for a dashboard view. You can enable Explorer by completing the **Explorer Setup** section. Once you have enabled Explorer, you can create a resource data sync by providing a data sync name and choosing which accounts and regions to sync resource use for, as shown in the following screenshot. Resource data sync centralizes OpsData from your AWS accounts to provide you with an aggregated view through SM Explorer:

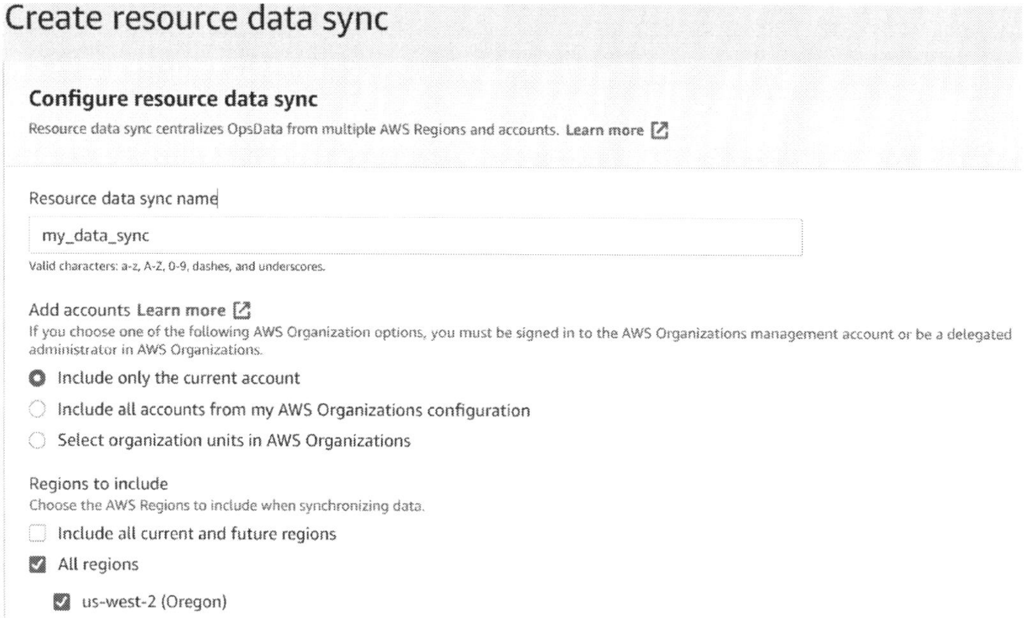

Figure 11.24 – SM Explorer data sync

Once you have created a data sync, you can configure your Explorer dashboard to configure OpsData sources. In the following screenshot, we are selecting the cost savings category and enabling the three OpsData sources to embed in our SM Explorer dashboard:

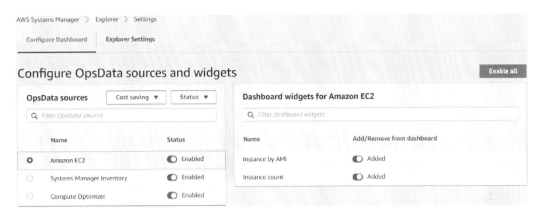

Figure 11.25 – SM Explorer OpsData dashboard configuration

When the data sync is complete, you'll be able to see Trusted Advisor checks on the **Explorer** page. Here, you can view a summary of all checks from different AWS accounts and regions. You can even view by AWS account ID:

Trusted Advisor Checks New

Actions ▼   ⓘ

Group By Source Category ▼

‹ 1 ›

Groups	Checks by status		
Performance	30 ⊘	0 ⚠	0 ⊗
Cost Optimization	20 ⊘	4 ⚠	0 ⊗
Security	40 ⊘	4 ⚠	7 ⊗
Fault Tolerance	42 ⊘	6 ⚠	3 ⊗
Service Limits	150 ⊘	0 ⚠	0 ⊗

Figure 11.26 – Trusted Advisor checks on SM Explorer

You can apply filters to search for specific items. For example, you can use the `AWS:TrustedAdvisor.ResourceCategory: Equal: Cost Optimization` filter to create a report on cost optimization, as shown in the following screenshot:

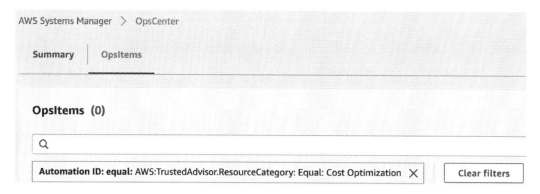

Figure 11.27 – OpsData filter showing Trusted Advisor recommendations

The filter allows you to access Trusted Advisor recommendations through the SM Explorer dashboard. This can help streamline managing OpsData as well as cost optimization findings in a single pane of glass. SM Explorer is meant to serve as a central platform for operations teams who can partner with a centralized FinOps to manage cost and resource usage across the organization.

Summary

In this chapter, we learned how to make the most out of AWS CUR by extracting insights using AWS analytics tools. We also learned about the enterprise-scale dashboards you can use as frameworks to provide cost and usage visibility for your business. You can partner analytics services such as Athena and QuickSight with CloudFormation as an IaC tool to create self-service deployments for teams to understand their costs.

We also learned about using the predictive capabilities of AWS Cost Explorer and Amazon Forecast to plan ahead. Although these estimates are subject to some prediction error, having some foresight usually bodes well compared to not knowing what the future entails at all. Planning helps to build trust within the organization and helps you prepare for unexpected cost and usage spikes.

Lastly, we saw how you can integrate Trusted Advisor with Systems Manager to operationalize your optimization efforts for your entire enterprise. This will help your central FinOps team look for optimization efforts across your organization.

In the next and final chapter, we'll focus on the ancillary efforts of FinOps teams such as messaging, communication, and workload reviews to support cost savings efforts for your business.

Further reading

To learn more about the topics that were covered in this chapter, take a look at the following resources:

- *Enterprise Dashboards*: `https://wellarchitectedlabs.com/Cost/200_Enterprise_Dashboards/Cost_Intelligence_Dashboard_ReadMe.pdf`

- *Cloud Intelligence Dashboards Workshops*: `https://catalog.us-east-1.prod.workshops.aws/workshops/fd889151-38aa-4fe2-a29d-d5fa557197bb/en-US`

- *AWS CUDOS Framework Deployment*: `https://github.com/aws-samples/aws-cudos-framework-deployment/`

- *What is AWS CloudShell?*: `https://docs.aws.amazon.com/cloudshell/latest/userguide/welcome.html`

- *Managed Spot Training: Save Up to 90% On Your Amazon SageMaker Training Jobs*: `https://aws.amazon.com/blogs/aws/managed-spot-training-save-up-to-90-on-your-amazon-sagemaker-training-jobs/`

- *Forecasting with Cost Explorer*, 2022: `https://docs.aws.amazon.com/cost-management/latest/userguide/ce-forecast.html`

Management Functions

In the previous chapters, we learned about the importance of establishing the right metrics to help us achieve our goal of cost optimization. We looked at defining useful metrics and learned about the tools and processes we can use to report on these metrics. These are key data-driven initiatives to help validate our work in cost optimization.

In this final chapter, we'll discuss other management functions that a centralized FinOps team might execute that are less analytical and more driven by people and processes. Given what we've learned thus far, a centralized FinOps team is already busy owning metrics, running analytics and reporting, forecasting, working collaboratively with tech teams to implement cost savings, and driving best practices across the organization. What we haven't explored yet are the soft skills needed to reduce spending in other areas such as negotiating contracts, managing purchase orders, and facilitating communication regarding cost optimization within the organization.

In this chapter, we're going to cover the following main topics:

- Leveraging AWS Solutions
- Conducting billing and administrative tasks
- Scaling FinOps for your organization

Leveraging AWS Solutions

The **AWS Solutions** library is a collection of curated solutions that address a specific technical or business use case. These use cases apply to various industries such as retail, travel and hospitality, financial services, and advertising, as well as various technological use cases such as data lakes, monitoring, and cost optimization. An AWS Solution is similar to the CUDOS dashboard, which we learned about in the previous chapter, in that you can deploy an AWS CloudFormation template and create a solution that's ready for use right out of the box. Additionally, you can customize the template to meet your needs.

The two solutions we'll learn about in this chapter are called **Instance Scheduler on AWS** and **Cost Optimizer for WorkSpaces on AWS**. The former helps automate the starting and stopping of your

Amazon EC2 instances and Amazon RDS database instances. This solution optimizes your costs by stopping resources that are not in use. Turning off AWS resources is the best way to save on cost, even more so than covering them with RIs or Savings Plans.

> **Important note**
>
> If you delete an Amazon EC2 instance that has an Amazon EBS volume attached, then deleting the instance may not necessarily delete the EBS volume, which will incur storage costs if you choose to retain them. Be sure to delete unused EBS volumes as part of your AWS environment hygiene.

The idea of the latter is similar but applies specifically to the **Amazon WorkSpaces** product. Amazon WorkSpaces is a desktop-as-a-service solution on AWS that allows users to remote access virtual desktops on the AWS cloud. Users can remotely access pre-provisioned desktops with all the software needed for them to perform their daily tasks. Administrators can securely install the applications that users need, monitor usage, and not worry about managing the underlying infrastructure of the virtual machines. Like Amazon EC2, you pay per hour (or month) for each WorkSpaces instance, and the best way to reduce waste on this service is to stop running the WorkSpace when not in use.

Let's look at these two solutions in detail.

Instance Scheduler in AWS Solutions

When you deploy the solution to your AWS account, you set *schedules* that specify when Amazon EC2 and RDS instances should run. You define the schedules with a unique name using a tag value. This allows you to create different schedules for different tag values that adjust to your variable workloads.

For example, you may have a fleet of Amazon EC2 instances that should run until the close of business while a different fleet of instances only needs to run for 6 hours during evening hours. These time, configurations are called *periods*. A schedule must have at least one period, and these define when the instances should be running.

The solution uses AWS Lambda to automate the starting and stopping of your instances. AWS Lambda will act based on the frequency of your configurations for scheduled periods. These configurations are saved in an Amazon DynamoDB table, which essentially acts as the data store for your configurations. Then, the solution uses the AWS Systems Manager maintenance windows (see the previous chapter), which helps trigger the Lambda invocations.

You will want to think through the design considerations when deploying this solution. First, you will want to consider the instance shutdown behavior. By default, the solution automatically stops your instances, rather than terminating them entirely. Stopping an instance still retains the attached EBS volume, which means you will not lose your data when you restart the instance. However, terminating an instance means that AWS will permanently take away the instance and any data stored locally. Also, data on the attached EBS volumes will be detached and deleted.

Stopping an instance is safer in terms of retaining data but if you have requirements to terminate the instance, you can change the instance shutdown behavior. You will not be charged for the instance, regardless of whether it is stopped or terminated since in both cases, they are shut off.

> **Important note**
>
> The solution automatically stops an Amazon RDS instance. You should have processes that automatically create RDS instance snapshots since losing data can detrimentally impact your organization.

Next, you may want to consider what types of instances you want to be automated on schedule, particularly for Amazon EC2. You can specify the instance type, such as smaller instance types on the weekend or larger instance types to support production workloads. Rightsizing the instance type adds another layer of cost optimization to this solution.

Also, you will want to consider the start and stop times for the Instance Scheduler. If you only specify a start time, then you will have to stop the instances manually or via some process outside of the solution. Conversely, if you only specify a stop time, then you must start the instance manually. You can also specify the time zone and the time of day for the solution to start and stop your instance.

The following screenshot shows the CloudFormation stack being used to deploy the solution. There are several parameter values you must specify when launching the stack. Here, we are specifying a tag value for the solution to associate with both our EC2 and RDS instances:

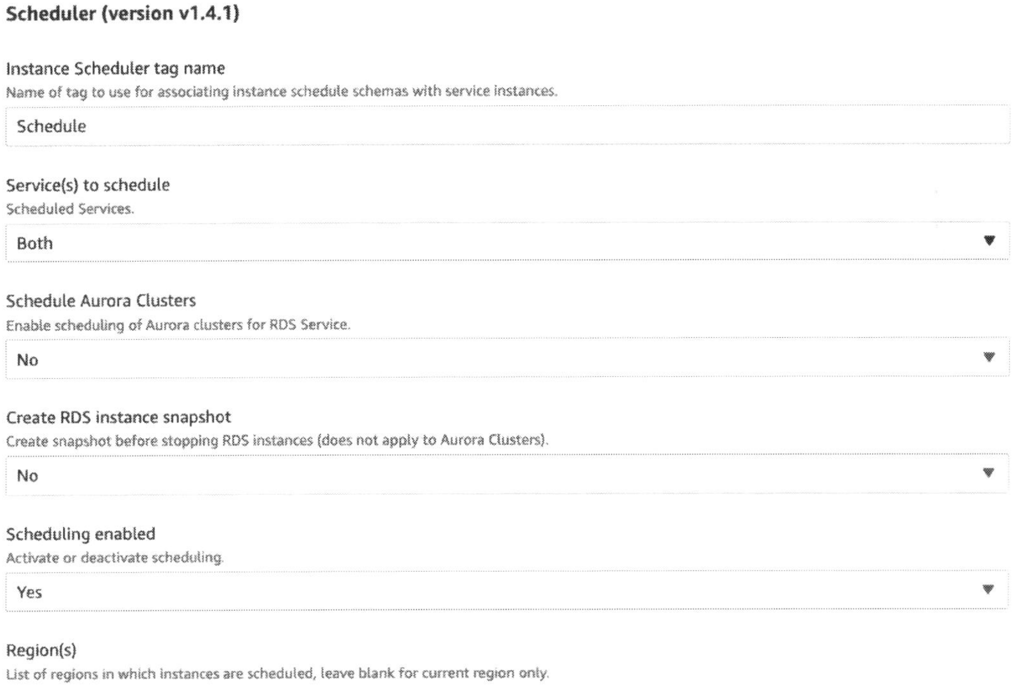

Scheduler (version v1.4.1)

Instance Scheduler tag name
Name of tag to use for associating instance schedule schemas with service instances.

Schedule

Service(s) to schedule
Scheduled Services.

Both ▼

Schedule Aurora Clusters
Enable scheduling of Aurora clusters for RDS Service.

No ▼

Create RDS instance snapshot
Create snapshot before stopping RDS instances (does not apply to Aurora Clusters).

No ▼

Scheduling enabled
Activate or deactivate scheduling.

Yes ▼

Region(s)
List of regions in which instances are scheduled, leave blank for current region only.

Figure 12.1 – Provisioning Instance Schedule with CloudFormation

We don't apply this schedule to Amazon Aurora instances and AWS' proprietary cloud database service. We also don't want the solution to automatically create RDS instance snapshots for us.

The following screenshot shows the configuration items we can set for the solution for monitoring and log retention. Note that not all fields must be specified:

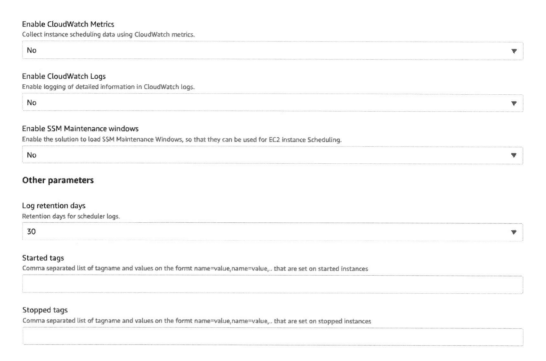

Figure 12.2 – Configurations for monitoring and log retention

We have not enabled CloudWatch metrics or logs but you may want to consider doing so in a production environment. These logs will inform you of the actions the solution takes on what resources, and at what times. You can use this information to adjust your schedules accordingly as things change.

You can see the results of the logs in a graph captured by CloudWatch, as shown in the following screenshot. You can select the CloudFormation's stack name and the `InstanceScheduler` namespace. The namespace will display all instances tagged with the Instance Scheduler solution to show as running or stopped:

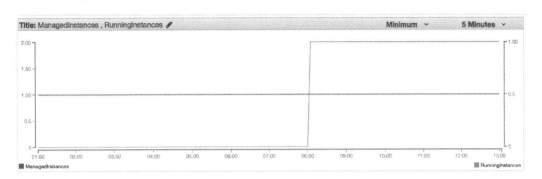

Figure 12.3 – Instance Scheduler metrics in CloudWatch

This graph shows the scheduling actions for a single instance. The 0 value shows that the instance was stopped, while the 1 value shows that the instance is running. CloudWatch displays the time on the *X*-axis.

Use this solution when you're considering ways to automatically start and stop EC2 and RDS instances. You can easily install the solution and set schedules that make sense to your teams quickly with CloudFormation or using the AWS **Command-Line Interface** (**CLI**). And remember, if it doesn't end up working well according to your needs, simply delete the CloudFormation stack to remove all resources.

Let's take a look at another solution that has a similar concept but works well with Amazon WorkSpaces.

Cost Optimizer for WorkSpaces in AWS Solutions

Amazon WorkSpaces is a fully managed service that provides a desktop-as-a-service experience for your end users. This is ideal for, say, organizations that are moving to remote-first work. You can provide a virtual desktop that employees can access over the internet with all the enterprise applications ready to go, rather than installing or making the applications available on workers' physical laptops (or desktops).

However, as with any AWS services, you will pay for WorkSpace per use, although you can choose between the monthly and hourly billing options. Hourly billing is as it sounds while monthly billing is better for workers that use WorkSpaces as their main workstation. With monthly billing, you pay a fixed rate, but with unlimited usage. Savings Plans discounted rates do not apply to WorkSpaces.

This is where the WorkSpace cost optimizer solution can be helpful. This solution monitors your WorkSpace usage and optimizes costs based on your usage patterns. It analyzes your WorkSpace usage data and automatically converts the WorkSpace pricing mechanism into the most optimized billing option. This is similar to how Amazon S3 Intelligent Tiering automatically optimizes your storage spending by placing the objects in the appropriate storage class (see *Chapter 7, Optimizing Storage*). The idea of automatically optimizing costs here is the same except that rather than it being a built-in feature of the service, you must deploy the solution separately.

We can easily deploy the solution using CloudFormation, which deploys resources in a stack. The solution performs several tasks:

- The solution uses CloudWatch to invoke an AWS Lambda function every 24 hours

- The Lambda function executes a containerized task and then gets all the WorkSpaces across all regions in the AWS Organization

- The task determines the usage for WorkSpace instances on an hourly billing model, and if the monthly usage threshold is met, it converts it into monthly billing to optimize costs

This task essentially determines if purchasing monthly member pricing is cheaper than paying on-demand. If you don't want the solution to immediately make these changes, but instead want more data to determine if the automated process first makes sense, then you can specify that in the CloudFormation **Dry Run Mode** parameter. This parameter, when set to *Yes*, runs this solution to gather metrics on WorkSpace usage. Once you have analyzed the patterns, you can manually implement the changes to switch billing options. By changing to parameter to *No* later, the solution will automatically make the changes moving forward.

For those instances where you don't want the solution to change the billing option, you can apply the `Skip_Convert` tag to the WorkSpace instances. The solution will identify this tag and ignore the billing conversion task to those tagged instances. You can remove the tag at any time to have the solution target those instances again for conversion. You can also opt out of specific regions if you don't want the solution to make changes to WorkSpaces in certain regions. You can change these parameters when deploying the solution with CloudFormation.

Similar to how you can choose among different Amazon EC2 instance types, you can choose the right WorkSpace instance type to meet your needs. For example, you may want to launch a Value WorkSpace bundle for testing purposes, but a GraphicPro bundle for graphics-intensive workloads. You can also switch between different hardware bundles as needed. You'll want to specify the optimizer schedules for the solution, depending on the hardware type.

You can set the number of hours a particular WorkSpace bundle needs to run before it's converted into the `ALWAYS_ON` billing option. This solution provides default values, but you can change these during deployment. For example, the `Standard Limit` parameter, when set to *80*, will ensure that the Standard WorkSpace bundle instance will be converted into the `Always_On` billing option after running for 80 hours.

By default, the solution creates a new VPC to run the solution, but you can also deploy it to an existing VPC if you like. The following screenshot shows deploying the solution via CloudFormation to a new VPC:

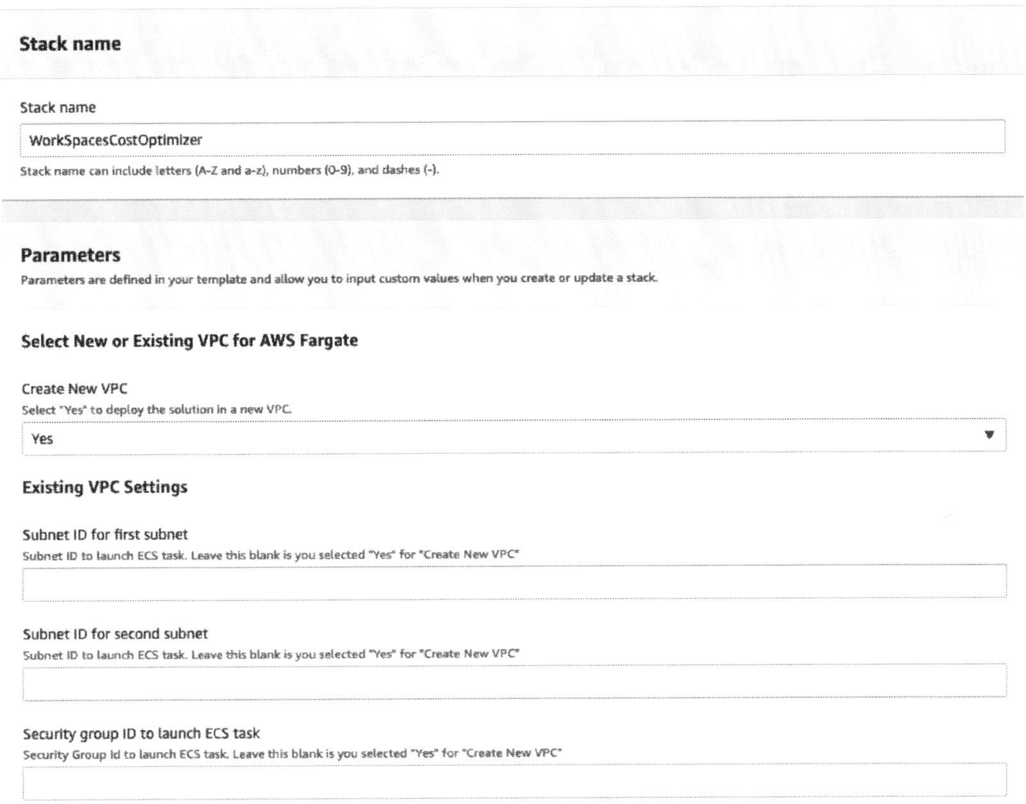

Stack name

Stack name

WorkSpacesCostOptimizer

Stack name can include letters (A-Z and a-z), numbers (0-9), and dashes (-).

Parameters

Parameters are defined in your template and allow you to input custom values when you create or update a stack.

Select New or Existing VPC for AWS Fargate

Create New VPC
Select "Yes" to deploy the solution in a new VPC.

Yes   ▼

Existing VPC Settings

Subnet ID for first subnet
Subnet ID to launch ECS task. Leave this blank is you selected "Yes" for "Create New VPC"

Subnet ID for second subnet
Subnet ID to launch ECS task. Leave this blank is you selected "Yes" for "Create New VPC"

Security group ID to launch ECS task
Security Group Id to launch ECS task. Leave this blank is you selected "Yes" for "Create New VPC"

Figure 12.4 – Creating a new VPC for the WorkSpace solution

If you want to deploy the solution in an existing VPC, you must ensure the **Amazon Elastic Container** (**Amazon ECS**) task is placed in a public subnet. The ECS task pulls the Docker image hosted in a publicly accessible AWS repository, so it needs to have an internet connection.

> **Important note**
> Amazon ECS is a container management service. When you use Amazon EC2, you are using virtualized hardware to run multiple operating systems. However, when you use Amazon ECS, you are using virtualized operating systems on a single instance. This is the difference between virtual machines and containers, with the latter being more lightweight and nimble.

After you have defined your networking infrastructure, you must define your optimizer schedule, as shown in the following screenshot. Here, you set the hourly limit for various WorkSpace instance types to instruct it when to change the billing mode from hourly to monthly. Depending on the workload patterns for each instance type, you may want to set different schedules to optimize your costs:

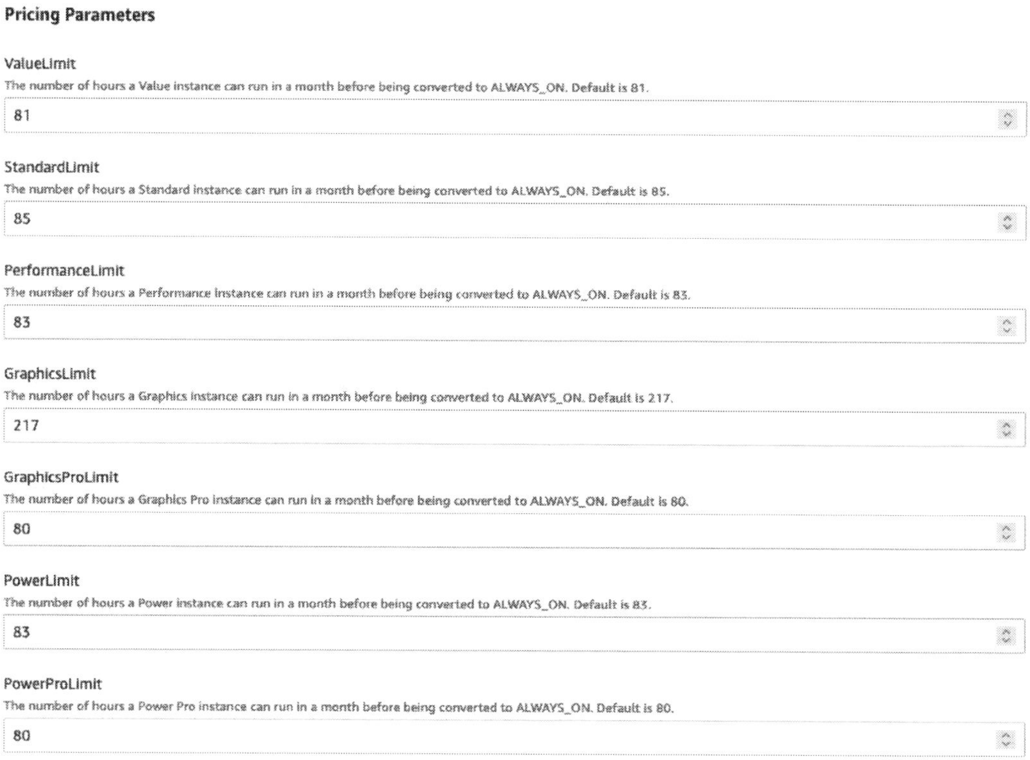

Pricing Parameters

ValueLimit
The number of hours a Value instance can run in a month before being converted to ALWAYS_ON. Default is 81.

| 81 | ⇕ |

StandardLimit
The number of hours a Standard instance can run in a month before being converted to ALWAYS_ON. Default is 85.

| 85 | ⇕ |

PerformanceLimit
The number of hours a Performance instance can run in a month before being converted to ALWAYS_ON. Default is 83.

| 83 | ⇕ |

GraphicsLimit
The number of hours a Graphics instance can run in a month before being converted to ALWAYS_ON. Default is 217.

| 217 | ⇕ |

GraphicsProLimit
The number of hours a Graphics Pro instance can run in a month before being converted to ALWAYS_ON. Default is 80.

| 80 | ⇕ |

PowerLimit
The number of hours a Power instance can run in a month before being converted to ALWAYS_ON. Default is 83.

| 83 | ⇕ |

PowerProLimit
The number of hours a Power Pro instance can run in a month before being converted to ALWAYS_ON. Default is 80.

| 80 | ⇕ |

Figure 12.5 – Configuring pricing parameters

Once you have deployed the solution, the WorkSpace optimizer will continuously monitor your WorkSpace usage and adjust the billing option according to your defined parameters. You can leverage these types of solutions to embed automation in your FinOps practices without having to build scripts.

In the next section, we will learn more about how to run billing and administrative tasks within the AWS Billing Console. These are geared toward finance and billing operators although they are still useful for technology teams to be aware of.

Conducting billing and administrative tasks

In this section, we'll learn about the billing and administrative tasks a FinOps team may need to conduct or partner with the finance department to complete. These tasks include managing cost and usage data through the AWS Billing Console. We'll learn about the AWS Billing Conductor, how to manage Free Tier usage, creating purchase orders, and leveraging private pricing to optimize AWS spending.

Simplifying billing with AWS Billing Conductor

The **AWS Billing Conductor** service supports your showback and chargeback efforts. You can customize your monthly billing data so that it represents localized versions of your AWS bill. Many AWS customers group their accounts into AWS Organizations because of the operational and financial benefits gained by grouping accounts into a single entity. However, we already know that by organizing your AWS accounts into one AWS Organization, you receive one bill (see *Chapter 2, Establishing the Right Account Structure*).

For some customers, this works well, but for others, they need to manipulate their billing data in ways that support their chargeback and showback mechanisms. This is particularly true for service providers using AWS to provide a platform for their customers. For example, if you're a company that deploys an AWS environment when a client onboards your service, then you may create AWS accounts unique to your end client – account A is for client A, account B is for client B, and so on. All the costs and usage roll up to your AWS account. Then, you work your magic to see how much to charge back to each client.

AWS Billing Conductor facilitates this process by allowing you to create mutually exclusive billing groups of accounts. You may have a single AWS account for a particular group, or you may have multiple AWS accounts for a particular group. You can have these settings to meet your use case and then you can see each billing group's standalone AWS bill.

Returning to our example, when using AWS Billing Conductor, we can create a billing group for client A (AWS account A) and a separate billing group for client B (AWS account B). Then, we can view the bills for each billing group, which facilitates our chargeback processes.

First, you must create a billing group to create your custom account groupings. Billing groups are mutually exclusive – that is, an AWS account can only be associated with a single billing group. If you want to move an account to another billing group, you must remove the account from the current billing group, then move it to the desired group. Doing so will refresh the billing data for that account, and you must wait up to 24 hours before billing data is refreshed. The following screenshot shows how to create an administration billing group with three AWS accounts selected:

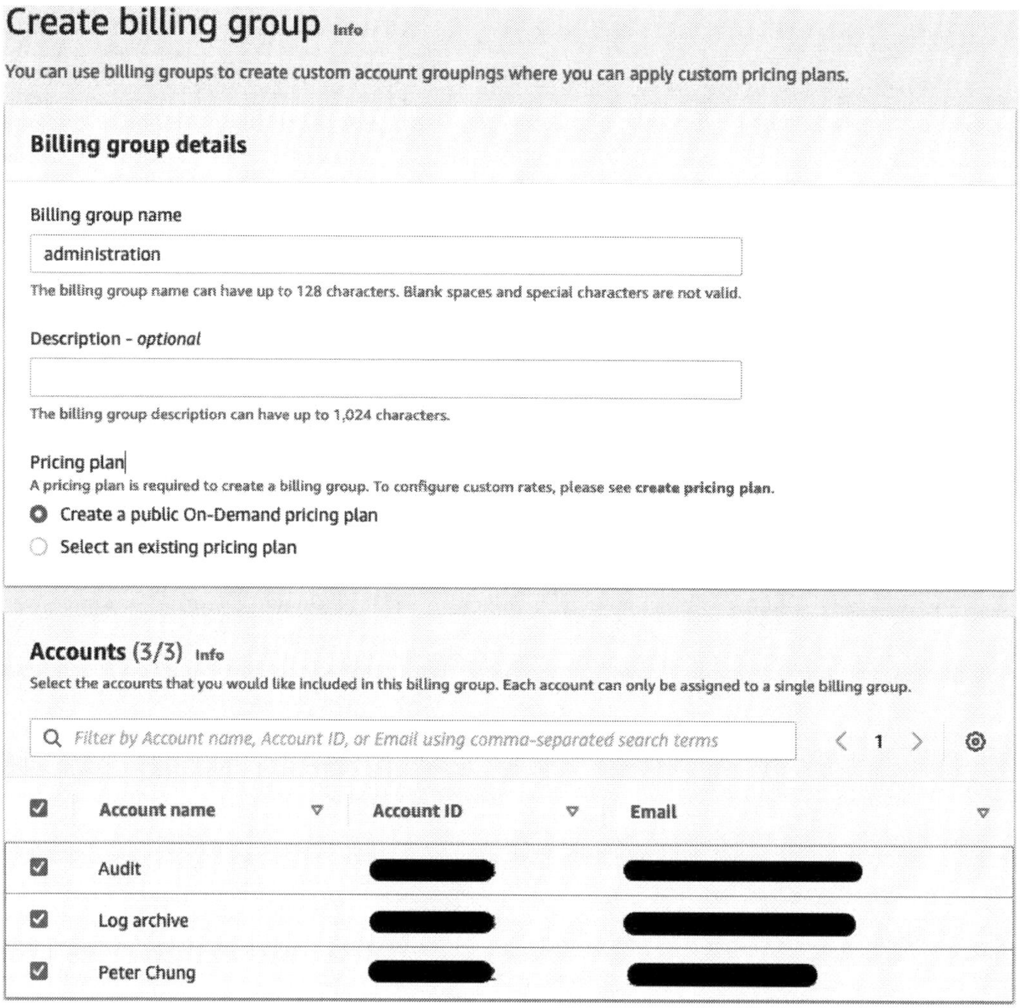

Figure 12.6 – Creating a billing group

The preceding example uses the public on-demand pricing plan. This means that the billing data that Billing Conductor will display will be based on public pricing and the account's usage. You may want to create custom pricing plans for your chargeback and showback efforts. For example, if you are a service provider and want to charge a 10% premium for your clients for using your platform, you can create a pricing rule that reflects the billing data with a 10% markup. Then, you can use this view for the billing group to see the adjusted pricing. The following screenshot shows how to create a pricing rule:

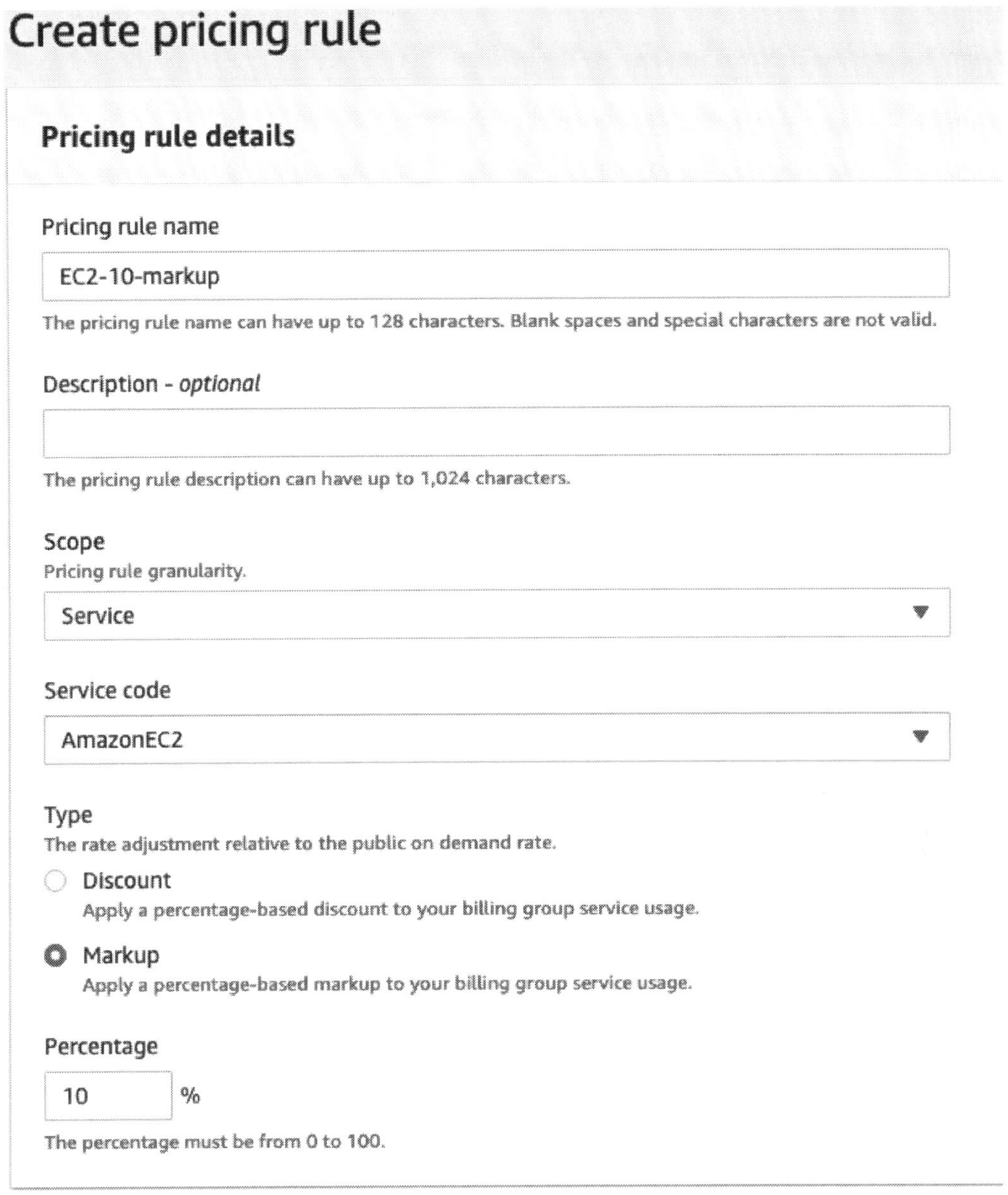

Create pricing rule

Pricing rule details

Pricing rule name

EC2-10-markup

The pricing rule name can have up to 128 characters. Blank spaces and special characters are not valid.

Description - *optional*

The pricing rule description can have up to 1,024 characters.

Scope
Pricing rule granularity.

Service ▼

Service code

AmazonEC2 ▼

Type
The rate adjustment relative to the public on demand rate.

○ **Discount**
   Apply a percentage-based discount to your billing group service usage.

● **Markup**
   Apply a percentage-based markup to your billing group service usage.

Percentage

10   %

The percentage must be from 0 to 100.

Figure 12.7 – Creating a pricing rule

We can create a set of pricing rules and define it as a pricing plan. Then, when we create a billing group, we can associate a pricing plan for that billing group to have the Billing Conductor present our billing data in ways that are most meaningful to our use case.

> **Important note**
>
> AWS Billing Conductor does not include data for AWS credits, taxes, nor support charges. If you need to access this data, then aim to use AWS Cost Explorer or the AWS CUR.

AWS Billing Conductor is a helpful tool for FinOps teams looking to modify their monthly bills to reflect their business needs. Billing Conductor can help with your chargeback and showback efforts if you need to allocate costs by AWS accounts and work around the limitation of receiving a single bill for your entire AWS Organization.

Managing your AWS Free Tier usage

AWS gives you Free Tier usage for select AWS services to help you gain hands-on experience without being charged. Newly created AWS accounts automatically benefit from **AWS Free Tier** for 12 months. At the end of the 12 months, the Free Tier expires, and usage is billed at normal rates.

You can track your AWS Free Tier usage in the AWS Billing Console. The following screenshot shows various AWS services eligible for Free Tier and the amount of monthly allocated Free Tier usage consumed:

Service	AWS Free Tier usage limit	Current usage	Forecasted usage	MTD actual usage %
AmazonCloudWatch	5 GB of Log Data Archive for Amazon Cloudwatch	5 GB-Mo	7 GB-Mo	100.00%
AWS Key Management Service	20,000 free requests per month for AWS Key Management Service	20,000 Requests	28,182 Requests	100.00%
AmazonCloudWatch	1,000,000 API requests for Amazon Cloudwatch	247,411 Requests	348,625 Requests	24.74%
Amazon Macie	$0.00 per GB first 1 GB / month of Sensitive Data Discovery US East (N. Virginia) region	0 GB	0 GB	21.49%
AmazonCloudWatch	5 GB of Log Data Ingestion for Amazon Cloudwatch	1 GB	1 GB	17.87%
AWS Lambda	400,000 seconds of compute time per month for AWS Lambda	12,231 seconds	17,235 seconds	3.06%
Amazon Simple Notification Service	1,000,000 Requests for Amazon Simple Notification Service (USE1)	14,065 Requests	19,819 Requests	1.41%
AWS Lambda	1,000,000 free requests per month for AWS Lambda	6,196 Requests	8,731 Requests	0.62%
AWS Systems Manager	Free Tier Automation Steps 100,000 in AWS Commercial Regions	151 Steps	213 Steps	0.15%
Amazon Simple Queue Service	1,000,000 Requests of Amazon Simple Queue Service	429 Requests	605 Requests	0.04%

Figure 12.8 – Viewing AWS Free Tier

You can integrate Free Tier tracking with automated notifications using Amazon SNS (see *Chapter 4, Planning and Metrics Tracking*). AWS Budgets automatically notifies you via email when you exceed 85% of your Free Tier usage for an eligible Free Tier service. But if you wanted to configure additional notifications, you can set message triggers when you reach 100%. This will ensure that your FinOps teams know when to expect billing charges as teams expend their Free Tier usage.

Although this is a small component of organization-wide cost and usage visibility, it is good to know that this exists if team members are curious about their Free Tier usage.

Creating purchase orders with AWS Billing

Another task that would be best handled by a centralized FinOps team is managing **purchase orders (POs)**. A PO is a legally binding document between a buyer and a seller. The buyer uses a PO to define a list of goods the buyer intends to buy and commits to purchasing the good or service for the agreed amount.

I've seen many AWS customers use POs when purchasing large, upfront RIs or Savings Plans commitments. Customers will reference the PO number and associate it with the AWS service purchase for reporting, chargeback, and accounting purposes. A central FinOps team may own the task of managing the PO or may work with a separate finance team to do so for the enterprise.

AWS provides a way for you to manage your PO details in the AWS Billing console. Adding a PO is a two-step process: first, you enter the PO details such as the billing/shipping address, the PO ID, and the expiration months, and then you configure your PO line items to define which invoices are to be associated with your PO.

With the PO configurations, you define how to map your invoices to your POs. This gives you greater control and visibility into charges associated with your AWS accounts. You can match the PO with charges on monthly recurring payments, subscriptions, or even AWS Marketplace invoices.

> **What is AWS Marketplace?**
>
> AWS Marketplace is a platform where you can find, test, buy, and deploy software that runs on AWS. Sellers and vendors across industries post products on the Marketplace to help you find solutions or services that you can buy instead of build.

The following screenshot shows how you can easily set up POs in the AWS Console. Simply select the **Purchase orders** option from the **AWS Billing** console to set up your details:

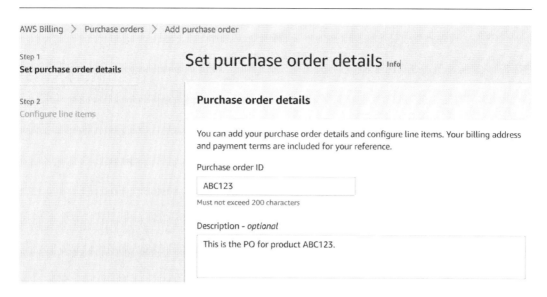

Figure 12.9 – Set purchase order details

When you configure line items, you can configure how they reflect on your invoices. For example, you can add multiple POs with multiple line items, or choose to have a single line item per PO. When AWS issues your invoices, AWS only associates active POs, removing any expired or suspended POs. For example, you may have a PO added for the AWS Inc. entity (PO1) and a second one for an AWS Marketplace purchase (PO2). If you purchase a product from the AWS Marketplace, only PO2 will be considered for invoice association.

Purchase orders can help manage your costs as your organization scales and you need stronger mechanisms to track invoicing and usage. However, this responsibility is best suited to a central FinOps team working collaboratively with the finance team, rather than putting the onus on developers and application teams to manage their own POs.

Next, let's look at how a central FinOps team would leverage longer-term commitments with a cloud provider to gain discounts for the business.

Engaging with enterprise discount programs

For many folks, *vendor lock-in* is a distasteful term. Many enterprises, including individuals, shun away from long-term commitments to a single vendor or service because they fear losing power or control in such a relationship. For example, vendor lock-in is often associated with certain **relational database management system** (**RDBMS**) solution providers simply because that was the only option at the time. Relational databases were practically the only means of storing enterprise data. Thus, there was a large imbalance of power for RDBMS-type relationships – the vendor would require long-term contracts and licensing fees with buyers, and given the lack of options, buyers would have no choice but to oblige.

With the rise and feasibility of open source technologies, buyers now have much more options than they were accustomed to having toward the end of the 19th century. Simultaneously, the licensing and lock-in type operating model is becoming an archaic and undesirable pricing method.

However, there are cases when long-term commitments to specific vendors do make financial sense. For instance, an individual or household may get a better monetary deal when they bundle home internet, television, and mobile device services with one provider. An **internet service provider** (ISP) may grant a better deal to the individual or household by bundling these services and committing to a specified term versus having a separate commitment per service renewed every month. Some households might defer the long-term commitment and change providers every month if they want that flexibility. However, for most households, the hassle of having to change mobile devices, login information to different providers' web applications for payment, and starting/stopping their internet service is simply not worth the effort.

You can apply the same principle to your enterprise's cloud infrastructure. Some enterprises are large enough to support multiple teams with different levels of expertise in different cloud platforms. You may have one business unit comfortable with AWS, and another business unit comfortable with another major public cloud provider. On the other hand, other enterprises struggle to get team enablement on a single cloud platform.

For enterprises that don't want to deal with enabling teams on multiple clouds, and that don't want to manage the hassle of migrating data and workloads back and forth between different platforms, a strategic and longer-term commitment program such as an **Enterprise Discount Program** (EDP) may make financial sense.

Engaging in an EDP with a cloud provider such as AWS gives you a blanket discount on all your AWS costs and usage under a contractual agreement. Of course, each contract between an organization and AWS will be distinct. Generally, an EDP states that you, as an organization, will commit to spending *XX* amount of dollars with AWS over an agreed number of years. Then, given that your organization meets that committed spend, AWS provides a discount. This is like the billing mechanisms of RIs and Savings Plans, but it covers all AWS services under the contract, not only specific instance types but services in the compute domain.

Not all organizations are keen to jump into a long-term commitment with AWS for several reasons. It could be in the business' interest to diversify cloud providers and use other services from other public clouds. It could be that the business is unsure of where it will be in the future and would rather pay for all IT resources on demand rather than under commitment. It could be that the business still has commitments to an on-premise data center and wants to fully exit the physical location before committing to a public cloud. It's understandable to have hesitancy. Not all organizations know where they will be in the future, and it's safer to be flexible and pivot when needed.

However, leveraging an EDP does make financial sense and will help you reduce costs if you're certain your cost and usage patterns with AWS won't fluctuate for even a year. With AWS, if you are spending at least $500,000 per year, then you are eligible to participate in the EDP program. You can commit to a 1-year/$500,000 EDP and get an approximate 3% to 4% discount on all AWS usage. This blanket discount applies to even RIs and Savings Plans commitments. You can essentially double-dip into savings by receiving a 25% discount via Savings Plans, and then a 3% discount on top of that through the EDP. A centralized FinOps function can help plan and determine whether an EDP makes sense. If there is enough historical data to show that the organization will reach a $500,000 per year spend on AWS anyway, then it makes little sense *not* to participate in the EDP program – if you're going to be spending that money anyway, why not get a discount on that?

A central FinOps function can help in negotiating these agreements with the cloud provider. The central FinOps team has the visibility to see historical data. They can project what the costs will be based on usage and forecasts. They can also see which services teams are using most to ensure that those services are subject to the discount terms of the EDP contract.

The FinOps team is best suited to have this level of visibility into the organization's use of AWS services. They possess the data, the historical spending and costs, and the usage patterns of all teams across the enterprise. Discount pricing, administrative tasks, and optimization efforts on the actual use of AWS services collectively contribute to reducing waste on the AWS cloud.

In the next section, we'll learn about how we can leverage a similar process to **EventStorming** as a helpful heuristic in approaching optimizing efforts for our organization. We'll also consider a training approach to enable your FinOps team by getting them FinOps certified.

Scaling FinOps for your organization

In this section, we'll move away from the technical aspects of cost optimization and consider some low-tech approaches that will help scale your teams and your FinOps efforts. You will learn about the **EventStorming** processes, how to facilitate an EventStorming workshop, and effectively share FinOps knowledge with other teams.

EventStorming, FinOps style

EventStorming is a low-tech activity typically associated with the domain-driven design of software architecture. This is a tactical tool that teams use to share business domain knowledge that helps to design the software components of a system.

During an EventStorming session, participants identify and map the business process to support a business function. They outline a series of domain events, represented by sticky notes over a certain period. As the participants work through the session, they model the stakeholders, commands, external systems, software dependencies, and more to cohesively tell the story of how a business process works.

Let's take the example of an online shopping website. There are *pivotal events* that can define the process of a user interacting with the website. EventStorming represents the events in past tense: a shopping cart initialized, an order initialized, an order shipped, an order delivered, or an order returned. EventStormers represent these events on sticky notes as pivotal events.

Then, EventStormers associate *commands* and *policies* with these events. Commands describe what triggered the event or flow of events. These can be *adding items* to a shopping cart, or *submitting an order* at the end of a transaction. Policies govern what command is automatically executed when a specific domain event occurs. These help with automation and governance to ensure your commands operate within strict boundaries.

By conducting this sort of workshop, participants are better able to understand the domain in which they operate. They can map out all possibilities of how the system works, how to handle errors, and who to call when things go wrong. As such, EventStorming is a collaborative workshop for modeling business processes that enable participants to synchronize their mental models of the business process and move toward using a common language.

> **Important note**
>
> Although I use the term EventStorming, I am *not* explicitly referring to it in the context of domain-driven design. I'm merely using it as a proxy for EventStorming from a FinOps perspective. Consider it as EventStorming in quotation marks.

Now, although EventStorming is intended for domain-driven design as a software design approach, we can use the same principles to model our FinOps processes. We can apply a narrow scope within the FinOps domain to enable business and technologies teams to identify FinOps processes and build a common language toward exercising the FinOps best practices we learned in this book.

You can use the following general steps as a guide for implementing an EventStorming exercise:

1. Brainstorm the domain events related to the FinOps domain. This *domain event* is something interesting that has happened that garners FinOps attention, whether that be a breach in the monthly budget, a cost anomaly, or a new workload launch. You can identify these events on sticky notes to share with the broader team. The intention is to brainstorm all the possible things that can happen as they relate to your AWS cloud costs.

2. Review the timelines. Based on the domain events you created in step one, you organize them in the order of how to respond to them. In the event of a *cost anomaly*, you can create a *happy path scenario* that looks something similar to anomaly detected → notification sent → anomaly confirmed/anomaly mitigated. The anomaly might have been in line with a new workload launch, or it might have been something that was created by accident but was mitigated by shutting down the resource. You can set a general workflow with the right owners to know how to respond (and quickly if needed) to cost events.

    Step two involves creating commands and policies associated with the events. These *commands* will be the actions the FinOps team takes to mitigate a cost problem or proactive work to optimize. The policies define the owner of the command and the importance of doing so. In other words, the command is the *what* while the policy is the *who* and *why* of a FinOps process. We want to ensure that our processes are in-line with our broader FinOps and business goal.

3. Identify pain points or processes that require attention. These can be bottlenecks, manual steps that may require automation, missing documentation, or missing owners. For example, if your teams struggle with purchasing Savings Plans promptly, this step allows teams to communicate this pain point and address it with other domain experts. It could be that teams may not understand the mechanics of Savings Plans, or they don't have the proper IAM permissions to purchase them. It's important to make these inefficiencies explicit to make things easy for teams to address them during the EventStorming process or afterward. As a facilitator, it helps to be aware of teams' pain points and document them for reference.

You should use this FinOps EventStorming exercise for several reasons:

- To build a common language. As the participants collaborate, they synchronize on the process, owners, and reasons for FinOps practices.

- To model the FinOps process. This builds a model for how FinOps works and what tasks need to be done to cost optimize your AWS environments.

- To identify cost savings. You can use this exercise to see how participants are on the same page on how cost optimization works on AWS and how they apply it to their running workloads.

- To share FinOps knowledge. Over time, FinOps knowledge can get lost and as new services and features launch from AWS, the knowledge gap can increase. This exercise helps keep everyone up to date.

- To improve optimization efforts. Identifying gaps and pain points can remove barriers that hinder your cost savings efforts.

- To onboard new members. No matter what team they are on, FinOps impacts the broader organization. Showing how FinOps impacts everyone can facilitate a FinOps culture, especially for new team members.

Now that you have a firm grasp of a FinOps-style EventStorming process and how it facilitates a strong communicative structure across teams, let's turn toward FinOps certification as a way to validate FinOps knowledge and upskill your internal team members.

Training for FinOps

We've covered many topics in this book around ways to reduce waste on our AWS cloud spending. We looked at optimizing our compute, storage, and networking costs, continuously monitoring our efforts, and visualizing our cloud and usage dashboard using various analytical tools. We also looked at leveraging AWS solutions and pricing programs to optimize our business and operations. So, how do we train our team members on FinOps? How do we enable teams to adopt new technologies and changes to existing systems and processes to maintain a lean AWS spend consistently?

To accomplish anything, you need a plan. Specifically, you'll want to develop a training plan. Typically, you must create a training plan to help meet a professional goal. Whether that goal is to develop the organization as a whole (say, improve financial margins by optimizing AWS spending by 20%), or just for employees to become FinOps certified, a training plan will help the manager and employee keep track and measure progress.

> **Important note**
>
> You can learn more about becoming a certified FinOps certified with the FinOps Foundation. There are several certification levels, such as certified Practitioner, Engineer, and Professional. Take a look at the FinOps Foundation website to learn more (`https://learn.finops.org/`).
>
> The FinOps Foundation's certifications are great ways to validate your teams' FinOps knowledge and bring accreditation to your organization. However, certifications are not the only benefit of the FinOps Foundation. The FinOps Foundations includes a community of FinOps professionals sharing best practices for FinOps across multiple cloud platforms. The FinOps Foundation also hosts events, talks, and community learnings where members can share best practices and learn from each other's experiences. Additionally, the FinOps Foundation provides several tools to help with managing container costs and creating cloud forecasts and multi-cloud tools, which are beyond the scope of this book.

When individuals improve themselves, it improves the organization as a whole. But there is a difference between an individual getting FinOps certified versus an individual getting certified so that the entire organization can benefit from FinOps practices. The training plan should aim to apply individual success to organizational success.

A training plan should be organized, detailed, and realistic. An organized plan is self-explanatory. A detailed plan is clear in its steps to accomplish the goal. For example, if the goal is to become FinOps certified, one of the steps could be to take a FinOps certification course. Another step could include setting up a learning path using other resources; the learning path can define the rest of the steps needed to accomplish the goal. A realistic plan ensures that the goals are obtainable. For example, it isn't realistic to set up a training plan and expect participants to become certified within 2 days with no practice if FinOps is entirely new. This is certainly possible, but it isn't realistic. Similarly, a realistic goal shouldn't be too far out – the goal shouldn't be to become certified in 2 years since studying and preparing for the exam should take less than that.

A useful acronym to know if a goal is organized, detailed, and realistic is SMART. You can use the following five questions to see if your goals are SMART:

- Is it **S**pecific? It should be written simplistically and defined well.

- Is it **M**easurable? Will there be tangible evidence that the goal was accomplished? This could be a successful FinOps deployment or a certification that a team passed the exam.

- Is it **A**chievable? There is little reason to set a goal to lower AWS cloud spending by 80% and still keep everything else the same. That's not a feasible goal.

- Is it **R**esults-focused? Is it a goal with a target at the end rather than the summation of activities?

- Is it **T**ime-bound? Setting a goal to take and pass the FinOps certification whenever team members get to it won't help your organization achieve its goal. Setting a realistic time limit on it will guide team members to work hard to meet a set deadline.

While a training plan can help with long-term training or new systems where there is time for training before implementing a FinOps practice, existing systems might not fit that model. In other words, a training plan might call for changes to be made to existing systems and processes. For example, an organization that looks at monthly financial reports may have to shift to daily or weekly reports, given that new cost and usage data is generated daily. This may also require changes in tools and training on how to use those tools for ingesting and presenting the data.

In this section, we looked at EventStorming from a FinOps perspective and how it helps your teams build a common language for FinOps. We also looked at considerations for getting your teams FinOps certified to help with their professional development and the long-term FinOps success for your organization. Merging personal professional development with strong communicative structures such as EventStorming provides your organization with a base from which you can operate the technical requirements when building a FinOps foundation.

Summary

In this chapter, we learned about the Cost Optimizer for WorkSpaces and Instance Scheduler AWS Solutions that you can use to quickly reduce costs for the WorkSpace and EC2 services on AWS. We learned how to deploy these solutions using AWS CloudFormation and their parameter considerations to meet your use case. These AWS Solutions can be quickly deployed by your FinOps teams out-of-the-box to realize cost savings across your numerous AWS accounts.

Know that you don't have to build a FinOps practice from scratch. You can certainly build upon solutions, whether those solutions are from AWS, AWS partners, or open sourced. Leverage these solutions to accelerate your FinOps practice without feeling the burden of having to build everything yourself.

This book presented the foundations for you to do that, starting with the right AWS account structure. Then, you learned about the various tools you can use to identify your cost and usage, monitor your spending, proactively identify anomalies, and apply governance across your environment to meet your FinOps goals.

You can use the strategies presented in this book to optimize your computing, storage, and networking infrastructure, as well as your cloud-native workloads. There are plenty of ways to optimize these architectural components, with the largest and easiest opportunities being choosing the right payment option for your workload needs. Purchase Savings Plans often and regularly to ensure you optimize your storage costs. Choose the right storage pricing tier to pay only for what you need, and if you're unsure of your access patterns, leverage Intelligent Tiering to experience automatic savings. Use RIs for your databases that will be running consistently. Understand your data transfer patterns. Knowing how your applications are communicating is the best way to know how to optimize your data transfer.

These are the technical ways you can optimize your AWS spending that the FinOps team can own. But we also covered the non-technical and administrative tasks a FinOps team must conduct when it comes to billing management and private pricing discussions. We learned how AWS Billing Conductor can help create a custom billing view for chargeback and showback purposes. We also learned about managing Free Tier usage and purchase order agreements. Finally, we learned about how private pricing works in the form of Enterprise Discount Programs and how to leverage these to experience blanket savings across AWS usage.

Lastly, FinOps practices will be most successful if they are tied to the right metrics. Build the right metrics and create the appropriate metrics visibility for your teams. This will enable your organization to track the success of your optimization efforts. Ensure that the teams have a common language on how you define the FinOps metrics as different terms can mean different things. EventStorming is an exercise you can use to share domain knowledge and create this common language. Consider becoming FinOps certified to solidify your FinOps knowledge and enable your team members to grow in their FinOps knowledge and career as well.

Remember, FinOps is an ongoing practice. Implementing a one-time Savings Plan purchase won't help your organization reduce waste in the long run. Embedding FinOps into your organization's operations and culture will be the best way to leverage the cloud efficiently.

Further reading

To learn more about the topics that were covered in this chapter, take a look at the following resources:

- AWS. *Automate starting and stopping AWS instances*, 2022: `https://docs.aws.amazon.com/solutions/latest/instance-scheduler-on-aws/welcome.html`

- AWS. *Monitor Amazon WorkSpaces usage and optimize costs with the Cost Optimizer for WorkSpaces on AWS solution*, 2022: `https://docs.aws.amazon.com/solutions/latest/cost-optimizer-for-workspaces-on-aws/overview.html`

- FinOps Foundation. *FinOps Certification and Training*, 2022: `https://learn.finops.org/`

- AWS. *What is Amazon Elastic Container Service?*, 2022: `https://docs.aws.amazon.com/AmazonECS/latest/developerguide/Welcome.html`

- AWS. *Best practices for AWS Billing Conductor*, 2022: `https://docs.aws.amazon.com/billingconductor/latest/userguide/best-practices.html`

- AWS. *Using the AWS Free Tier*, 2022: `https://docs.aws.amazon.com/awsaccountbilling/latest/aboutv2/billing-free-tier.html`

Index

A

U

V

W

Other Books You May Enjoy

If you enjoyed this book, you may be interested in these other books by Packt:

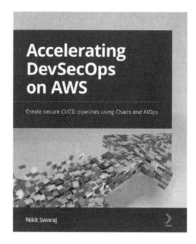

Accelerating DevSecOps on AWS

Nikit Swaraj

ISBN: 978-1-803-24860-8

- Use AWS Codestar to design and implement a full branching strategy

- Enforce Policy as Code using CloudFormation Guard and HashiCorp Sentinel

- Master app and infrastructure deployment at scale using AWS Proton and review app code using CodeGuru

- Deploy and manage production-grade clusters using AWS EKS, App Mesh, and X-Ray

- Harness AWS Fault Injection Simulator to test the resiliency of your app

- Wield the full arsenal of AWS Security Hub and Systems Manager for infrastructure security automation

- Enhance CI/CD pipelines with the AI-powered DevOps Guru service

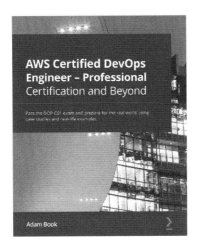

AWS Certified DevOps Engineer - Professional Certification and Beyond

Adam Book

ISBN: 978-1-801-07445-2

- Automate your pipelines, build phases, and deployments with AWS-native tooling
- Discover how to implement logging and monitoring using AWS-native tooling
- Gain a solid understanding of the services included in the AWS DevOps Professional exam
- Reinforce security practices on the AWS platform from an exam point of view
- Find out how to automatically enforce standards and policies in AWS environments
- Explore AWS best practices and anti-patterns
- Enhance your core AWS skills with the help of exercises and practice tests

Packt is searching for authors like you

If you're interested in becoming an author for Packt, please visit `authors.packtpub.com` and apply today. We have worked with thousands of developers and tech professionals, just like you, to help them share their insight with the global tech community. You can make a general application, apply for a specific hot topic that we are recruiting an author for, or submit your own idea.

Share Your Thoughts

Now you've finished *AWS FinOps Simplified*, we'd love to hear your thoughts! Scan the QR code below to go straight to the Amazon review page for this book and share your feedback or leave a review on the site that you purchased it from.

`https://packt.link/r/1803247231`

Your review is important to us and the tech community and will help us make sure we're delivering excellent quality content.

Made in the USA
Las Vegas, NV
17 December 2023

82994950R00162